EVERYTHING

YOU NEED TO KNOW ABOUT...

Shakespeare

PETER RUBIE

David & Charles

A DAVID & CHARLES BOOK

David & Charles is a subsidiary of F&W (UK) Ltd.,

an F&W Publications Inc. company

First published in the UK in 2004

First published in the USA as The Everything® Shakespeare Book,

by Adams Media Corporation in 2002

Project Manager Ian Kearey

Cover Design Ali Myer

A catalogue record for this book is available from the British Library.

ISBN 0 7153 1951 5

Printed in Great Britain by CPI Bath

for David & Charles

Brunel House   Newton Abbot   Devon

Visit our website at www.davidandcharles.co.uk

David & Charles books are available from all good bookshops;

alternatively you can contact our Orderline on (0)1626 334555

or write to us at FREEPOST EX2110, David & Charles Direct,

Newton Abbot, TQ12 4ZZ (no stamp required UK mainland).

EVERYTHING

YOU NEED TO KNOW ABOUT...

Shakespeare

Contents

Introduction

In a scene from the special millennium episode of the BBC TV comedy *Blackadder,* the hero, played by Rowan Atkinson, travels back in time to the days of Queen Elizabeth I and meets William Shakespeare walking the corridors of the royal palace. Before Shakespeare realizes what is happening, Blackadder punches him. As the Bard lies on the floor, totally mystified, Blackadder says, 'This is for every schoolboy and schoolgirl for the next 400 years!', and marches off.

The point is that many a potential fan has been put off forever by being forced to read Shakespeare at school, or dragged to see a badly staged and acted version of one of his plays. Nearly all of us as schoolchildren were compelled to suffer turgid study sessions of Shakespeare plays because it was 'good for us'.

There is a light at the end of the tunnel, however. Some fantastic versions of Shakespeare's plays have been produced,with great actors taking what seems to be incomprehensible language and making it sing. Also available are terrific radio productions that are sold as audio tapes. If you look carefully you can find not only extracts but also full audio versions of the plays on the Internet for free. If you're going to study a Shakespeare play, you may want to get hold of one of these audio tapes and follow the text while listening to it.

There is no question that studying Shakespeare requires some effort. He takes us into a different world, introduces us to some very different people, and makes us listen to them talk in a way that at first seems almost unintelligible. But the key word here is *almost*. The truth is, his characters are, in fact, very recognizable. You only have to pick up the newspaper or turn on the TV to see variations on the people he populated his plays with.

Shakespeare's genius was to capture, perhaps for the first time in the English language, the deep and troubling complexities and passions that we are all slave to. It took another 300 years for Sigmund Freud and the advent of psychology to allow us to fully appreciate how perceptive were Shakespeare's observations of the human condition. Are the passions of Othello, driven to murder his wife by a blinding jealousy brought on by his consuming love for her, really so different from those of the man who arrived at his ex-lover's house on her wedding day and shot her? Most of us can identify with the frustrations of a tormented Hamlet. We learn to feel great compassion for a mighty man fallen as King Lear descends further and further into madness, grief and homelessness. The ambitious , brutal Gordon Gekko, who declares 'Greed is good' in the 1988 Oliver Stone film *Wall Street* can't hold a candle to the naked, murderous ambitions of Macbeth and his wife.

But more than this – as if this weren't enough – Shakespeare also helped to invent the language we now know as English. He wrote at a time when English was evolving from a form called Middle English, which was part Germanic and part French, into the version we recognize today. He invented words and played with the language. Don't think for a minute that audiences in his day understood everything he wrote any better than we do. He was a challenge then and now. As a poet with a poet's sensibilities, his use of language and his inventiveness reflect this.

But Shakespeare was also an actor and knew well how to entertain the 'groundlings' or common folk who flocked to his plays. The scripts are filled with double entendres, dirty jokes, blood and gore – the end of *Hamlet* is bloodier than even *The Godfather*, and *Titus Andronicus* is literally a complete bloodbath, with bodies and dismemberments all over the place. Shakespeare also includes bawdy sex, drunkenness, humorous idiots, and evil characters who all but twirl their moustaches as they rejoice in revealing their wicked plans.

So, let's investigate the world of the man who once wrote 'All the world's a stage, and all the men and women merely players' (*As You Like It*), and see if he can't teach us a thing or two about ourselves and our fellow men and women, and enjoy ourselves at the same time.

PART 1

The Life and Times of William Shakespeare

Chapter 1
Shakespeare's World

Shakespeare is an enigma. Back in Elizabethan times not too many people could write, so records are sketchy. However, a bit of detective work in church records and court case records, and a few personal reminiscences, give us the bones of a skeletal life story on which we can conjecture some 'meat'.

The Early Years

It is commonly agreed that England's greatest poet and playwright was born and died on the same day of the month, St George's Day – born on 23 April 1564, and died on 23 April 1616. (It was a notion of fame at the time that great men were born and died on the same date.) His birth date is calculated from an entry in the parish register for a William Shakespeare baptized on 26 April; baptisms usually took place about three days after a child's birth because infants often died in those first two days.

Spelling was hit or miss in the days before English was standardized, so Shakespeare's name can also be found spelled as Shackerpere, Shaxpeare and many other variations. This discrepancy has to be taken into account in the hunt for the real William Shakespeare.

Shakespeare was born at Stratford-upon-Avon in the county of Warwickshire about 100 miles northwest of London. In the 16th century, Stratford was a market town of some 1,500 people. In the agrarian society of the time, communities were limited in size by the character of the surrounding countryside. They were dependent on rivers and streams to transport local produce such as wool, cheese and grain. The population of London in 1564 was about 100,000. In comparison with London, Stratford can be considered quite a large town.

Shakespeare's Family

Shakespeare was the eldest son of a glovemaker and leather worker, John Shakespeare, and the third child of eight. John was of yeoman stock, which meant his family was reasonably well-off and middle-class, but he still rented his farms and worked them himself. Shakespeare's mother's maiden name was Mary Arden, and her family was from the gentry – that is, they were landlords rather than tenants and lived off the income from their property. In fact, John's landlord was Mary's father. Along with the properties that Mary brought to the marriage and the leather and tanning business, which was a very respectable trade in those days, John also bought and sold grain.

John was active in local government and was appointed to positions of increasing responsibility, culminating in his election as bailiff, or mayor, of Stratford. However, as his son's fortunes rose, John's began to decline. In 1586 he was replaced as an alderman, and by 1592 he was being rebuked in writing for not attending church and was in fear of being jailed for debt.

Historians speculate that John may have held onto old Roman Catholic beliefs and suffered for this. England had become Protestant under Henry VIII, and after he died, his daughter Mary had tried to reintroduce Catholicism by rather bloody means. When Elizabeth I became queen in 1558, she established the Church of England as a Protestant church, though she also strove for religious tolerance.

Shakespeare's Education

As the son of a local official, Shakespeare would have been entitled to free schooling (mandatory schooling was not yet the law), and it is likely he was educated at Stratford Grammar School, which had an excellent reputation. His lessons would have included Latin grammar. After a few years of training in basic literacy, boys from well-off families spent the rest of their education learning to read, recite and converse in Latin and possibly some Greek. The influence of Latin authors such as Pliny, Ovid and Seneca, as well as Greek authors such as Homer and Plutarch, is clear in Shakespeare's works.

As John's debts grew, the family properties were mortgaged; Shakespeare did not go on to a university, but the grammar school curriculum must have given him a formidable linguistic and literary education. As was common at the time, he attended classes from dawn to dusk six days a week, and was probably whipped if he was inattentive or lazy in his studies. Some researchers think that the character of Sir Hugh Evans, in *The Merry Wives of Windsor,* is a caricature of Shakespeare's old headmaster, Thomas Jenkins.

Marriage and Children

According to the parish records, 'William Shagspere' married Anne Hathaway in 1582, when he was 18 years old. Anne was eight years his senior and from the nearby village of Shottery. Her father Richard was a fairly well-to-do farmer. The couple were forced to ask for a waiver of the banns from the Bishop of Worcester so that the wedding could take place quickly before the holiday season, when marriages weren't performed. Their daughter Susanna was born six months later.

Their marriage does not seem to have been particularly happy, and it may have been what we would now call a 'shotgun' wedding, urged on by Shakespeare's father because of the financial improvements to the family that would result from the union. It's also worth remembering that in those days marriage was considered as much a business proposition as a union of two people who had fallen in love. Moreover, historians estimate that one in three Elizabethan brides was pregnant on her wedding day, so this situation was not out of the ordinary by any means.

Anne gave birth to Susanna in 1583. Two years later, in January 1585, twins were born. They were named in honour of two family friends, the baker Hamnet Sadler and his wife Judith. Hamnet Shakespeare died in 1596, at only eleven years old. Some historians think that the lines spoken by Constance in *King John*, which was written the following year, refer to Shakespeare's heartsickness at losing his only son:

> Grief fills the room up of my absent child,
> Lies in his bed, walks up and down with me,
> Puts on his pretty looks, repeats his words,
> Remembers me of all his gracious parts,
> Stuffs out his vacant garments with his form;
> Then have I reason to be fond of grief.
> Fare you well. Had you such a loss as I,
> I could give better comfort than you do.

Is there any connection between Hamnet and Hamlet?
Some critics have suggested that in *Hamlet*, when Hamlet talks to his father's ghost at the beginning of the play, it is a psychological inversion of Shakespeare talking to his son's ghost. Hamlet's father is also named Hamlet.

The Effects of War

Not a lot is known of Shakespeare between the ages of 18 and 25. Some stories say he had to flee Stratford after being caught poaching deer on a nobleman's estate, while others, less fanciful, have him working as a schoolmaster, either in a small town or for the family of a local nobleman. Be that as it may, he arrived in London in 1587 as a member of a troupe of actors called Lord Leicester's Men.

Newly Anglican (i.e. Protestant) London was the capital of a nation at war, engaged in a drawn-out fight with the Catholic Spanish empire, which controlled a great deal of Europe, either directly or by alliance. The Lowlands of the Netherlands (Holland and Flanders) were the battlefields of constant engagements between the armies of Spain and small companies of men from Holland, France and England.

At sea, meanwhile, Sir Francis Drake and Sir Walter Raleigh, among others, were harrying Spanish ships bringing back gold and exotic trade goods from the New World. Although really pirates or privateers, they received a blessing from the Queen, who turned a blind eye as long as money filled the royal coffers. It all came to a head in 1588, when the English crushed a vastly superior Spanish Armada. The war dragged on, though, and the English lost Calais to the Spanish in 1596. For days, it was said, you could hear the sounds of the cannons as far as London.

Shakespeare wrote a lot about nations at war, or existing in an uneasy peace, at a time when religious strife and bigotry could result in a treason trial and your head stuck on a pike at Traitor's Gate in London. As the medieval guilds (which operated like unions in some ways) began to founder, unemployment grew, and beggars and homeless people filled the streets and prisons of towns and cities. Something of a baby boom also occurred as the country recovered from the ravages of the Black Death over the previous 100 years.

There is very little information about Shakespeare's activities from 1582, when he married, until 1587, when he pops up in London. This time is often called 'the lost years'.

But as the riches of the Renaissance began to pour forth, the notion of being an Englishman was steadily taking hold. This growing pride in nationhood and military might, particularly after the defeat of the Armada, is a key to understanding a lot of Shakespeare's work.

Life in Theatre

It is unlikely, but a commonly held belief is that Shakespeare's first job in the theatre was holding horses at the stage door. Instead, he was probably some sort of stage manager. But as he began journeyman play-editing and copying, and collaborating with other playwrights and actor/managers, he started to learn his craft.

By 1592 he was well established as an actor/playwright in London. Shakespeare worked at the Globe Theatre and appeared in many small parts. However, a bitter rival, Robert Greene, accused Shakespeare of stealing techniques from other playwrights to further his own career, and added, '... there is an upstart crow, beautified with our feathers [that is, he stole our stuff], that with his Tygers hart wrapt in a Players hyde [a possible reference to a line from *King Henry VI, Part III*, an early play, but also referring to Shakespeare as an untalented person pretending to be a playwright and actor], supposes he is as well able to bombast out blanke verse as the best of you [that is, he thinks he's pretty hot stuff as a writer]; and being an absolute Johannes fac totum [that is, Jack-of-all-trades (and the rest of the insult implies a master of none)], is in his own conceit the only Shake-scene in a country [in other words, he *really* thinks he's hot stuff].'

Greene was a university-trained writer who resented 'uneducated' low-lifes like Shakespeare becoming more successful than he. It's easy to think of Shakespeare now as eclipsing his contemporaries, but he wrote alongside other famous names – Marlowe, Kyd and Jonson, then the younger generation of Webster, Beaumont and Fletcher.

We don't know exactly what roles he played, but authorities on Shakespeare think they were cameos, such as the Ghost in *Hamlet* and Chorus in *King Henry V*. He seemed to play older men, and is also in the cast list of a Jonson play, *Sejanus*.

The troupe did well, no doubt partly as a result of their in-house writer, and performed for Queen Elizabeth I several times a year. They also put on productions in the courtyards of inns for law school teachers and students (whose courtyards are known to this day as Inns of Court), and at theatres such as the Swan.

The sonnets, though some of Shakespeare's most moving and personal pieces, were never written for publication, nor have scholars determined when and to whom they were written.

In 1592 the plague broke out again, and the authorities in London closed all the theatres because of the risk of infection spreading through the audiences. In an attempt to bridge the gap in his sudden loss of income, and probably also to get himself a noble patron, as well as establish himself as a legitimate poet (poetry was considered a higher calling than playwriting), Shakespeare published two major lyric works, *Venus and Adonis* in 1593 and *The Rape of Lucrece* in 1594.

When the theatres reopened in 1594, the 30-year-old actor/playwright joined an acting company, led by Richard Burbage, which called itself the Lord Chamberlain's Men.

The Master of the Revels

Anyone involved in the production of plays in Elizabethan England, from the playwrights to the theatre owners, knew that the Master of the Revels was the man to impress and fear, for he auditioned acting troupes, selected the plays they would perform, and controlled the scenery and costumes to be used in each production. During the reign of James I, the Master of the Revels reached the apex of his power and had complete authority over both the production and the publication of plays.

The Master of the Revels, deputy to the Lord Chamberlain, headed the Revels Office, the department of the royal household responsible for the coordination of theatrical entertainment at court. To perform at court was the goal of every Elizabethan theatre company. When the Master of the Revels organized an upcoming season of performances, he would summon the acting troupes so that they could audition before him and his three subordinate officers. The Master would then choose which companies would perform and which plays they were allowed to produce. If the Master saw fit, he would delete lines or passages, and even request that entire scenes be inserted into the original material.

The Master of the Revels's power included issuing licences to provincial acting troupes, which led to a gradual corruption of the office; it was common for the Master of the Revels to earn ten times his yearly salary through bribes. However, following the Civil War in 1642, the Puritan government closed all the theatres and the Office of the Revels became redundant; it was formally eliminated by 1737.

Once the Master had selected the plays to be produced before the royal court, he arranged for all the required costumes and scenery to be created by his own seamstresses and workmen. Much time and money was spent on elaborate wardrobes, and only the finest fabrics were used.

Profile of the Bard

By some accounts Shakespeare was a good-looking, witty young man, probably not unlike Joseph Fiennes's portrayal of him in the 1998 film

Shakespeare in Love. He could probably be pretty intense, had a real eye for the dramatic in a situation, was extremely knowledgeable about stagecraft, and almost certainly paid great attention to the world and the people around him, initially listening more than talking.

He wouldn't have been above taking someone else's idea if he liked it, and rewriting it for himself and his company. Shakespeare's version, of course, would have been uniquely his. For example, the *King Lear* story did not have an unhappy ending until Shakespeare rewrote it. In those days, plagiarism wasn't a crime. A lot of his work, for example the stories of Macbeth, King Lear and Hamlet, can be traced back to stories by Chaucer, Plutarch and Holinshed, and also to folk tales.

Shakespeare might have been the quiet one in a crowd at first, sitting in the corner entertaining himself and perhaps a friend or two by watching everyone coming and going, and making pithy, witty comments in a low voice. But once the party got going, he was probably just as animated and passionate as others. Pity the poor man who found himself in an argument with Shakespeare. A nimble mind, a way with words and a sharp tongue no doubt helped him win a lot more arguments than perhaps he should have won.

Shakespeare the Businessman

Shakespeare was a businessman, and the theatre was the television of its time. As an actor and a writer who owned a stake in the company, Shakespeare received a percentage of the proceeds. He earned fees from his plays being performed, from acting in his own and others' works, and as the owner or part-owner of several theatres and the acting compamy. He did not, however, own his own plays – these were owned by companies such as the Lord Chamberlain's Men. Shakespeare was careful with his money, and most of the records that mention him deal with legal cases. Having invested his money wisely in property both in London and Stratford, he ended up a wealthy man. As he grew older, he still liked to hang out with his theatre pals, drinking and swapping stories of days gone by, keeping his hand in, so to speak, while being relatively removed from the hurly-burly of everyday theatre life.

A great deal is still missing from Shakespeare's biography. We have no evidence, for example, that he travelled around the country or abroad, although it's certainly possible, given his knowledge of other countries and the things he wrote about in his plays.

Performing for Royalty

Shakespeare's time spent writing and performing entertainment for Queen Elizabeth and later King James I no doubt helped him to write convincingly about royalty, and it does not stretch the imagination too much to think that as the leading playwright and poet of his time, he was often in the company of his betters – that is, noble men and women and leading political and social figures of the time.

In 1599 the Lord Chamberlain's Men built the Globe Theatre on the south bank of the River Thames near the Swan. It held about 3,000 people – a huge place for its day, and fairly substantial even by today's standards – charging a penny for the standing-room-only groundlings, and more for those with the cash to buy a cushioned seat. Most of the great tragedies, such as *Hamlet* and *King Lear*, were probably performed there for the first time.

In 1603 Elizabeth died and was succeeded by James VI of Scotland, known as James I of England. He took Burbage and company under his wing, and the Lord Chamberlain's Men changed its name to the King's Men and soon became established as the premier troupe of the day, performing often at court for King James.

The Works

Shakespeare wrote for nearly 20 years, and at the height of his powers probably completed as many as two or even three plays a year. He began writing plays in 1595, and of the 38 plays that comprise the Shakespearean canon, 36 were published in the First Folio of 1623. Eighteen plays had been published in his lifetime in the quarto publications. Scholars have identified evidence of his involvement in other playwrights' works as well.

King Henry VI, King Richard III, Titus Andronicus and *Love's Labour's Lost* appear to be among the earliest works, followed by *The Comedy of Errors, King Richard II, The Two Gentlemen of Verona* and *Romeo and Juliet.* Then followed *The Taming of the Shrew, King John, The Merchant of Venice, A Midsummer Night's Dream, All's Well That Ends Well, King Henry IV, The Merry Wives of Windsor, King Henry V, Much Ado About Nothing, As You Like It, Twelfth Night, Julius Caesar, Hamlet, Troilus and Cressida, Othello, Measure for Measure, Macbeth, King Lear, Timon of Athens, Pericles, Antony and Cleopatra, Coriolanus, Cymbeline, The Winter's Tale, The Tempest, King Henry VIII, Cardenio* and *The Two Noble Kinsmen.*

King Henry VIII may have been a collaboration with John Fletcher, an up-and-coming playwright who was working as a dramatist with the King's Men, and who probably also collaborated with Shakespeare on *Cardenio* and *The Two Noble Kinsmen.*

The Final Years

Shakespeare retired from writing in 1611, although *King Henry VIII* was performed at the Globe in London in 1613. During the performance sound-effect cannon were fired in a shed on the roof and the thatching caught fire. Someone tried to douse it with a flagon of ale, which fuelled the flames, and the Globe burned to the ground. No one was hurt, except a man whose doublet and hose caught fire. The Globe was rebuilt and reopened in 1997.

Shakespeare returned to Stratford to live in a house he had built for his family as part of his substantial property holdings in the area. In 1607 his daughter Susanna married a Stratford doctor, John Hall, and their home, called Hall's Croft, is today preserved as one of the Shakespeare Properties and administered by the Shakespeare Birthplace Trust.

In 1616, a few months after his daughter Judith (Hamnet's twin) was married, Shakespeare died at the age of 53 and was buried in the Church of the Holy Trinity, the same church in which he was baptized. Tradition has it that he died of a fever after an evening's drinking with Ben Jonson and some of his other theatre friends. His gravestone bears the words that are thought to be the last he ever wrote:

> Good frend, for Jesus sake forebeare
> To digg the dust encloased heare.
> Bleste be ye man yt spares thes stones,
> And curst be he yt moves my bones.

Judith married Thomas Quiney and had three children, all of whom died young without leaving heirs. John and Susanna, who received the bulk of Shakespeare's estate when he died, had a daughter, Elizabeth, who died in 1670, leaving no heirs.

CHAPTER 2

The Elizabethan Stage

In order to appreciate both what Shakespeare wrote and why it's as brilliant as it is often said to be, it's useful to know something about the Elizabethan stage and how it developed. It is also important to note that Shakespeare and his companions invented what we now consider to be the modern theatre. Today's West End shows are the direct descendants of the early plays presented in Elizabethan theatres.

The Evolution of Elizabethan Theatre

When Shakespeare reached London around 1587, the Elizabethan theatre was slowly taking shape. It was evolving from the religious pageants and morality plays of the Middle Ages that had been the norm until then. London at that time was an exciting place for a young dramatist. John Burbage opened the first public theatre – the Theatre – in Shoreditch, east London, in 1577. The old religious drama was dying out, but two plays, written shortly before Shakespeare's birth, *Ralph Roister Doister* (the first recognized comedy in English) and *Gorboduc* (the first recognized tragedy in English), were helping to shape a new Elizabethan drama.

The precursor of this theatre was a type of religious pageant performed on the front steps of cathedrals with repetitions and chants, as seen in the *Quem Queritis Trope*. Later, amateur actors took on roles and the stories were broadened for entertainment's sake. One such play depicted the character of Noah's wife as a shrew, though she is not portrayed as such in the Bible. This kind of expansion into entertainment made the church nervous of drama, and it began to keep it at arm's length. Eventually, most of the morality plays were performed only for the nobility because of their abstract concepts.

The Elizabethan theatre competed for its audience with public executions, where victims were hung, and sometimes drawn and quartered, or butchered. Traitors were beheaded, and their heads were left to rot on pikes at the city limits. Another form of entertainment for the public was baiting, where dogs were pitted against other dogs, or bulls and bears, to fight to the death.

Morality Plays

Roaming groups of acrobats, mimes and musicians of varying talent performed in the first theatre. Their plays, known as mysteries, were heavily influenced by religious morality and took place in inn courtyards, town squares, village halls and fairgrounds, or anywhere enough boards could be rested on barrels or trestles to create a stage. (That's where the expression 'treading the boards' comes from.)

Private performances for noble folk were held in great dining halls lit by tall candles. A curtain ran behind the boards, forming an area hidden from public view where the actors could change costumes and make ready their entrances and exits. They used few props and little scenery, and because the casts were small, actors often played two or more roles during a production.

These morality plays about vice and virtue used archetypes to put their points across. Characters were the vices and virtues –Death, Kindness, Virtue – while the human protagonists were called Everyman. In contrast, as the theatre developed throughout the reign of Elizabeth I and went from a travelling fairground act to something housed in a permanent structure, distinctive stories about recognizable characters with sometimes ambiguous purposes and personalities developed.

The Players

Actors, or as they were called, players, were all men. Women were forbidden to step on the stage, so boys played women's roles, as they still do in Kabuki and Noh theatre. (In 1642 the Puritans shut down the theatres for 20 years; when they reopened after the restoration of the monarchy under Charles II, women were finally allowed to act.)

It is interesting to note that of all the people in Shakespeare's companies, only one, Will Kemp, actually had a performing background. All of the others were from merchant families, as was Shakespeare. The itinerant troubadours generally went about their business on the roads. Players needed a licence to act, and the travelling types couldn't acquire one, as they were generally considered to be among the lowest of the low in society, akin to cutpurses (thieves), vagabonds and beggars.

But it's also true that as the theatre developed, Elizabethan actors became well skilled in singing, dancing, swordsmanship, throwing knives and axes, juggling and performing sleight-of-hand tricks. There was no faking it. If a playwright needed a song, a player would sing it; if he needed a thrilling sword fight, there was no fumbling, clumsy jabbing and poking at arm's length – the players should give the playwright and the audience the real thing without anyone getting hurt. However, the only skill you really needed in order to become an actor was the ability to memorize lines.

Journeyman actors would be paid five shillings a week (20 shillings equals £1), and more experienced actors would be paid ten shillings a week or 15 shillings on the road.

The players in *Hamlet,* for example, pretty accurately recreate what acting troupes were like during Shakespeare's time:

HAMLET: Speak the speech, I pray you, as I pronounced it to you, trippingly on the tongue. But if you mouth it, as many of your players do, I had as lief the town-crier spoke my lines. Nor do not saw the air too much with your hand, thus; but use all gently: for in the very torrent, tempest, and, as I may say, whirlwind of your passion, you must acquire and beget a temperance that may give it smoothness. O, it offends me to the soul to hear a robustious periwig-pated fellow tear a passion to tatters, to very rags, to split the ears of the groundlings, who, for the most part, are capable of nothing but inexplicable dumb shows and noise…. Pray you, avoid it…. Be not too tame neither, but let your own discretion be your tutor. Suit the action to the word, the word to the action, with this special observance, that you o'erstep not the modesty of nature. For anything so overdone is from the purpose of playing, whose end, both at the first and now, was and is, to hold, as 'twere, the mirror up to nature, to show virtue her own feature, scorn her own image, and the very age and body of the time his form and pressure. Now this overdone or come tardy off, though it make the unskilful laugh, cannot but make the judicious grieve, the censure of the which one must in your allowance o'erweigh a whole theatre of others…. And let those that play your clowns speak no more than is set down for them; for there be of them that will themselves laugh, to set on some quantity of barren spectators to laugh too, though in the mean time some necessary question of the play be then to be considered. That's villainous, and shows a most pitiful ambition in the fool that uses it.

The Playwrights

The playwrights were often anonymous hacks, labouring in obscurity either in collaboration with others or in ill-paid isolation. But even if they had 'little Latin and less Greek' – as Ben Jonson, the university-educated playwright, said of his contemporary and friend William Shakespeare, the writer who had *not* gone to university – they could still get hold of a copy of Holinshed's history book, *The Chronicles of England, Scotland and Ireland*, North's translation of the Greek writer–philosopher Plutarch's *Lives of Noble Greeks and Romans*, Florio's translation of the Frenchman Montaigne, and many French and Italian romances that were making their way into English.

Shakespeare's knowledge of people combined with his poetic skill made him the greatest of playwrights. In building his plays he seldom wrote a speech that did not forward the action, develop a character or help the imagination of the spectator.

Shakespeare was also particularly influenced by Golding's translation of Ovid's *Metamorphoses*, not to mention the new translations of the Bible. It's in the *Metamorphoses* that Shakespeare found the seeds of *Romeo and Juliet*, *Othello*, *Measure for Measure*, *As You Like It* and *The Winter's Tale*. He transformed old folk tales, similar to those about King Arthur, into dark tales of tragedy – *King Lear* and *Macbeth*.

Reaching Modern Audiences

Copyright laws did not exist in Shakespeare's time, and playwrights were free to borrow plots and dialogue from other sources. Some experts, for example, think parts of *King Henry VI* were borrowed, while some of his

Roman plays, such as *Julius Caesar* and *Antony and Cleopatra*, have been linked to North's translation of Plutarch's *Lives of Noble Greeks and Romans*. Playwrights thought nothing of wholesale adapting or stealing events, characterization and even lines from previous works.

As a result, there was a disincentive for acting companies to publish the plays they commissioned until they had stopped performing the play. The versions sold by printers were called quartos, and about half of Shakespeare's plays were first published in this way, sometimes in pirated editions like the Bad Quarto of *Hamlet*. Not until Ben Jonson oversaw the publishing of his own folio of dramas was the publishing of plays treated with some care and respect.

A number of Shakespeare's contemporaries remain well known, and occasionally their plays are performed. Chief among them are Ben Jonson and Christopher Marlowe, who in their day were in some ways more famous than Shakespeare. Now considered to be Shakespeare's greatest literary rival, Marlowe died in a pub brawl at the age of 29, leaving behind several famous plays: *Doctor Faustus* (the text of which is very corrupted and has to be reassembled by whoever produces it), *Edward II*, *The Jew of Malta* and *Tamburlaine the Great* (in two parts). Marlowe's work has passed the test of time. It is an important part of most standard English degrees, and it continues to challenge modern-day actors and directors, who still are able find new relevance and meaning in the plays when they are performed for contemporary audiences.

Many of Shakespeare's plots seem far-fetched today, but the Elizabethans were romantics who loved poetry. People did not go to the theatre to see real life, but to be carried away to other times and places or to a land of fancy. The imaginative reader today loves him for the same reason.

Little Fame, Little Glory

Just as it is today, the actors, not the authors, were the stars who drew the audiences. Usually, playwrights would propose their ideas to a theatre company. If the manager liked the idea, the writer would be commissioned to write the play. Sometimes the company manager would come up with the idea and approach a well-known dramatist to put the idea into play form. It was not uncommon for a company to commission several writers to write about the same idea, then the manager would cut and paste the versions into one play, or another writer would be hired to revise the work.

The going rate was about £4 a play (in today's money that would be many times as much, perhaps the equivalent of around £750). Once it had been paid for, a play became the property of the company. Authors of successful plays – ones that ran more than the average ten performances – might get bonuses.

To Play or Not to Play

As the theatre developed, the need for sponsorship from the great lords diminished. Although they still needed a licence to operate, actors began to be able to support themselves through their craft. A large part of this independence was due to the growth of theatres in London, an increasingly thriving city nestling against the banks of the River Thames. As the century drew to a close, ships sailed up the Thames from foreign ports and departed on the turn of the tide, as London sent its sons and daughters as far afield as newly colonized Virginia in the New World, while welcoming travellers from all over the known world.

The Queen's Protection

Presiding over the growth of art and drama and maritime adventure was the ageing Queen. Elizabeth was childless and unmarried; her advancing years and the likelihood that the throne would soon stand empty threatened the peace and security of the nation with potential civil wars or the imposition of foreign potentates. Shakespeare wrote about all these fears and wonders in his own way.

Most plays were staged during the daytime, and the local authorities often cast an unwelcoming eye on players and their audiences. The city alderman and constables feared that the theatres would become meeting places for mobs and disaffected groups, as well as dangerous centres of infection in times of plague. The Earl of Essex's attempted coup against Elizabeth was to have been preceded by a performance of *King Richard II*. Luckily Shakespeare and company suffered no after-effects except stiff questioning from the authorities.

Meanwhile, disease was constantly forcing the theatres to close and the acting troupes to take to the road. The actors were allowed to follow their vocation under sufferance, however, because the rich, and particularly the Queen, demanded their entertainment.

Attacking Moral Purity

The Protestant clergy considered the theatre a threat to the moral purity of the populace, particularly the young. In 1583 in his *The Anatomie of Abuses*, religious leader Philip Stubbes declared that far from teaching men and women how to be better people, plays offered instruction in how to lie, cheat, steal and deceive: 'If you will learn to jest, laugh and leer, to grin, to nod and mow [fornicate]; if you will learn to play the vice, to swear, tear and blaspheme both Heaven and Earth; if you will learn to become a bawd, unclean, and to devirginate maids, to deflower honesty wives; if you will learn to murder, flay, kill, pick, steal, rob and row...' You get the idea. The Puritans, to give them their due, also didn't approve of animal-baiting, which also took place at the theatres.

Because of the official hostility to plays and players, most companies consisted of about a dozen or so regular actors and looked for protection through patronage. Shakespeare began his career with Lord Leicester's Men, then joined a troupe called the Lord Chamberlain's Men with acting stars such as Richard Burbage and Will Kemp, a famous comedy actor. The troupe was renamed the King's Men when James I came to the throne. Rival companies had names such as the Lord Admiral's Men, which starred Edward Alleyn.

Choice Theatres

In 1576 James Burbage, father of Richard, a former carpenter and then the actor/manager of Lord Leicester's Men, leased a piece of land in Shoreditch, just northeast of the London city limits, and built the first permanent theatre, called, appropriately enough, the Theatre. A second theatre was built nearby the next year. Building permanent theatres within the London city limits was prohibited.

Other theatres on the north bank of the Thames soon followed, including the Curtain and the Fortune. Builders of permanent theatres sought to avoid the interference of the local authorities, so they also built on the south bank of the Thames, free of London's jurisdiction, in what could be thought of as a sort of downtown or entertainment area in Southwark, where you could also find brothels, gambling dens and bull- and bear-baiting arenas. Here you could find the Rose, the Swan and eventually the Globe flourishing.

As people entered the Globe, they would drop their admission fee into a box. The practice is reflected today in the name 'box office' at the front of a theatre.

In 1598, Richard Burbage lost the lease to his father's theatre, which fell into disrepair. At dead of night, he and his players had to sneak the building timbers off the property before the landowner confiscated them. They dismantled the building, transported it piece by piece across the frozen Thames, reassembled it on the south bank of the river and called it the Globe.

The theatre provided a good annual profit of several hundred pounds – a comfortable amount for Elizabethan times – for a consortium of people that included Burbage and Shakespeare. In 1613, however, during a performance of *King Henry VIII* some wadding from the sound-effect cannon set the thatched roof alight, and the theatre burned to the ground.

Different companies adopted particular theatres as their 'homes', even if they toured the countryside and gave performances in the houses of noble patrons. The Blackfriars, for instance, was a small indoor theatre that housed a troupe of boy actors, offering highbrow theatre for nobles (as did other boy companies) until it was taken over by Shakespeare's King's Men after the Globe burned down. Scholars speculate that some of Shakespeare's later plays, particularly more contemplative works such as *The Tempest* and *The Winter's Tale*, may have been composed for the more intimate setting of the Blackfriars, and its richer, more sophisticated audiences.

Stage Construction

The stage still had little scenery, no front curtain to hide the bare boards and little or no stage machinery for special effects. A chorus, or dialogue, established the scene. Entrances and exits were through two doorways to the tiring house (a corruption of 'attiring house') backstage.

The Stage

However, the theatre was by no means a drab affair. A lack of scenery was compensated for by magnificent costumes. Even if the action was supposed to take place in ancient Egypt (*Antony and Cleopatra*) or some mythical far-off island kingdom, the audiences knew that the plays were really about themselves, and so there was little attempt to make the costumes fit the time or style of the setting.

Battle scenes were accompanied by loud bangs and smoke, with braying trumpets sounding the start and announcing the arrival of important characters. Music played a large part in Elizabethan theatre, and often incidental music that included jigs and reels and clowning was used, even when the main event was a tragic play such as *King Lear*.

The 'dead' were carried off in dramatic flourishes because there was no other way to get the bodies off the stage. Some stages had a curtained alcove set off to one side, for small, more intimate or intense scenes, such as the murder of Desdemona in *Othello*. There might also be an open gallery or balcony high on the back wall of the stage where Romeo could climb up to pursue his love Juliet.

The groundlings were left open to the elements, but the stage was covered by a roof; the exposed underside would sometimes be painted with a moon and stars. A trapdoor in the stage would allow a 'ghost' to arise, as in *Macbeth*, or for the gravedigger scene in *Hamlet*.

The Audience

Unlike the modern theatre, where the expensive seats put you almost on the stage, and certainly near the front of the theatre, the 'cheap seats' were at the front. In fact they weren't seats at all, but a courtyard open to the sky, where the groundlings, or common folk, stood. These were usually an opinionated, often drunken, unruly mob of labourers, less-skilled artisans, and prostitutes who lived near the theatre and saw an opportunity to make some money when a play was being performed.

The groundlings stood in a rough semicircle 20m (60ft) or more in length in front of a stage that stood about 1.5m (5ft) off the ground, was about 12m (40ft) in width, and had a jetty-like piece that jutted into the audience by 6m (20ft) or more. The vertical walls of the theatre in front of the stage had a number of boxes or galleries that were reached by steep staircases. On a good day, a packed house could have more than 3,000 people in the audience.

Given the nature of the audience, we can presume that feedback was instantaneous, with shouts of encouragement and applause for what worked, and boos and rotten fruit and vegetables thrown onstage for what didn't work. The groundlings would have paid a penny, which was close to a day's wages for an unskilled labourer, to see the play, and they wanted value for their money. The price was at least double for the boxed seats.

CHAPTER 3

Did Shakespeare Write Shakespeare?

O f all the great writers in the Western literary canon, Shakespeare presents a unique enigma. Despite several hundred years of scholarship, doubts still remain that the man from Stratford wrote what have long been considered to be 'The Collected Works of William Shakespeare'.

The Oxfordians and the Stratfordians

Was there really a William Shakespeare of Stratford? Or was Shakespeare someone else, for example, Edward de Vere, the 17th Earl of Oxford? There are two main schools of thought: the Oxfordians, who promote the idea of de Vere as the author of the plays and poems, and the Stratfordians, who contend that Shakespeare wrote Shakespeare. All told, some 60 candidates vie for the honour of having written Shakespeare's works.

The Oxfordian Stance

In the last century and a half, sincere and intelligent people have believed that strong evidence exists to prove that Shakespeare did not write Shakespeare. Among them are Walt Whitman, Mark Twain, Sigmund Freud, Helen Keller, Orson Welles, Muriel Spark and Black Muslim leader Malcolm X. As Ralph Waldo Emerson put it, 'I cannot marry the life to the work.'

The Oxfordians claim that those who support the Stratford man are blinded to the evidence by a vested self-interest. More extreme Oxfordians claim that Stratfordians are engaged in an active conspiracy to suppress pro-Oxford evidence. The truth, however, is far more mundane. Oxfordians are not taken seriously by the Shakespeare establishment because most of them do not follow basic standards of scholarship, and the 'evidence' they present is either distorted, taken out of context or just plain false.

Thomas Looney's *Shakespeare Identified in Edward de Vere, 17th Earl of Oxford* is the first work to claim that de Vere was the Bard. On the other side of the argument, Dave Kathman's articles, which can be found on the Internet, put forward strong reasons why Shakespeare was really the Shakespeare who wrote the plays.

The Stratfordian Argument

The Stratfordians maintain that one of the greatest difficulties with the argument that Earl of Oxford wrote Shakespeare's plays is that de Vere died in 1604, yet still managed to produce some of his greatest plays post-mortem, as it were. These plays include *King Lear* (c. 1605–6), *Macbeth* (c. 1606–7), *Antony and Cleopatra* (c. 1606–7), *Coriolanus* (c. 1608), *Cymbeline* (c. 1608–10), *The Winter's Tale* (c. 1609–11) and *The Tempest* (c. 1611). Most Oxfordians concede that these plays post-date de Vere's death, but argue that de Vere wrote the plays before he died, and that they were brought out as needed for performance, sometimes with added references to events after 1604 in order to make them look contemporary.

In 1769, the actor/manager David Garrick staged a Shakespeare Jubilee at Stratford, and from that time on Stratford became the mecca for those pilgrims who worship the Bard.

The problem with this argument is that when you examine the body of Shakespeare's plays as a whole, it's possible to trace a definable stylistic development. As David Bevington, Professor of English Language and Literature at the University of Chicago, said in a 1989 US public television *Frontline* documentary about this issue:

> The argument [that de Vere wrote Shakespeare] has to posit a conspiracy of staggering proportions. Shakespeare, according to this scenario, agreed to serve as a front man for Oxford because the writing of plays was below the dignity of a great man. Shakespeare's friends in the company agreed to serve up his plays in the years after Oxford's death, publicizing the plays as by Shakespeare. Persons who knew Shakespeare well, like Ben Jonson, went along with the fiction, writing ecomiastac verses for Shakespeare after his death in 1613. The acting company, especially Shakespeare's colleagues John Heminges and Henry Condell, supervised the publication of all of the plays (except *Pericles*, *Cardenio* and *The Two Noble Kinsmen*, which are regarded as collaborations) in a handsome Folio volume in 1616, essentially the first of its kind to recognize a dramatist. Many writers poured out their praise for England's great national poet and

playwright, and some of them knew Shakespeare. All of these people had to be either deceived by the presumed cover-up or, in many cases, accessories to a hoax.

Lack of Formal Education

That Shakespeare wasn't Shakespeare didn't occur to anyone before the 19th century. Until then, everyone celebrated Shakespeare as the great English writer of genius. The debate can be couched in terms of an early form of class warfare.

As a newly emerging Victorian middle class arose, and a liberal university education became the distinguishing mark of a gentleman, people began to reinforce the superiority of their own status by believing that Shakespeare's plays and poems could have been the work *only* of a university-educated gentleman, rather than the genius of a partially self-taught middle-class glover's son. What's more, to add fuel to the controversy, writers such as Christopher Marlowe and Ben Jonson *did* attend university, although others, such as John Webster and Thomas Dekker, apparently did not.

The point that many scholars miss is that writing is about observing and reflecting the human condition. It is also about reading, and a great deal was being printed for the first time in English around Shakespeare's time, as we've seen. What's more, if you examine the careers of great writers throughout history, their formal academic education could often be the least relevant aspect of their success as a writer.

Playwrights did not have to be courtiers themselves to accurately portray court life, just as journalists today can recreate and interpret what happens in Parliament or 10 Downing Street without being in government or elected officials themselves.

In fact, many writers have come primarily from social classes below those of the privileged class. For example, James Joyce, D. H. Lawrence, Harold Pinter, Sam Shepard, John Arden and Arnold Wesker all came from the working classes or middle classes. In pre-19th century times, John Webster was the son of a merchant tailor; Edmund Spenser's father was a cloth-maker; Christopher Marlowe's father was a shoemaker in Canterbury; Ben Jonson's stepfather was a bricklayer. While these promising young men were well educated at places such as Merchant Taylor's School and Westminster School in London, not all of them went on to university.

However, they had enough education to challenge the concept of 'knowing their place' and to move to thinking 'outside the box', as it were, and beyond society's expectations of them, and they became writers in London. There, the theatre, among other opportunities, provided them with both employment and intellectual stimulation and drew them into a world of urbane events. They either observed, or became peripheral participants, in the goings-on of kings and nobles, and were able to write compelling pictures of courtly life in their plays.

Is Hard Evidence Needed?

The lack of manuscripts or handwriting samples, and the uncertainties about certain periods of Shakespeare's life are all in keeping with a playwright of the period. We may have some of Shakespeare's handwriting in some additions made to several pages of a play, *Sir Thomas More*, he was either editing or collaborating on, but which was never produced)

Play scripts, like many film scripts today, existed solely so that an acting company could stage a play. The wonder is that so many of Shakespeare's plays were published at all. We have no definitive manuscripts of plays by Marlowe or Jonson or Webster, even though some of their plays rival those of Shakespeare in their literary and dramatic qualities, yet their authorship is not generally questioned.

No one suggests that Marlowe wasn't written by Marlowe or Jonson by Jonson. So why is Shakespeare singled out? The answer lies mainly in his greatness. True geniuses are few and far between, and there are those such as Einstein and Shakespeare who defied their backgrounds as their genius flowered. Shakespeare is among the greatest of our thinkers and creators, and so he is the subject of intense speculation.

Influence of Society

Some people believe that the question of authorship is intensified by today's society. We live in an era where democracy and being yourself, particularly in the arts, have sometimes come to mean mediocrity and licence, with little real artistic merit needed if you have the ability to command attention in the moment.

Some men known personally to Shakespeare – for example, Francis Meres and Ben Jonson – did recognize his worth. And to argue that an obscure Stratford boy could not have become the Shakespeare of literature is to ignore the mystery of genius.

'Great art' is sometimes defined by how much money something is worth, and we seem to live in a society where everyone, as the artist Andy Warhol said, 'will be famous for fifteen minutes'. Shakespeare has thus become an icon of Western literature who must be toppled so that the rest of us can feel that what we do has some worth.

Too Many Questions, Not Enough Answers

What could be more exciting than solving a mystery? What happened to the crew of the *Marie Celeste*? Is there a Bermuda Triangle? What really happened in the Kennedy assassination? Who wrote Shakespeare's plays? Such detective work appeals to all manner of people who like to pursue Shakespeare as a hobby.

Imagine, if you can, an enthusiastic amateur showing the professional scholars that all Western culture has been bamboozled over the centuries by a hoax, and that Shakespeare is really the Earl of Oxford.

As David Bevington writes, 'If Oxford was so eager that someone should "Report me and my cause aright/To the unsatisfied", why did he leave such enigmatic clues? Was the stigma of being a playwright so huge that he could tell no one, not even write it down for his friends? Ultimately the case collapses on lack of motive as well as lack of evidence, for it presupposes a social history of how playwrights got to be playwrights that is simply not in keeping with historical reality.'

Candidates for Shakespeare

Why are there so many candidates, and why should we choose de Vere over such illustrious figures as Sir Francis Bacon or Christopher Marlowe? Actually, of all Elizabethans put forward since the middle of the 18th century as the 'true Shakespeare', only four have merited serious consideration: Sir Francis Bacon (Lord Verulam), Christopher Marlowe, William Stanley (Sixth Earl of Derby) and Edward de Vere (17th Earl of Oxford).

Irvin Leigh Matus's *Shakespeare, In Fact* is a good examination of the authorship question. Charlton Ogburn's *The Mysterious William Shakespeare* is generally considered the most thorough exposition of the Oxfordian case. In 1997 Joseph Sobran's *Alias Shakespeare* introduced many newcomers to the Shakespeare authorship question.

Since the 1800s different scholars have attempted to prove either that Shakespeare did not write the plays, or that others did. For a long time the leading candidate was Sir Francis Bacon. In fact, nearly every famous Elizabethan has been named. Some people even claim that 'Shakespeare' was an assumed name for a whole group of poets and playwrights.

The contest, summed up by US TV correspondent Al Austin, 'comes down to this: those who believe de Vere was Shakespeare must accept an improbable hoax as part of it, a conspiracy of silence involving, among others, Queen Elizabeth herself. Those who side with the Stratford man must believe in miracles.' Or, it might be added, accept the nature of genius for what it is – a rarity of generational proportions.

CHAPTER 4

Shakespeare's Rivals

Shakespeare was not the only playwright of his time, and was not even the most famous for most of his writing career. After the success of the Theatre and the Globe, quite a few new theatres sprang up and playwriting became a way to fame and fortune. Would-be playwrights flocked to London, much in the same way that aspiring screenwriters today head to Hollywood.

Christopher Marlowe

It's generally acknowledged that the greatest of Shakespeare's rivals was Christopher Marlowe (1564–93). Marlowe was the second child and eldest son of John Marlowe, a Canterbury shoemaker. Nothing is known of his first schooling, but on 14 January 1579 he entered King's School, Canterbury, as a scholar. A year later he went to Corpus Christi College, Cambridge, and received his Bachelor of Arts degree in 1584.

A group of playwrights who became known as the University Wits sprang up in the closing years of the 16th century. They all, in some way or another, helped pave the way for Shakespeare's success. One of the pioneers was John Lyly, and others included Thomas Lodge, George Peele, Christopher Marlowe, Robert Greene and Thomas Nashe. Another of the Wits, though not university-trained, was Thomas Kyd.

Marlowe continued in residence at Cambridge, which may suggest that he was intending to take Anglican orders. However, according to university records, Marlowe disappeared frequently during his last years at college, putting his degree in jeopardy. The university's doubts were apparently set at rest after the Privy Council sent a letter declaring that Marlowe had been employed 'on matters touching the benefit of his country' – apparently in Elizabeth's newly created secret service.

It's likely that a lot of this time was spent in Rheims, France, among the Catholics who were plotting against Queen Elizabeth's Protestant regime. It's also possible that Marlowe fought in the wars in the Low Country after graduation.

Marlowe's Playwriting Career

What is certain is that by 1587 Marlowe was living in London and had begun his career as a playwright – although he may still have been working for William Cecil in the secret service. Marlowe also earned a dangerous reputation for atheism. In Robert Greene's deathbed tract,

Greenes groats-worth of witte, he calls Marlowe a 'famous gracer of Tragedians' and reproved him for having said, as did Greene himself, 'There is no God.'

The young man was quickly in the heady company of other poets and adventuring soldiers such as Sir Philip Sidney and Sir Walter Raleigh. He roomed with fellow playwright Thomas Kyd, and often frequented the taverns of London with the likes of Robert Greene and Thomas Nashe. His magnificent appearance, impulsiveness and bejewelled costumes soon became the talk of the town.

In a playwriting career that lasted not much more than six years, Marlowe's achievements were remarkable. Before leaving Cambridge he had already written *Tamburlaine the Great* (a two-part play performed by the end of 1587 and published in 1590). He also translated Ovid's *Amores* (*The Loves*) and the first book of Lucan's *Pharsalia* from Latin, and co-wrote the play *Dido, Queen of Carthage* (published in 1594) with Thomas Nashe. It was *Tamburlaine the Great*, the first notable English play in blank verse, that won him recognition and acclaim. None of his other plays, poems or translations were published during his life, but his unfinished *Hero and Leander* is considered by many to be one of the finest examples of nondramatic Elizabethan poetry composed before Edmund Spenser's *Faerie Queene*.

Scholars argue about the order of Marlowe's plays after *Tamburlaine* was written. Many think *Dr Faustus* was next, followed by *Edward II* and *The Massacre at Paris*. Marlowe's last play may have been *The Jew of Malta*.

It wasn't until Marlowe and Shakespeare began their careers in the 1580s that dramatic poetry began to flourish. England took pride in her poets, and a new breed of actor appeared who was able and willing to give dramatic life to the new style of play that was developing. The Lord Admiral's company, one of the premier acting companies in London, presented Marlowe's plays. While his contemporaries were watching their work performed by church boys, Marlowe saw his dramas staged by full-grown men such as the 2.1m (7ft)-tall, outstanding actor Edward Alleyn, who played Tamburlaine, Faustus and Barabbas the Jew.

Dr Faustus is Marlowe's most famous play, but it has survived only in a corrupt form. It was first published in 1604, and another version appeared in 1616. Nevertheless, no playwright had previously invoked the world, the flesh and the devil so magnificently and with such powerful and lyrical language. However, while the acclaim piled up, the money didn't, and Marlowe became more and more restless and irritable, until even his friends began to lose patience with him.

Heresy and Death

In 1593, after pointing out what he considered to be inconsistencies in the Bible, Marlowe fell under suspicion of heresy. His housemate Thomas Kyd was tortured into giving evidence against him. On 18 May 1593, the Privy Council issued an order for Marlowe's arrest; two days later the poet was ordered to give daily attendance on their lordships 'until he shall be licensed to the contrary'.

On 30 May 1593, the 29-year-old poet went to Dame Eleanore Bull's tavern in Deptford to have dinner with some friends: Ingram Frizer, Nicholas Skeres and Robert Poley. According to witnesses, there was a quarrel over the bill and Marlowe drew his dagger on Frizer, who defended himself by driving the dagger back into the young poet's eye, mortally wounding him.

John Lyly

John Lyly (c. 1554–1606) is considered the first English prose stylist to leave a lasting impression upon the language. He was educated at Magdalen College, Oxford, and went to London in 1576. He gained recognition with the publication of two prose romances, *Euphues: the Anatomy of Wit* (1578) and *Euphues and His England* (1580). These works made him the major writer of the 1580s. The *Euphues* are stories told in letters interspersed with general discussions on religion and love. Lyly's style became known as euphuism.

In 1583 he gained control of the first Blackfriars Theatre, in which his comedies were produced. The players in the comedies were the Children of Paul's, a company that periodically played for Elizabeth I. The finest of his plays is considered to be *Endimion* (1588), which some critics hold as a masterpiece.

Lyly's popularity waned with the rise of Thomas Kyd, Christopher Marlowe and William Shakespeare, and his appeals to Queen Elizabeth for financial relief went unheeded. He had hoped to succeed Edmund Tilney in the court post of Master of the Revels, but Tilney outlived him and Lyly died a poor and bitter man.

Lyly's comedies marked an enormous advance in English drama. Their plots are drawn from classical mythology and legend. While his characters are often engaged in euphuistic speeches filled with flowery Renaissance pedantry, the charm and wit of the dialogues, and the skilful construction of the plots set standards that younger and more gifted dramatists could not ignore.

Thomas Kyd

The details of Thomas Kyd's life (1558–94) are obscure, though it's known that he shared a room with Christopher Marlowe for a while. He is best known for *The Spanish Tragedie* (1589) (sometimes called *Hieronimo* or *Jeronimo*, after its protagonist), which initiated the Elizabethan revenge tragedy genre. The son of a professional copyist or scrivener, Kyd was educated at Merchant Taylors' School in London. There is no evidence that he attended a university before turning to literature. He seems to have been in service for some years with Ferdinando, Lord Strange, the patron of Lord Strange's Men.

It is not known which company first performed *The Spanish Tragedie*, nor when, but Strange's company played it 16 times in 1592, and the Admiral's Men revived it in 1597, as did the Chamberlain's Men. The play became the most popular and influential tragedy of its day, and was even more so than Shakespeare's plays. It continued to be performed throughout the Elizabethan period.

Many critics believe that Hieronimo in *The Spanish Tragedie* prepared the way for Shakespeare's psychological study of Hamlet. Kyd did not share Marlowe's towering poetic ability, but his brilliance came from an instinctive grasp of the tragic form and what worked best on the stage. By 1589 he had written a lost *Hamlet* – sometimes referred to as the Ur-*Hamlet* – which may have been the model for Shakespeare's tragedy.

The only other play that can be attributed to Kyd with certainty is *Cornelia* (1594), which was adapted from a French play by Robert Garnier. *Soliman and Perseda* is usually attributed to him as well, on the basis of style and the fact that it has the same plot as *The Spanish Tragedie*.

Another play sometimes attributed to Kyd is *Arden of Feversham*, a dramatization of a crime that had been reported in Holinshed's *Chronicles*. Kyd's authorship of this play has come into doubt, but if he is indeed the author, then Kyd is the founder of middle-class tragedy as well as the revenge play.

In 1593, after falling under suspicion of heresy, his rooms were searched and certain 'atheistical' disputations denying the deity of Jesus Christ were found. He was arrested for atheism and tortured into giving evidence against his housemate Marlowe. Kyd denied the charge of atheism, claiming the offending evidence belonged to his friend. The situation is rich with irony. The innovator of the revenge genre may well have been set up by Marlowe, Kyd may have returned the favour, and Marlowe's subsequent death could have been a covertly arranged murder.

Kyd was eventually released from prison, but had been broken by his imprisonment, torture and disgrace. He died in poverty in December 1594, not yet 36 years old, and even his debt-ridden estate was repudiated by his mother.

Ben Jonson

A close friend of his rival, Ben Jonson (1572–1637) is generally regarded as the second most important English dramatist of the Jacobean period after William Shakespeare. His Protestant father, who had been imprisoned and deprived of his estate during the Catholic reign of Mary Tudor, died when Jonson was young. His mother, left penniless and with no means of supporting her young son, was forced to marry a bricklayer.

Though his stepfather was a working man, by good fortune the boy was able to attend Westminster School. The scholar Camden recognized Jonson's exceptional literary ability and took the young man under his wing. Though Jonson never received a formal university education, because of Camden's instruction he became one of the most learned men of Elizabethan and Jacobean times, and eventually received honorary degrees from Oxford and Cambridge universities.

His formal education, however, ended early, and at first he followed his stepfather's trade, then fought with some success with the Protestant English forces in the Netherlands. The Orange Men were defending their religious and political freedom against Catholicism and Spanish rule. The fiery young poet proved to be a formidable soldier. In one particular incident, advancing before the English volunteers, he challenged a Spaniard to a single combat sword fight, killed him, and then, in an act straight out of Homer's *Odyssey*, stripped the corpse of its armour.

In 1596, his wife gave birth to a son whom Jonson called his 'best piece of poetry'. He was devastated when the boy died of the plague at the age of seven. Jonson plunged himself into the bohemian life of the city, drank a lot and got into fights.

Jonson returned to England in 1592, married a woman whom he would later describe as 'a shrew, yet honest', and became an actor and playwright, though how good an actor was open to debate (but good enough to play the leading role of Hieronimo in Kyd's *The Spanish Tragedie*, it seems). By 1597 he was writing plays for Philip Henslowe, London's leading impresario. With one exception (*The Case Is Altered*), these early plays are known only by their titles – nothing of the text remains.

Rising Above

It was not until 1598 that Jonson finally emerged from the crowd of unrecognized playwrights with *Every Man in His Humour*. Dedicated to Master Camden, *Every Man in His Humour* is a comedic masterpiece that paints a telling portrait of the Elizabethan age. Presented by the Lord Chamberlain's Men, legend has it that Shakespeare himself recommended his friend's play to them.

That same year Jonson got into a quarrel with the actor Gabriel Spencer and, in a duel, killed the man, though his blade was 25cm (10in) shorter than his opponent's. He was imprisoned and only escaped capital punishment by pleading benefit of clergy – the ability to read a passage from the Latin Bible. He was, however, branded on the thumb and his property was confiscated.

In 1606 Jonson and his wife were brought before the Consistory Court in London to explain why they failed to go to church. He denied that his wife was guilty, but admitted that his own religious opinions held him aloof from attendance. The matter was resolved by his agreeing to debate learned men, who might persuade him if they could.

His release was celebrated by the performance of his new play *Every Man Out of His Humour* (1599). It was the longest play ever written for the Elizabethan public theatre, but it proved a disaster, and Jonson had to look for a different type of venue to present his work. The obvious place was a private theatre, in which only young boys acted. The high price of admission meant a select audience, and they were willing to try strong satire and formal experiment. Jonson then wrote *Cynthia's Revels* (1600) and *Poetaster* (1601).

He made a mark second only to Shakespeare's in the public theatre. His comedies, *Volpone* or *The Foxe* (1606) and *The Alchemist* (1610), were among the most popular and acclaimed plays of the period, and are still performed today. Both plays are eloquent, compact and satirical.

Collaborations

Although constantly quarrelling with his fellow playwrights, Jonson managed to collaborate with John Marston and George Chapman on *Eastward Ho!* (1605), a play that landed them all in prison. The play contained an unflattering reference to Scottish royalty, and the new king, James I (formerly James VI of Scotland) took offence. Chapman and Marston were thrown into prison, and Jonson joined them there voluntarily, claiming equal responsibility for the play. In the end, they were spared – probably because of the new-found popularity Jonson was beginning to enjoy as a writer of masques for the court. Jonson also won royal attention with his *Entertainment at Althorpe*, presented to Anne, the new Queen, as she journeyed to England from Scotland in 1603.

The masque was a quasi-dramatic entertainment, primarily providing a pretence for a group of strangers to dance and sing before an audience of guests and attendants in a royal court or nobleman's house. During the reign of James I it became an elaborate affair, partly because the architect Inigo Jones provided increasingly magnificent costumes and scenic effects for masques at court.

The Restoration dramatists' (post-1660) use of type names for their characters came directly from what was called 'Jonsonian humour'. In the late Jacobean and Caroline years, Jonson, Shakespeare and Francis Beaumont and John Fletcher provided all the models. But it was Jonson, and Jonson alone, who gave the essential impulse to dramatic characterization in the comedies of the Restoration and well into the 18th and 19th centuries.

It was Jonson, in collaboration with Jones, who gave the Jacobean masque its characteristic shape and style. That the two men should quarrel seemed inevitable, and the friction led to a complete break. Jonson wrote the *Twelfth Night* masque for the court in 1625, but then had to wait five years before his services were asked for again.

Death

In 1628 Jonson suffered what was apparently a stroke, and as a result was confined to his room and chair, then ultimately to his bed. That same year he was made City Chronologer and, theoretically, responsible for London's pageants. In 1634 his salary for the post was made into a pension. Jonson died in 1637 and was buried in Westminster Abbey.

John Marston

John Marston (1575–1634) came from a good family and would have been considered a gentleman. He was one of the first Elizabethan satirists, and helped pave the way for Jonson's later success. A good definition of a satire is a play where human faults and vices are exposed to public view and made ridiculous.

In 1605, *Eastward Ho!* got him and his co-authors Chapman and Jonson a jail sentence for insulting the new king, James I. He wrote one other play, in 1606, after which he seems to have retired from the theatre. Later in Marston's life, he joined the church and took orders. Marston was a great satirist and was in constant competition with Ben Jonson.

Beaumont and Fletcher

The names Francis Beaumont and John Fletcher go side by side in English literature, partly because of their collaborations and partly because they were asked to append introductory poems to Jonson's *Volpone*.

According to John Aubrey, the notorious 17th-century gossip and diarist, the two playwrights 'lived together on the Banke side, not far from the Play-house, both batchelors. They lay together... had one wench in the house between them... the same cloathes and cloake, &c., betweene them.'

Of the 54 plays with which their names or the names of their other collaborators are associated, one or two were written by Beaumont alone and only nine or ten were Beaumont and Fletcher collaborations. Beaumont's hand also probably appears in three other plays written together with Fletcher and Philip Massinger.

Attempts to disentangle the various shares of Beaumont and Fletcher in any given work are complicated by the fact that Beaumont sometimes revised Fletcher's scenes, and Fletcher edited some of Beaumont's work.

In the three masterpieces of the Beaumont and Fletcher collaboration, *The Maides Tragedy*, *Philaster* and *A King and No King*, scholars assume that Beaumont had the controlling hand, since the plays manifest a firmer structure than Fletcher's single or collaborative efforts.

John Fletcher

John Fletcher's (1579–1625) father, Richard Fletcher, was a successful clergyman who became the bishop successively of Bristol, Worcester and London, gaining a measure of fame as a tormenting accuser in the trial of Mary, Queen of Scots, and as the chaplain who sternly officiated at her execution.

When not quite 12 years old, Fletcher was accepted at Corpus Christi College, Cambridge, and two years later became a Bible clerk. From the time of his father's death (1596) until 1607 nothing is known of him, although the evidence of his later plays indicates that he did not inherit his father's religious bigotry.

After 1613, Fletcher collaborated with or had his plays revised by Philip Massinger, who succeeded him in 1625 as chief playwright of the King's Men. Other collaborators included Nathan Field and William Rowley. Throughout his career he also wrote plays unaided.

In 1625, while the plague raged in London, Fletcher lingered in the city to be measured for a suit of clothes, instead of making his escape to the country. He died, along with some 40,000 others.

Francis Beaumont

Francis Beaumont (1585–1616) was the son of Francis Beaumont, Justice of Common Pleas in Charnwood Forest, Leicestershire. Beaumont arrived at Pembroke College, Oxford, in 1597, but on the sudden death of his father left the university without a degree. In November 1600 he entered London's Inner Temple, with the intention of studying law, but instead began to frequent the Mermaid Tavern.

In 1602 he published *Salmacis and Hermaphroditus*, a lush rewriting of a poem by Ovid. By 1607 Beaumont and Fletcher had begun to collaborate on plays for the Children of the Queen's Revels and its successor, and then from 1609 until Beaumont's retirement in 1613, mainly for the King's Men at the Globe and Blackfriars theatres.

In 1613 Beaumont married an heiress, Ursula Isley of Sundridge in Kent, and retired from the theatre. He died in London in 1616, a month before Shakespeare, and was buried in Westminster Abbey. As a playwright, Beaumont remains a shadowy figure whose contributions to drama are not as clear as Fletcher's.

John Ford

Because of his disdain for orthodoxy and his sympathetic treatment of unorthodox love, John Ford (1586–1639) is often considered the most modern of Elizabethan and Jacobean dramatists. He first appeared in print with *Fame's Memorial* (1606), a long elegy on the death of the Earl of Devonshire, followed by other occasional pieces before he finally concentrated on drama. His first attempt was most likely the writing or revising of *A Bad Beginning Makes a Good Ending*, which was acted by the King's Men at court in 1612, and was one of the four unprinted plays by Ford that were accidentally destroyed.

His career as a playwright took off in 1621, when he co-authored *The Witch of Edmonton* with Thomas Dekker and William Rowley.

He collaborated with Dekker on several other plays and with John Webster on at least one. After 1624, however, he worked alone, and his reputation rests chiefly upon his three tragedies of forbidden love, *'Tis Pity She's a Whore*, *The Broken Heart* and *Love's Sacrifice*.

Thomas Middleton

As a teenager, Thomas Middleton (1580–1627) published *The Wisdom of Solomon Paraphrased* (1597) and *Micro-Cynicon, Six Snarling Satires* (1599), but didn't graduate from Queen's College, Oxford, until 1598. There is no record of his connection with the theatre until 22 May 1602, when impresario Philip Henslowe records in his diary a payment made to him together with Munday, Drayton and Webster 'in earnest of a book called *Caesar's Fall*'.

While he sometimes wrote alone, more often he wrote in collaboration with other well-known dramatists, notably Dekker and Rowley. Two satirical tales, *The Black Book* and *Father Hubbard's Tale* (1604), show his early interest in the underside of London life, which he was to turn to good account in his comedies of manners, which were written between 1604 and 1611.

The temporary amalgamation of the companies of Princess Elizabeth and Prince Charles in 1614 or so brought Middleton and Rowley together, and their period of collaboration began shortly thereafter. *The Changeling*, the best of Middleton and Rowley's joint efforts, written in 1622 and performed at Whitehall in 1624, was not published until 1653.

Middleton's one unaided tragedy, *Women, Beware Women*, written around 1612, was followed in 1613 by his first masque, *The Triumphs of Truth*, and until his death he was in demand as a writer of this type of entertainment.

Middleton possesses no great poetic gift, but his strengths were in his ability to structure a play and his well-honed dramatic sense.

John Webster

John Webster (c. 1580–c. 1625) was the last of the great Elizabethan playwrights. Like many of his contemporaries, little of certainty is known about him. A John Webster was admitted to the Middle Temple on 1 August 1598 to study law. If this is the dramatist Webster it would explain the legal bent of many of his plays, including trial scenes in *The White Devil*, *The Devil's Law Case* and *Appius and Virginia*.

The earliest known records of Webster's employment as a playwright are found in the diary of impresario Philip Henslowe, who noted in 1602 payments to Webster, Anthony Munday, Thomas Middleton, Michael Drayton 'and the rest' for a play entitled *Caesar's Fall*. Over the next decade, Henslowe's records show Webster collaborating with Dekker and Heywood, writing a prologue to Marston's *Malcontent*, and composing two masterpieces, *The White Devil* and *The Duchess of Malfi*.

Webster's scope has been criticized as limited, as he wrote mostly about anguish and evil. But his poetry is of a high standard and holds its own with the best of Marlowe and Shakespeare. T.S. Eliot described Webster as the poet who was 'much possessed by death, and saw the skull beneath the skin'.

After *The Duchess of Malfi*, Webster lapsed into mostly second-rate work. His death c.1625 marked the decline of the Elizabethan theatre. The stage was filled with mediocre writers such as Glapthorne, Brome, Markham, Suckling and D'Avenant, the last reputed to be Shakespeare's illegitimate son. Then, in 1642, the Puritans closed the public theatres, and there was darkness.

CHAPTER 5

How to Understand Elizabethan English

The thought of dealing with Shakespeare's work can be quite daunting, and can seem about as accessible as Japanese Noh theatre. Probably misperceptions about Shakespeare's language cause these hang-ups – all those old 'thees' and 'thous' and 'prithees' and 'fol-de-rols' – fol-de-*what*?

Shakespeare's Language

Shakespeare was a poet, and he used words not only to explain the plot but also to create word images, lots of them, to tell us what the characters were really feeling. For example, he writes, 'Now is the winter of our discontent, made glorious summer by this son of York...' (*King Richard III*) to describe the murderous bleakness of the Wars of the Roses – a civil war that went on for decades between two major contenders, the Dukes of Lancaster and York, for the throne of England – as 'winter'. That one word conjures up cold, rain, snow, damp, bleakness, hardship and so on. He then describes the winner of the war at the time of the play's beginning, the Duke of York, as a 'son of York' and his victory a 'glorious summer', using 'summer' to create images of warmth, peace, prosperity etc., that contrast directly with the 'winter' it was about to replace.

If you're going to enjoy Shakespeare, it's important to see the plays or at least listen to audiotapes of them, not just read them on your own. Plays are difficult enough to read at the best of times, and while the poetry of Shakespeare does spring from the pages, it helps to either see them performed or hear them spoken.

And what's really great about Shakespeare is that he does in two lines, with two potent words, what it just took me several sentences to try to explain. Does reading Shakespeare take effort? Yes it does, but like every new accent or language that seems foreign at first, after a while, a certain familiarity allows you to make sense of what is being said.

The Context of Language

We take very much for granted that English is the universal global language, despite the fact that statistically many more people speak Chinese, for example. But have you stopped to think that the English you speak today would be hard for someone living in Shropshire in 1900 to follow? 'After the move, I'm going to the shopping centre to get a new modem for my computer. I'll probably pop into a cybercafé while I'm there and check my e-mail because I'm expecting my travel agent to confirm my flight to New York tonight.'

Language is all about context. And Shakespeare's language has a context you need to be familiar with in order to make sense of what's going on, and why people say and do the things they do in the plays. Good productions of the plays try to address these points by drawing parallels with our own time. That's why Shakespeare is sometimes done in modern dress or set in particular periods of modern history. It's an aid to help us follow what's going on and what's being said.

Shakespeare's English

Many people unfamiliar with the world of William Shakespeare think he wrote and spoke a form of Old English. But Shakespearean English is remarkably close to the language we use today. In fact, he is credited with inventing words and phrases that are now part of our everyday speech, such as laughing stock, hot-blooded, ill-tempered, cold-blooded, puppy dog, eyesore, sea change, salad days, bated breath and bag and baggage, to mention but a handful.

It is true that Shakespeare's syntax is not always the 'subject-verb-object' sentence structure with which we are familiar. And although he was a writer who was very aware of words and their meanings, some of his subtleties of language are difficult for modern audiences to appreciate, because the words have changed meaning. For example, naughty now means badly behaved, but in Shakespeare's time it meant wicked.

Some of the words he used are now archaic, as well. The plays assume some sort of rudimentary knowledge of Elizabethan events and history, and they are filled with references to Renaissance learning: Greek and Roman mythology, astrology, alchemy and the theory of 'humours'.

Elizabethans believed that a person's physical and mental attributes were the result of a balance of four fluids or humours – blood, phlegm, choler and bile. Imbalances in these fluids accounted for mood swings and personality traits (a choleric person, for example, was bad-tempered).

The Evolution of the English Language

The English language evolved from a combination of sources. Before 1066, Britain was invaded and colonized mainly by Angles, Saxons and Jutes from Denmark and Germany, who overran the Celtic-speaking natives, many of whom fled either west to Wales and Ireland or north to Scotland. Anglo-Saxon was a Germanic-sounding language, and perhaps the most important piece written in it was the epic poem *Beowulf*.

When the Norman king, William the Conqueror, defeated Harold at the battle of Hastings in 1066 and made himself king of England, the language underwent a drastic change. While the natives continued to speak Anglo-Saxon, their new lords and masters spoke Norman French. By 1400 a melding of languages had taken place, and thousands of French and Latin words had become absorbed into the Germanic Anglo-Saxon to create a language that is called Middle English.

By Shakespeare's time, thousands of new words were entering the language from the publication of Greek and Latin texts, as well as books in Italian, French and Spanish. Of the approximately 25,000 different words that Shakespeare used in his plays, 2,000 of them were ones he either invented or recorded for the first time.

The major change was one of structure, however. The basis of all modern European romance tongues – French, Italian and Spanish – is Latin. Word order is not very important in Latin (or Anglo-Saxon) because the words take their meaning from the differing endings or inflections they can have, which depend on the work they're supposed to do in a sentence.

Middle English became a language that more closely resembles our own, in terms of sentence structure. The parts of a sentence (subject, verb, object etc.), became more dependent on word order than word form. One of the masterpieces of this period was Geoffrey Chaucer's *The Canterbury Tales*. Two hundred years later, by the time Shakespeare was born, English men and women were speaking Early Modern English. Later Modern English, which is essentially what we speak today, is considered to date from the middle of the 17th century, when the concepts of grammar and spelling were codified and made uniform.

Elizabethan English

Perhaps because English was still in flux, Elizabethans – even the unschooled groundlings – were fascinated with language, and they delighted in puns. In *Romeo and Juliet*, for example, as Mercutio dies he says, 'Ask for me tomorrow, and you shall find me a grave man.' The pun, of course, is a play on grave meaning serious and grave meaning dead. In *King Henry IV, Part II*, the Lord Chief Justice tells off the fat knight Sir John Falstaff, one-time drinking companion of Prince Harry, soon to be Henry V:

> Lord Chief Justice: Your means are very slender, and your waste is great.
>> ('Waste' is a pun on the size of Falstaff's waist, that is, on his being fat. It is also a reference to the fact that he doesn't have much money because he's wasted the rest on drink, women and gambling.)

> Sir John Falstaff: I would it were otherwise; I would my means were greater and my waist slenderer.
>> (Falstaff cleverly turns the wordplay around.)

So what did Elizabethan English sound like? In Shakespeare's day English was not the Received English of the upper and middle classes that we hear now in many plays and films, nor the clipped Cockney accent of the south. Surprisingly, it was probably closer to the accents of northern England, Scotland and Ireland, and some dialects of the rural eastern and southern parts of the United States. The renowned British director Sir Peter Hall has proposed an American Shakespearean theatre company, partly to try to re-create the authenticity of the sound of the language. Language experts say that the inhabitants of Ocracoke Island, part of the Outer Banks of North Carolina, which was originally founded by

Elizabethan sailors and their families, speak the closest to Elizabethan English today.

> As English developed from Middle English to Modern English, it underwent what is called the Great Vowel Shift. The pronunciation of vowels in modern-day continental romance languages (ah/eh/ee/oh/oo) changed to what is now considered the received pronunciation of the English middle and upper classes (eh/ee/eye/oh/yew).

The reason Sir Peter Hall and others want to try to recapture the original pronunciation as much as possible is because the lines sometimes make much more sense when spoken in the original dialect. For instance, if you can imagine an Irish accent speaking the following lines from *Julius Caesar* you would not hear Cassius say, 'Upon what *meat* doth this our Caesar *feed*, that he hath grown so great'. Instead, you might well hear, 'Upon what *mate* doth this our Caesar *fade*...', and now we have a clever play on words (mate, also meaning friend; fade, meaning of lessening importance).

Playing with Words

In Shakespeare's day, the syntax of the language and grammar themselves were still evolving, so some lines need more careful reading than others. Like many Elizabethans, Shakespeare loved to play with words. What's more, because there were no rules as to how to write English yet and Shakespeare felt the need for his lines to have the rhythm of poetry, or to scan, he used a rather stretched-out sentence structure.

New Words, New Meanings

Because of the changes in the structure of language as English developed from Middle English to Modern English, writers were able to invent new uses for words. Shakespeare often used nouns as verbs or adjectives as nouns, for example. But the massive flow of foreign words into the

English language during the 16th century created a multitude of variations for nearly every word. Shakespeare used this expanded vocabulary to make his language both more precise and more evocative.

In *Love's Labour's Lost* Berowne's ingenious comment, 'Light, seeking light, doth light of light beguile', plays upon four different senses of *light* – meaning, in order: intellect, wisdom, eyesight and daylight – so the sentence can be interpreted as reading: wisdom can be as enticing to intellectuals as daylight to a sighted person.

A lot of words have disappeared from use. For example, who says *micher*, meaning a petty thief, or *slubber*, meaning clumsy and messy? In Chaucer's time *nice* meant ignorant or licentious; by Shakespeare's time it meant precise, as in a 'nice distinction', and today it means pleasant.

Shakespearean Style

Shakespeare wrote in blank verse, that is, the lines do not have to rhyme. When they do, it is usually to mark the end of a scene, because there were no curtains. The rhyme itself gave the clue to the audience that they were about to experience a scene change. The plays' language did have a rhythm, however, commonly called an iambic pentameter. This is a technical way of saying that a typical line has five two-syllable units, with the emphasis on the second syllable. It's considered one of the most successful ways to write poetry that has a natural spoken form.

But Shakespeare also wrote in prose, which he often ascribed to the lower classes and the low-born, while his kings spoke verse. However, King Lear speaks in prose as he goes mad (*King Lear*), and *The Merry Wives of Windsor* is mainly in prose.

Shakespeare used a lot of metaphors and similes. Everyone drew on the Bible, using phrases such as 'strong as Samson' or 'wicked as Herod', and comparisons were also made to the widely known Robin Hood and King Arthur stories. Members of the upper-middle class and nobles sprinkled their speech with references to the Greek and Roman classics, such as 'beauteous as Venus' or 'bright as Phoebus Apollo'. Shakespeare also personified inanimate objects, saying that trees blushed or seas were angry.

Elizabethan Pronunciation

Because pronunciation is challenging, it's best to see and hear the plays before you read them, if you can. Perhaps the most obvious sound is that of the rolled *R*, as in *mother*. Think of a drawn-out pirate 'ARRGH'. In general, try to think Irish, or southern United States. The following list of word pronunciations will give you a flavour of Shakespearean language as it was spoken.

Father – the long *a* sounds like *a* in favour: f-ay-th-u-rrr.

Want – the *a* here sounds like the *a* in apple.

Make – the *a* sounds like *mek*.

Head – the *eh* sounds like someone from the deep south of the United States, as in *haid*, or *daid* for dead.

I – pronounced (like a 1950s doo-wop singer) in two vowels, as in the *u* in cup and the *ee* in bee, thus *uh-ee*. This is the quintessential peasant sound. Die becomes 'duh-ee', my becomes 'muh-ee'.

Down – another doo-wop sound, pronounced *uh-oo* with the *oo* as in soon, also as in *abuh-oot* for about.

Mercy – the *ur* sound is pronounced *mayor-cy*.

Neither – pronounced *neigh-ther*.

Lord – drawn out *oo* sound, as in lured.

Cup – a short and rounded *o*, as in coop.

'Thee' and 'thou' were informal pronouns used to anyone who was your equal and intimate. One is the subject, the other the object of the sentence. For example, 'I prithee (a contraction of 'I pray thee') take a sip', and 'thou hast a fair face'.

Elizabethan Vocabulary

It helps to be familiar with some basic vocabulary words when reading or listening to Shakespeare. The following is a list of some of the more common Elizabethan words and their definitions.

Anon – until later

Arise – to stand up or get an erection

Aroint – away

Aside – a speech revealing the character's innermost thoughts, spoken directly to the audience

Aye/yea – yes

Banns – notice of intent to marry

Beef – meat or prostitute

Broadside – a sheet of paper printed on one side, often used for proclamations and ballads

Certes! – certainly!

Cod – fish or male organ (hence a codpiece is a cup that covered the male genitals)

Count – numbers or a pun on female genitalia

Cousin – friend

Dear – significant or expensive

Die – to pass away or have an orgasm

E'en – evening

Enow – enough

Fare-thee-well – goodbye

Fie – a curse

Fond – foolish

Get – to create or bring into existence

Grammarcy/gramercy – thank you

Green – inexperienced, or a colour of virility

Head – army or source

Hell – Hades or female genitalia

Hello! – not a greeting, but an exclamation of surprise

Jade – jewel or prostitute

Marry – a mild curse contracted from 'by the Virgin Mary'

Mayhap/perchance/belike – maybe

Morrow – day

Nay – no

Ne'er – never

Nice – trifling or silly

Oft – often

Poppet – doll or child

Prithee/pray – please

Privy, jakes or ajax – toilet

Rub – to strike against something, or an obstacle

Sad – serious

Soliloquy – a speech, rather like an aside, revealing a character's thoughts

Sonnet – 14-line poem with iambic pentameter construction

Stay – to wait

Still – always

Sweeting – a term of endearment

Ta'en – short form of taken or mistaken for

Tell – to count

Thane – Scottish earl

Thing – object or male genitalia

Verily – very or truly

Wherefore – why

Will – name or sexual desire

CHAPTER 6

Scenes from Elizabethan Life

W hat follows are thumbnail sketches of everyday life in Shakespeare's England that will give you a better sense of what the world was like during his time. Knowing what coins were used, how beggars were treated, and so forth, provides a context in which to appreciate Shakespeare's brilliance in drawing timeless universal truths from what would have been entirely familiar to contemporary audiences.

Servants and Masters

Male servants in a large household were called grooms or serving men. Women were called serving maids or just maids. The term valet or manservant came into use in English in about 1567. In *Romeo and Juliet*, for example, Benvolio refers to Romeo's ever-present servant as 'his man'.

As a noble, it was undignified to fetch and carry for yourself. As a noble's servant, it was undignified to let your master or mistress do their own fetching and carrying. Everyone knew their places in the social order and were comforted by its predictability. Servants tried to take advantage of the social hierarchy. They would use their wits to rise in the world, to create an even better place for their children. A potboy, for example, might aspire to become a butler or steward in a great house.

Servants expected vails (tips) or douceurs (sweeteners) for services rendered. Taking a tip was only a problem if it created a clash of loyalties. A good master was paternalistic but stern. His superior station was God-given, and ideally he maintained it by honorable behaviour, not debate.

Rules of Working in a Great House

This list of 'rules' comes from *A Book of Orders and Rules*, written by Sir Sibbald David Scott in 1595.

A servant must not be absent from morning or evening meals or prayers lest he be fined two pence for each time.

Any man waiting table without a trencher [a small tray] in his hand, except for good excuse, will be fined one penny.

For each oath, a servant will be fined a penny.

Any man provoking another to strike or striking another will be liable to dismissal.

For a dirty shirt on Sunday or a missing button, the fine will be sixpence.

After 8:00 a.m. no bed must be found unmade and no fireplace or candle box left uncleaned, or the fine will be one penny.

The hall must be cleaned in an hour.

The whole house must be swept and dusted each Friday.

Any man leaving a door open that he found shut will be fined one
penny unless he can show good cause.

Patronage

As we've seen previously, young men sought patrons for their advancement.
Nobles drew gentlemen like honey attracts flies, creating a feudal
relationship based on personal loyalty, gifts and favours. Some of the gentry
put their sons into great houses for their education and advancement.

The lord also maintained retainers or personal attendants, some of
whom were armed and dangerous – bodyguards by any other name. The
noble put them in his livery and gave them nominal positions in the
household, such as gentleman or yeoman usher.

A noblewoman drew her cortège from relatives and the daughters of the
gentry. Her gentlewomen joined her in sewing, minding the children,
dispensing charity in the neighbourhood and taking charge of her clothing
and jewellery. She would also help unmarried girls of good families find
suitable husbands.

Military Life

There was no standing army in England until the restoration of Charles II
in 1660, so armies had to be raised when needed from the general
population. When necessary, a recruiting officer would travel from town to
town, enticing men to enlist and 'take the Queen's shilling'. The recruiting
officer was responsible for making sure that recruits were fit for duty, and
were not only sons (for reasons of inheritance) so that small businesses
and farms could keep working. Sometimes he earned a bounty for every
man he enlisted.

New soldiers received their first payment immediately – the Queen's
shilling, which was sometimes sunk at the bottom of a tankard of ale.
Once the recruit drank the ale, he was committed to serving and received
a uniform (the cost of which was usually deducted from his pay), took an

oath to the Queen, and then with little training went off to fight overseas. Life expectancy was short. Lord Mountjoy, Elizabeth's General in Ireland in 1601, commented that, 'it has ever been seen that more than three parts of the four of these [men] do never return'.

Foreigners and Travel

During Elizabeth's reign, partly because of the many armed skirmishes that were taking place in Europe, England became wary of foreigners. As a result, unless they were in the armed forces, young people were discouraged from going abroad, although only the wealthy could really afford to travel anyway. A poor person worked as a servant or on the land, or became a bandit or beggar.

Yet, ironically, during the last 20 years of Elizabeth's reign in particular, the number of soldiers engaged in military service meant that more Englishmen travelled overseas than ever before.

Italy, especially, was off-limits – because the Pope, a powerful political figure at this time, lived there, and because Catholicism was considered to be heretically infectious. Young men could lose their inheritance and social standing, and come under serious official scrutiny, just for travelling to Italy.

Selected for Service

When recruits were urgently needed, however, men were conscripted, or pressed, often against their will. In *King Henry IV, Part I*, Falstaff describes the tricks he used to get extra money from those he pressed:

> I press me none but good householders, yeomen's sons, inquire me out contracted bachelors, such as had been asked twice of the banns – such a commodity of warm slaves as had as lief hear the devil as a dru ... and they have bought out their services.

In other words, he pressed only those who were willing to bribe him to let them go, ending up with the leftovers, a group of such 'scarecrows' that he was ashamed to be seen with them.

All men between the ages of 16 and 60 were eligible to serve and had to appear at musters in town squares, on village greens and at other places, where unlucky individuals would be selected for service. Moreover, most of these men were used as 'food for powder' [cannon fodder], according to Falstaff (*King Henry IV, Part I*). Only about 20 per cent of the army was trained. The rest were simply given equipment and had to learn how to be a soldier while in the field.

A soldier's rank often dictated whether or not he would live or die. The untrained common soldier often ended up as cannon fodder because the better-trained, more professional army was considered too valuable to send to a possible death overseas, and was held back for the defence of England.

The Nature of Warfare

The medieval feudal system was breaking down, and the development of gunpowder ushered in a new era of warfare. The maces and lances of knights in armour, and the longbows and crossbows of archers, gave way to the more accurate cannons and mortars and ranks of soldiers wielding fuse-lit muskets and small arms. This changed the nature of warfare.

Many experienced soldiers, however, were reluctant to give up their bows, partly because the technology of gunpowder weaponry was still in its infancy. Guns often exploded after being fired a few times because of poor metal working, and the stress and heat of continued, compressed explosions inside the breech. For good reason, many soldiers took to turning away their heads while firing, thus missing their targets. It was much easier to train musketeers than bowmen, although a bow could be more accurate in the hands of an expert.

Country Life

In Shakespeare's day, England was still very much an agrarian society. The comic image in *Monty Python and the Holy Grail* of peasants spending their days grubbing about in the mud and dung heaps is an exaggeration of what it was like to be poor in Elizabethan times, but it makes a point worth remembering. It was a hard life. People lived off land they didn't own and were considered virtual slaves by the wealthy landowners they rented their property from.

Peasants were totally at the mercy of the whims of their betters. They knew their place in the social order and were grateful for what they had. Peasants were given a scrawny piece of land on which to build their one- or two-room shacks and to scratch out a subsistence level of living from their own crops and animals.

In exchange for having a place of his own, a peasant worked on the owner's land at least three days a week. An overseer made sure the peasant and his family did everything required. The rest of the time, the peasant worked on his own land, banding together with other families to cope with big jobs such as bringing in the harvest and haymaking. Women and children helped, though they often worked indoors cooking, cleaning and taking care of babies.

At harvest time the owner received a portion of the peasant's crops. If the crops failed, everyone starved. If the peasant needed to grind his grain, he did it at the owner's mill, leaving behind a portion for the owner. If he needed to bake his bread, he could use the owner's ovens if he left behind a loaf of bread or two.

Peasants, like Bottom and his companions in *A Midsummer Night's Dream*, were at the bottom of the social ladder. They could not marry or travel without the landlord's permission, and were expected to return home if they did travel. Of course they could leave the estate for good whenever they wanted, but how could they make a living without land? Besides, travel was dangerous. There were few roads, particularly through the forests that still covered much of the countryside, and virtually no organized police force of any description, so if a thief stole their possessions or attacked them, the chances are that nobody would help.

Except for Sundays and Holy Days, peasants worked long and hard in the fields, regardless of the weather. A lot of families didn't have enough food to feed themselves, so it shouldn't be a surprise to learn that on average peasants lived only into their thirties. Diseases were many, and medicine was rudimentary and expensive. Babies and children often died.

Peasants had only two legitimate ways to gain their independence: to save enough money to buy their own piece of land, or to marry a free person, but only with the landowner's permission – and there was no guarantee that he would give it.

Town Life

In exchange for an annual tax, townspeople received a royal charter that allowed them to govern themselves. Once chartered, they were able to make their own laws, form trade guilds and raise taxes. In most towns the people elected a mayor or bailiff and a local council to govern them.

The streets of the town, which were often noisy, chaotic places during the day, were filled with bustle and business. Tradesmen cried their wares at markets as they wandered through the streets. Here are some examples of town life, recorded in *Street Cries* by Orlando Gibbons:

'Buy any ink, will you buy any pens, very fine writing ink, will you buy any ink?'

'I ha' ripe peascods, ripe. Ripe damsons, fine ripe damsons. Hard garlic, hard. Fine potatoes, fine.'

'What is't ye lack? Fine wrought shirts or smocks. Perfumed waistcoats, fine bone lace or edgings, sweet gloves, silk garters, very fine silk garters, fine combs or glasses. Old doublets, ha'ye any old doublets?'

'Ha' ye any corns on your feet or toes? Will ye buy any starch for a clear complexion, mistress?'

'Ha' ye any rats or mice to kill?'

Merchants and Craftsmen

The growing middle class was composed of merchants and craftsmen who were freemen and generally had a more comfortable life than country peasants. Merchants tended to be either traders or factory owners (i.e. craftsmen). Merchants traded with other merchants both at home and abroad, and often owned their own ships. Many hired mercenary soldiers to protect the goods that were being shipped.

It was particularly important that the craftsmen doused any fires they used during the day, because houses were made from wood and plaster and were so packed together in narrow streets that if a house caught fire it was almost guaranteed that large parts of the town would burn, too.

Craftsmen deliberately set up shop in towns so that they could take advantage of the population's needs. Their houses were usually fair-sized, sometimes of two to three storeys, and craftsmen often worked at windows that opened out onto the street, giving them the chance to show off their skills to passers-by, as well as to get the best light to work by. Crafts included confectioner, blacksmith, shoemaker, buttonmaker, saddler, porter, boxmaker and soap-boiler.

Markets were held once or twice a week in the town square. They were always crowded, busy, noisy, smelly and dirty, with people shouting, pushing and generally trying to make money among the wooden stalls and carts displaying wares. At sunset, town bells tolled a curfew, and everyone finished their business and went home.

Entertainment

There was little in the way of entertainment besides drinking in pubs and alehouses and gambling, often at animal-baiting or cockfights, or some other kind of blood sport. Town fairs were held once or twice a year and were filled with contests, sports and games. Guilds sometimes staged plays; peasants needed their master's permission to attend.

Merchants and craftsmen came from far and wide to sell their goods at these fairs. Jugglers, dancers, acrobats and minstrels would stroll through the crowds or set up a booth somewhere. The minstrels, in particular, wandered from town to town strumming a cittern, lute or viol, singing ballads and telling stories such as the legend of Robin Hood, the outlaw of Sherwood Forest.

Towns also competed with each other on Sunday afternoons with games such as bladder ball (an early form of football), rounders, archery, wrestling and so forth. Nobles played real tennis (an indoor sport) or battledore and shuttlecock (badminton), as well as going in for fencing and horse riding.

Guilds

Rather like the peasants during harvest in the countryside, town merchants and craftsmen decided they could improve their lot by working together rather than separately. They started banding together, forming clubs, or unions, called guilds. If you were a member of a guild you were able to vote for the head of the guild, who would serve a limited term of office. Guilds were important in local economies, maintaining product quality and industry standards. They also formed the basis of political power and, potentially, a guild leader had a lot of power that could be abused.

tips

Apprentices were treated strictly, and were punished if they stepped out of line. At a 1561 Christmas celebration, for example, a young apprentice was found strutting about in the clothes of 'his betters' (i.e. someone of a higher social standing) and was fined for celebrating in ruffs and a silk hat.

Guilds were divided into hierarchies, with masters at the top, journeymen in the middle and apprentices at the bottom. A boy in his early teens would often be apprenticed to a master, who would be paid by the boy's family to care for him and educate him in his trade.

After seven or eight years the young man would rise to the rank of journeyman and receive a wage. After a journeyman acquired sufficient experience, he would create a 'masterpiece' that was judged by other masters within his guild. If the piece won their approval, he joined the ranks of the Guild Masters.

Few guilds included women, although there was a guild of laundresses. In London, a law called the Widow's Law stated that if a guild member died, his widow could take his place as long as she employed a journeyman to do her husband's work and she split the profits with him.

The Urban Poor

The number of urban poor had been increasing before Elizabeth's reign, and kept increasing during it. The trend toward the enclosure or private ownership of what was previously considered common farm land forced many people to turn to begging for their livelihood.

By Shakespeare's time, a large, shifting population of landless unemployed men and women lived in London. 'Masterless men' threatened the stability of society. They had no place in the social order, and were the most likely to commit crimes to stay alive. Soldiers fortunate enough to return home from fighting overseas, but unlucky enough to be injured and unable to work, invariably became beggars on crutches.

The rural poor consisted mainly of widows and children who did not have the means to support themselves, and landless labourers, often unemployed in the winter once the harvests were done. Passing vagrants were likely to be ignored, or persecuted for fear that they might squander the charity of the community or commit crime.

By the last decade of Elizabeth's reign the booming English economy was in decline, and crime and vagrancy worsened. Poor harvests, outbreaks of the plague and other ills caused agricultural prices to rise while wages plummeted. Nearly 80 per cent of the English population fell below the subsistence level. Church and government aid was meagre. Laws criminalized poverty, and the poor were punished brutally for the often desperate acts they committed to stay alive.

In the towns, the poor were considered a public nuisance, a potential threat to public welfare and a burden on the greater community. Local authorities often tried to curb the practice of begging and discouraged the establishment of tenements – houses divided into many small suites to be rented to poor individuals or families.

Coins and Money

The values of the many different types of coins changed depending on the value of the metal used to make them. When the coinage was 'debased', that is, when the amount of gold or silver in the coin was reduced, the value of the coin itself was reduced.

Halfpennies (pronounced hay-pennies) and farthings were made of brass, lead and occasionally even leather. Some merchants issued tokens that were redeemable as payment for goods and services by themselves and other merchants, though certainly not by all.

Value of the Coins

The following are some Elizabethan denominations with very rough current decimal equivalents. The translation of money values is a tricky subject, and while we can generalize that a penny was close to 60–65p today, in truth it varied dramatically. At different times it could be worth only 30p or as much as £3.50 or more, depending on the variations of precious metals used to cast the coin (combinations of either brass, copper, silver or gold), economic ups and downs, and a proportional value defined by the cost of goods and services against wages earned.

Monetary Unit	Modern equivalent
Farthing	25p
Halfpenny piece	50p
Three-farthing piece	75p
Penny	£1
Half groat	£2
Threepenny piece	£3
Groat	£4
Sixpence	£6
Shilling	£12
Half-crown	£30
Crown	£60
Angel	£80–100
Noble	£80–120
Royal	£120–200
£1	£250
Sovereign	£250

The Cost of Living

A soldier's shopping list (based on a Tudor soldier's food allowance):

0.33kg (1lb 8oz) wheat bread: 1 penny
3l (2/3gal) beer: 1 penny
0.9kg (2lb) beef or mutton (cod or herring on Fridays): 2 pence
0.22kg (8oz) butter: 1½ pence
0.45kg (1lb) cheese: 1½ pence
Total: 7 pence
(Note the lack of vegetables and fruit.)

Average wages:

Skilled journeymen could earn sixpence a day (sometimes as much as a shilling), with food and drink included.
Actors were paid a shilling a day, but it is unlikely that they received food.
Apprentices received food, drink and lodging.

Farm workers got about threepence a day; women were paid less and often supplemented their earnings by spinning thread.

Permanent servants were paid annually, with board and food included – often no more than six shillings a year, or just over a penny a week.

The Cost of the Theatre

The average fees for attendance at a public theatre were:

The lords' room: 1 shilling (12 pence)
The gentlemen's rooms: sixpence
The galleries: two pence
The pit (for the groundlings): one penny

The cheapest seats in the private theatres were usually sixpence, thus effectively excluding all but relatively wealthy patrons.

Impresario Philip Henslowe paid £3–5 for a play; on a good day his gross gate for a performance of a new play would be over £3. On 28 November 1595 he took in £4/6s for the first performance of *The Famous Victories of King Henry V.*

Outsiders

Unfortunately, Shakespeare's time wasn't lacking prejudice and injustice. Some ethnic and religious groups were mistreated due to their minority status. The following sections give a brief description of two such groups – Jews and blacks – who were portrayed in Shakespeare's plays.

Jews

In 1290, under Edward IV, the Jews in England were deported en masse to France. It was not until 1656, in Oliver Cromwell's Commonwealth, that Jews were again allowed to establish communities in England.

In 1593, Dr Rodrigo Lopez, a convert from Judaism and physician to Queen Elizabeth, was condemned to death for treason. Neither Elizabeth nor Robert Cecil, Secretary of the Privy Council, believed that Lopez was guilty, and he died proclaiming his innocence. However, the trial instigated a lot of anti-Semitism. Against this backdrop, Christopher Marlowe wrote *The Jew of Malta*. Interestingly, Marlowe's villainous Jew was even treated badly by the Christians in Malta – as was Shakespeare's Shylock in *The Merchant of Venice*.

Shylock was a challenging character for Elizabethans. Although he is the villain, he has some wonderful speeches about the way that he is mistreated, including one of the great statements that define humanity:

> Hath not a Jew eyes?
> Hath not a Jew hands, organs, dimensions, senses,
> affections, passions; fed with the same food, hurt with
> the same weapons, subject to the same diseases, healed
> by the same means, warmed and cooled by the same
> winter and summer as a Christian is? If you prick us
> do we not bleed? If you tickle us do we not laugh? If
> you poison us do we not die?

Amsterdam and Venice, for example, flourished as centres of commerce, partly because they tolerated large, open communities of practising Jews. Elsewhere in Europe, Jews were forced to pretend they had converted to Christianity to avoid persecution and deportation. The Jews in London were forced to worship in secret and attended Christian churches.

Henry VIII passed a law allowing interest rates of up to 10 per cent, but his son Edward VI repealed it. (More accurately, it was repealed by one of his regents, because Edward was too young to make decisions for most of his short life.)

Because Jews were banned from almost all kinds of work, they became moneylenders by default. But moneylending was a complicated profession. For centuries, usury (lending money and charging interest) had been illegal and considered contrary to the law of God. But the rise of capitalism made banning the practice impractical.

Blacks

Othello is called a Moor, which suggests someone of Arab descent. Yet his physical description is that of a black man from central Africa, rather than an Arab. (Rodrigo describes Othello as having 'thick lips', for example.) Black people were already living in London during Elizabeth's reign. Ships carrying black slaves passed through London, and many blacks stayed, working as 'exotic' servants or in the brothels that sat cheek by jowl with the theatres and gambling and baiting arenas. As foreigners, they were regarded with a mixture of curiosity and suspicion.

To be black was not just to be foreign, but also something of an oddity. There were too few blacks in London for prejudice in the modern sense, but the colour black was traditionally associated with ugliness, savagery and sin. (Caliban in *The Tempest* is a classic example.)

It is remarkable that Shakespeare chose to make Othello, a black man, the protagonist of one of his great tragedies. Regardless of whether or not Othello is seen as noble or foolish, the play treats him sympathetically and explores the concept of how an outsider can be ill treated and demonized by society for no good reason.

CHAPTER 7

The Sonnets and Poems

One of the defining aspects of great writers is that they are also great philosophers, which is certainly true of Shakespeare. Four hundred years ago he was able to express profound thoughts and feelings in words of great beauty and power that still have meaning for us today.

Becoming a Poet

Shakespeare's plays are as great as they are because, beyond his love of language, his humour and his technical skills as a dramatist, Shakespeare was a poet. He was able to capture the speech of common men and the language of philosophers and distil it into his work to create some of the finest poetry that has ever been written in the English language.

The meter of his plays used the unrhymed iambic pentameter called blank verse, which originated in Italy. English poets embraced it during the reign of Henry VIII. The University Wits, especially Christopher Marlowe, developed it into a dramatic verse form that Shakespeare perfected. In the company of John Milton, Shakespeare made it the greatest metre in English.

Shakespeare was established as a playwright and actor in London by 1592, but that year, the bubonic plague broke out again and the authorities in London closed all the theatres because of the risk of infection spreading among members of audiences. (A certain number of plague deaths in a given week automatically closed them.) Left without an income in London, Shakespeare had to consider what to do while the theatres were empty.

Poetry was considered far superior to mere public entertainment, even if that did happen to also be in verse. The writing of what was thought of as poetry proper was considered the highest form of literature. Edmund Spenser's unfinished allegorical poem, *The Faerie Queene*, which was being published throughout the 1590s, was a prime example.

It's clear that Shakespeare was interested in gaining social prestige, as the purchases of property in Stratford tell us. What's more, in 1596 he became a gentleman when his father, John, after various reverses (probably due to his being a Roman Catholic), was finally granted a coat of arms.

The profession of poet, though usually by no means as lucrative as that of playwright, could come close with some luck. If the poet was not a nobleman, then he (only a very few women were poets) required the patronage of a nobleman and all the gifts that went with it. Edmund Spenser, for example, worked hard to gain the favour of Queen Elizabeth.

Not only was non-dramatic poetry considered a higher form of art, it also attracted social prestige. Being a playwright, just of itself, certainly did not. Most playwrights (Jonson, Chapman, Marston, Marlowe, but never, it seems, Shakespeare) spent periods in prison for annoying the authorities, and the young Christopher Marlowe, the boldest, most gifted and most recklessly subversive of them all, was stabbed to death in an alehouse brawl in 1593.

In an attempt to bridge the gap in his sudden loss of income, and undoubtedly to get himself recognized as a legitimate poet, Shakespeare published a major lyric work, *Venus and Adonis*, in 1593. It had a somewhat obsequious dedication to Henry Wriothesley, Earl of Southampton and Baron of Titchfield (1573–1624) who was just 19 years old at the time, but already a wealthy and influential patron of the arts. The poem described itself as 'the first heir of my invention' while promising 'some graver labour' to come.

Rising to Fame

Venus and Adonis, a funny and erotic narrative poem loosely based on Ovid's *Metamorphoses*, was published by Richard Field, a Stratford neighbour of Shakespeare and most probably a childhood friend, who was fast becoming one of London's leading bookseller/publishers.

A far more serious narrative poem, *The Rape of Lucrece*, published in May 1594, was based on an ancient legend recounted by the Roman poets Fasti and Livy, among others. This poem was also dedicated to the Earl of Southampton, but the formal tone of the first poem's dedication was replaced by a certain warm familiarity.

One of the curious facts of Shakespeare's life is that in his day he was famous, not as the creator of Lear, Othello, Prospero or Hamlet, but as the playwright of *Titus Andronicus* and the author of *Venus and Adonis*. The poem was reprinted at least nine times during his lifetime and was the model for many imitators.

Both *Venus and Adonis* and *The Rape of Lucrece* are full of gorgeous imagery and pagan spirit and very obviously the work of an intense young man. The fame that these two poems brought Shakespeare no doubt substantially raised his profile as a serious writer and, when the theatres reopened in 1594, helped the 30-year-old actor/playwright join Richard Burbage's acting company, the Lord Chamberlain's Men.

There is a story that the Earl of Southampton rewarded Shakespeare for his poetic labours with £1,000, a huge sum of money in those days. The biographer A. L. Rowse (*Shakespeare the Man*) is one of the few scholars who believes this story. Others seem to think it a bit fanciful.

Exactly what Shakespeare felt about a life in the theatre is pure conjecture of course, and yet there is some evidence that his ambition was to be known as a poet, not a dramatist. Sonnet 111 says:

> O for my sake doe you wish fortune chide,
> The guiltie goddesse of my harmfull deeds,
> That did not better for my life provide,
> Then publick means which publick manners breeds.
> Thence comes it that my name receives a brand,
> And almost thence my nature is subdu'd
> To what it works in, like the Dyer's hand.

Scholars generally agree that Shakespeare was being both sarcastic and ironic. But most scholars also agree that 'harmful deeds' refers to his success in the theatre, and the reference to his name receiving a 'brand' (in the sense we would talk about a brand name today) because of his theatrical associations is unmistakable. The American scholar O. J. Campbell (*A Shakespeare Encyclopaedia*) said there was 'little doubt for which achievement he wished to be remembered: the preservation of the plays is owed to the efforts of others [meaning the people who published the First Folio], the [two early narrative] poems Shakespeare seems to have seen through the press himself.'

Venus and Adonis

In short, *Venus and Adonis* describes the unrequited infatuation of Venus, the Roman goddess of love and beauty, for Adonis, a somewhat self-absorbed golden boy. All he wants to do is get on with his hunt, but Venus pursues him regardless. She pulls him off his horse, kisses him all over, and aggressively chases him up hill and down dale until the hunter has become the prey. She makes it very clear that she wants him, although he is not interested. 'No, lady, no; my heart longs not to groan,/But soundly sleeps while now it sleeps alone' he says. He returns to his hunt and is killed by a wild boar. In her grief, Venus puts a curse on love for all eternity:

> Sorrow on love hereafter shall attend.
> It shall be waited on with jealousy,
> Find sweet beginning, but unsavoury end...
> The strongest body shall it make most weak,
> Strike the wise dumb, and teach the fool to speak...
> It shall be raging-mad, and silly-mild;
> Make the young old, the old become a child.
> It shall suspect where is no cause of fear;
> It shall not fear where it should most mistrust...
> It shall be cause of war and dire events,
> And set dissension 'twixt the son and sire...
> Sith in his prime death doth my love destroy,
> They that love best their loves shall not enjoy.

She turns Adonis into a purple and white flower and vows to wear this nosegay day and night.

Are any of Shakespeare's poems especially famous?
Perhaps one sonnet is more famous than the other 154 because of the sheer number of times its lines have been quoted. Sonnet 18 begins, 'Shall I compare thee to a summer's day?/Thou art more lovely and more temperate:/Rough winds do shake the darling buds of May,/And Summer's lease hath all too short a date...'

The Rape of Lucrece

The Rape of Lucrece is more serious. It tells the story of Lucretia, an aristocratic Roman matron who is raped by Tarquin, the son of the Roman king. He steals into her bedroom determined to have his way with her, and the first half of the poem is told from his point of view as she begs to be spared. Nothing moves him. He tells her:

> This night I must enjoy thee.
> If thou deny, then force must work my way
> For in thy bed I purpose to destroy thee.

The last half of the poem is told from her point of view, and focuses on the terrible experience she has just endured. Despite her distress she proclaims 'I am the mistress of my fate', and decides to tell everyone what has happened to her before she kills herself. She tells her husband, father and the Roman lords what has been done to her and demands vengeance. Then she stabs herself in the heart to allow her soul to escape, and her bloody corpse is paraded through the streets of Rome. Tarquin is banished; and, according to legend, the political fallout of the rape of Lucretia ended the rule by kings and led to the establishment of the Roman Republic.

Lesser-known Poems

In 1599 a volume of poetry entitled *The Passionate Pilgrim* was published and attributed to Shakespeare. However, only five of the poems are definitely considered his, two appearing in other versions in the sonnets and three in *Love's Labour's Lost*. A love elegy, *The Phoenix and the Turtle*, was published in 1601, though pretty much ignored, as was *A Lover's Complaint*, which was published along with the sonnets in 1609 to fill out the pages of the volume.

A Lover's Complaint is a monologue delivered to an old shepherd by a distraught young woman who has been betrayed by her lover. He was handsome and intelligent, but she realized by the number of illegitimate children he fathered that he was not the marrying kind. She should have known better, but she let him have his way with her anyway, and he dropped her for someone else soon after.

In the 1980s and 1990s many Elizabethan scholars concluded that *A Funeral Elegy,* a poem published in 1612 and signed 'W.S.', exhibits many Shakespearean characteristics of style, although it has yet to be included in the canon.

The enigmatic lyric *The Phoenix and the Turtle* (published in *Love's Martyr,* 1601) leaves many scholars bewildered. Is it a joke, obscene or deadly serious? What is the 'bird of loudest lay'? There has been little agreement on, and relatively little commentary about it.

The Sonnets

Shakespeare's sonnets were first published in 1609, but there is no clear evidence of when they were written. Scholars generally date them from 1594 to about 1599 (some fix on 1597). In *Palladis Tamia* (1598) Francis Meres mentions that 'honytongued Shakespeare, witnes his *Venus and Adonis,* his *Lucrece,* his sugred Sonnets among his private frinds.'

The sonnet is a formal rhyme scheme of 14 lines where each line is usually in iambic pentameter (meaning each line has ten syllables), denoting different thoughts, moods or emotions, sometimes summed up in the last lines of the poem. The two main forms of the sonnet are the Petrarchan (Italian) and the Shakespearean (English).

The Italian Sonnet

While the Italians had been using the form for almost 200 years prior to Shakespeare's time, Sir Thomas Wyatt and Henry Howard, Earl of Surrey, were among the first to introduce the sonnet into England. William Shakespeare's first few years in London were spent writing in the Italian style.

There's no easy way to explain this, but here goes: the Italian sonnet form has an eight-line stanza (or octave) followed by a six-line stanza (or sestet). The octave has two quatrains, rhyming ABBA, ABBA, but avoiding a couplet. The first quatrain gives the theme, and the second develops it. The sestet is built on two or three different rhymes; the first three lines reflect on the theme, and the last three lines bring the whole poem to an end. Got that?

The English Sonnet

The English sonnet differs from the Italian in that it is divided into three quatrains, each rhymed differently, with an independently rhymed couplet at the end. The rhyme scheme of the English sonnet is ABAB, CDCD, EFEF, GG. Each quatrain takes a different approach to the idea or develops a different image to express the theme. Except for a few early poems, all of Shakespeare's sonnets were in this form.

Are these rhyme schemes confusing? Don't worry about them unless you're going to study the theory seriously. It's easy enough to enjoy the sonnets as they are, without having to delve into the technicalities.

Personal Poetry

Sonnets were personal poetry, usually circulated among one's friends and close acquaintances. It was thought bad form to publish sonnets, and undesirable to write them for the purpose of being published. They were private thoughts for a select few. William Wordsworth wrote, 'With this key [the sonnet form], Shakespeare unlocked his heart.'

Because there were no copyright laws in 16th-century England, a printer named Thomas Thorpe was able to obtain copies of the sonnets and publish them without Shakespeare's knowledge or consent, although it is also suggested that given a *fait accompli*, Shakespeare may have decided to work with Thorpe.

Are the Sonnets Autobiographical?

Shakespeare wrote 154 sonnets. As not much is known about his private life, scholars have searched his plays, and the sonnets in particular, for hints, without much success. They have attracted more attention than anything else he wrote except *Hamlet*. As poetry alone, they are superb. However, people are just as interested in them because they may tell a story.

 Some scholars feel the sonnets are literary exercises without a personal theme. A middle view is that they explore personal relations in friendship and in love, and rehearse themes later dramatized in the plays. It's also not known if the order of the sonnets is what Shakespeare intended, although most scholars see little reason to question it.

The story is hinted at, rather than told, and concerns the poet's feelings toward a young nobleman who wronged him by stealing the affections of a sweetheart and by transferring his friendship to another poet. (Some think it might have been Kit Marlowe, though that is unlikely, given the dates.) In the end the young nobleman is forgiven. Critics and scholars disagree among themselves about whether the sonnets are autobiographical.

The first 126 sonnets are addressed to a man with the initials W. H. Scholars conjecture that W. H. may be the inverted initials of Henry Wriothesley, third Earl of Southampton, to whom Shakespeare had dedicated his earlier poems, or they may stand for William Herbert, Earl of Pembroke, or for someone else entirely.

The remaining poems are addressed to the so-called Dark Lady of the Sonnets, since it is made clear that she is dark in hair and complexion. Guesses have been made as to who she might be. Some think it was Mary Fitton, a maid of honour at court and mistress of William Herbert. A. L. Rowse believed her to be another poet, Aemelia Lanyer. Neither supposition has enough evidence to prove it.

Recurring Themes

Only by analysing the entire set of sonnets, some critics say, is it possible to fathom Shakespeare's intent. For example, a sonnet with a certain meaning may be followed immediately by a sonnet conveying the opposite message. The first cannot be discussed without discussing the second because the contradiction defines the nature of its meaning.

The sonnets build on, cancel out and are formed by each other. The meanings of the sonnets are all relative, but in general they are marked by the recurring themes of beauty, youthful beauty ravaged by time, and the ability of love and art to transcend time and even death.

In the first 27 sonnets, Shakespeare proposes one method to outwit the passage of time. He urges the young man to have children so that his beauty will be preserved in posterity and therefore time will not have won the battle. The first two lines of the first sonnet present this theme:

> From fairest creatures we desire increase,
> That thereby beauty's rose might never die.

In Sonnet 11, Shakespeare tells the young man that when he grows old he will be young in his children and that:

> Herein lives wisdom, beauty and increase;
> Without this, folly, age and cold decay.

The poet goes on to explain to the young man that nature has given him a gift of beauty so that he may reproduce it. The couplet sums it up:

> She [mother nature] carved thee for her seal, and meant thereby
> Thou shouldst print more, not let that copy die.

Shakespeare's suggestions to the young man sometimes turn into accusations that he is hoarding the beauty which he was lent, and therefore abusing the lease. After Sonnet 17, when it becomes apparent the young man is unwilling to marry, Shakespeare presents another way in which to wage war against time.

He says that his poetry will always exist and be read and that through his poetry his love will be forever alive. In Sonnet 15, Shakespeare writes in the last four lines:

Where wasteful time debateth with decay
To change your [the young man's] day of youth into sullied night;
And all in war with time for love of you,
As he [time] takes from you, I engraft you new.

Homosexuality or Platonic Love?

The rest of the sonnets discuss aspects of the love between Shakespeare and the young man, and the poet and his mistress. They describe a number of circumstances in the poet's relationship with these people. The final opponent of time is presented in Sonnet 116:

Love is not love
Which alters when it alteration finds,
Or bends with the remover to remove.
O no, it is an ever fixed mark
That looks on tempests and is never shaken;
It is the star to every wand'ring barque,
Whose worth's unknown although his height be taken.
Love's not time's fool, though rosy lips and cheeks
Within his bending sickle's compass come;
Love alters not with his brief hours and weeks,
But bears it out even to the edge of doom.

Some scholars suggest that the sonnets betray homosexuality between Shakespeare and another. (The Elizabethans made a distinction between homosexual love and sodomy, which was against the law.) While it may or may not be true, such arguments don't really take into account the concept of platonic love that was prevalent in the Renaissance.

Hallet Smith, writing in *The Riverside Shakespeare*, commented that, 'the attitude of the poet toward the friend [the handsome young man] is one of love and admiration, deference and possessiveness, but it is not at all a sexual passion. Sonnet 20 makes quite clear the difference between the platonic love of a man for a man, more often expressed in the 16th century than the 20th, and any kind of homosexual attachment.'

 William Shakespeare was the first writer to be commemorated at Westminster Abbey's Poet's Corner, where there is still a bust of him over a door.

Regardless of the uncertainty about the who, where, when and why, when it comes to Shakespeare, scholars agree that several of these poems are among the most perfect ever written.

CHAPTER 8

An Introduction to the Plays

Since his death, Shakespeare's plays have been performed almost continually, in English and in other languages, and he is quoted more than any other single author. The plays have been constantly examined by critics trying to explain their timeless appeal, with each criticism a reflection of the era that the critic lived in.

Shakespeare and Elizabethan Theatre

Critics have sometimes faulted Shakespeare's inconsistency in holding to any particular philosophy, religion or ideology. For example, *A Midsummer Night's Dream* includes a burlesque of the kind of tragic love that he treats idealistically in *Romeo and Juliet* and somewhat more cynically in *Troilus and Cressida*.

The strength of Shakespeare's plays lies in the wealth of complex characters and their eloquent, vivid and lyrical speech. Shakespeare's characters are neither all good nor all bad, and it's their flawed, inconsistent nature that makes them so memorable. Hamlet fascinates us because of his ambivalence over whether or not to avenge his father's death, and our uncertainty over how mad he really is. As well as being genial, openhearted and witty, Falstaff is also boisterous and cowardly, but is ultimately moving.

One thing about the Elizabethan theatre worth remembering is that it was a much more intimate experience than going to the theatre nowadays. While the costumes were lavishly rich and colourful, the Elizabethan stage was bare, except for a couple of props, and relied heavily on the actors' ability to connect with the audience.

The limited use of settings and props made it easy to take a play on tour. But more importantly, it allowed the audience to focus on the play, not its trappings, and brought the actors in closer contact with the audience than a modern proscenium stage often does. An Elizabethan player would be almost able to touch the nearest of the spectators, whether it was from the apron that thrust into the audience, or because the play was performed in the cleared courtyard of an inn or in a great hall in a Tudor mansion, with the chairs and heavy wooden dining table pushed to one side to make room. The actor played almost from the audience, not just to it from above. Today, this effect can be achieved to an extent by staging plays in the round, that is, with the audience sitting 360° around the action of the play, not just viewing it from in front of a stage.

The Four Time Periods

Shakespeare's plays can be broadly divided into four time periods:

1. Pre-1594 (*King Richard III*, *The Comedy of Errors*, etc.)
2. 1594–1600 (*King Henry V*, *A Midsummer Night's Dream*, etc.)
3. 1600–08 (*Macbeth*, *King Lear*, etc.)
4. Post-1608 (*Cymbeline*, *The Tempest*, etc.)

The first period (pre-1594) has its roots in Greek, Roman and medieval drama – the plays show a certain obviousness, leaning towards cliché. It's possible that Shakespeare was influenced at this point by Christopher Marlowe, whose writing was gaining recognition as Shakespeare's playwriting career began.

The second period (1594–1600) shows a clearly maturing author, and the plays are less laboured and predictable. The histories of this period portray royalty in human terms rather than as ciphers to move along a plot, and he experiments with blending comedy and tragedy, considered a trademark of Shakespeare that would eventually become a stylistic signature.

The third period (1600–08) includes the great tragedies. At this point he wrote the plays that would earn him his place in history. Lear, Hamlet, Macbeth and Othello are classic tragic Greek theatre characters in the best dramatic sense. The comedies, meanwhile, are never less than moody and ambiguous.

Scholars still debate whether these last plays show Shakespeare writing in a form of dramatic shorthand, or whether the plays reflect an evolving theatrical trend from Elizabethan tastes to Jacobean ones as James I's reign took hold.

The last period is one of cynical plays and symbolism. At the end of his career and facing middle age, Shakespeare seemed preoccupied with stories of redemption. The plays show Shakespeare at his most symbolic.

Chronological Order of Plays

Despite the above, dating and grouping Shakespeare's plays is problematic. In 1598 the commentator Francis Meres created a kind of literary marker when he wrote that Shakespeare was 'the greatest English playwright' and listed his plays to date. This list has helped scholars distinguish the earlier plays from the later ones.

Meres also lists a play named *Love's Labour's Won,* which may have been revised and turned into *All's Well That Ends Well.* A reasonable approximation of the order of the plays has been deduced from dates of publication, references in writings of the same time, allusions in the plays to then-current events, thematic relationships and stylistic comparisons.

The Early Plays (Pre-1594)

Some scholars consider the first plays to be the three parts of *King Henry VI*; it is uncertain, however, whether *Part I* was written before or after parts *II* and *III*. *King Richard III* is related to these plays and is usually grouped with them as the final part of a first quartet of historical plays. Others think *The Comedy of Errors* was Shakespeare's first play. Some evidence suggests it might have been *King Edward III*, a new play now being considered by many critics as part of the canon.

After the early Henrys come, in probable order, *The Comedy of Errors, Titus Andronicus, The Taming of the Shrew, The Two Gentlemen of Verona, Love's Labour's Lost* and *Romeo and Juliet*. Some of the comedies of this early period are parodies with strong elements of farce. The two tragedies among the plays, *Titus Andronicus* and *Romeo and Juliet*, were both very popular in Shakespeare's own lifetime. *Romeo and Juliet*, in particular, shows a departure from genre and cliché, with a substantial development of minor characters.

After these early plays and before his great tragedies, Shakespeare wrote *King Richard II, A Midsummer Night's Dream, King John, The Merchant of Venice, King Henry IV Parts I* and *II, Much Ado About Nothing, King Henry V, Julius Caesar, As You Like It* and *Twelfth Night*. *King Richard II*, each part of *King Henry IV*, and *King Henry V* form a second quartet of historical plays, although each can stand alone. *King Henry IV* introduces the fat knight Sir

John Falstaff, one of Shakespeare's classic creations who has enjoyed immense popularity from the beginning.

The Great Tragedies (1600–08)

Shakespeare's great tragedies and the 'problem plays' (meaning that they are hard to categorize and critique) date from 1600 with *Hamlet*. Following this are *The Merry Wives of Windsor* (written on the request of Elizabeth I, who wanted to see another play featuring Falstaff), *Troilus and Cressida*, *All's Well That Ends Well*, *Measure for Measure*, *Othello*, *King Lear*, *Macbeth*, *Antony and Cleopatra*, *Coriolanus* and *Timon of Athens*.

Othello, *King Lear* and *Macbeth* deal with the conflict of order and chaos, good and evil, and spirituality and hedonism. *Pericles*, *Cymbeline*, *The Winter's Tale* and *The Tempest* are considered tragicomedies. The main characters seem to encompass a tragic potential to rival that of Lear or Othello, but the plays can be considered comedies because they end happily, often through magical means.

The Lost Plays

Little is known about *Cardenio*, considered a lost play and possibly developed from an episode in Cervantes's *Don Quixote*. In fact, *The Norton Shakespeare* is the first edition of Shakespeare's works to include a separate description of it. We know that on 20 May 1613, John Heminges, who ran the King's Men, was presented with a sum of money for performing six plays, one of which was entitled *Cardenio*. In 1728, Lewis Theobald published a play called *Double Falsehood*, or *The Distressed Lovers*, based on the story of *Cardenio*, 'revised and adapted' from the play 'originally written by William Shakespeare'.

Shakespeare's 'retirement' to Stratford was spent collaborating with John Fletcher, who essentially took Shakespeare's place as the primary playwright of the King's Men. Fletcher was known to be a great admirer of Cervantes, and probably read *Don Quixote* in its original Spanish.

Historian Charles Hamilton claims to have reconstructed Shakespeare and Fletcher's *Cardenio*, in *Shakespeare with John Fletcher: Cardenio or The Second Maiden's Tragedy*. Two more plays, *King Henry VIII* and *The Two Noble Kinsmen*, may also be collaborations with John Fletcher, and the canon is now considered by some scholars to include *King Edward III,* which fits into the sequence of Wars of the Roses plays chronologically before *King Richard II*.

There are several pages of a play called *Sir Thomas More* that include what appear to be the only extant examples of Shakespeare's handwriting apart from legal documents. A brief summary of the play is included later in this book.

King Edward III was first published anonymously in 1596, but it was not until Edward Capell re-edited the play in his *Prolusions* (1760) that Shakespeare was said to be the author. The Arden Shakespeare series, the leading publisher of William Shakespeare's works, has taken the new play into its canon, as have the Cambridge University Press and American Riverside Press, although Oxford scholars are still holding out.

Appreciating Shakespeare's Greatness

As with any exceptionally popular author, Shakespeare's work was appreciated differently over time. In his own day, for example, according to Ben Jonson, *Titus Andronicus*, a bloodthirsty revenge melodrama now regarded as one of Shakespeare's least interesting plays, was particularly enjoyed. The poet John Dryden (1631–1700) in his *Essay on Dramatic Poesy*, preferred *King Richard II*; and Samuel Johnson (1709–84), in his *Preface to Shakespeare*, admired the comedies.

It makes sense that *Titus Andronicus* would have suited the more vulgar tastes of the groundlings in an age where bloody executions were popular spectacles. Dryden and Johnson both belonged to neoclassical periods, and it's not surprising, given the taste of the time, that Shakespeare was criticized for mixing comedy and tragedy and failing to observe the unities of time and place prescribed by Aristotle's rules of classical drama. Dryden and Johnson were among the critics who claimed that he had corrupted the language with false wit, puns and ambiguity. These views are in direct contrast to those of modern critics, who have praised their use in later plays especially for adding depth and resonance of meaning. Johnson's good nature no doubt caused him to respond to the comedies.

It's also worth noting that both Ben Jonson and Dryden were ahead of their time in being able and willing to promote Shakespeare's genius, despite the rigid insistence on how things should be done by the now-forgotten arbiters of taste of their age who disagreed with them.

Besides A. C. Bradley's seminal text on *Shakespearean Tragedy*, published in 1904, the 20th century was by far the most prolific in appreciating and commenting on Shakespeare's greatness. Wilson Knight (*The Imperial Theme* and *The Crown of Life*), Harley Granville-Barker (*Preface to Shakespeare*) and others have contributed to our understanding of the plays and poetry.

The first collected edition of Shakespeare is the First Folio, published in 1623, which includes all the plays except *Pericles* and *The Two Noble Kinsmen*. Eighteen of the plays exist in earlier quarto editions, eight of which are extremely corrupt, probably reconstructed from an actor's memory. In 1709, Nicholas Rowe was the first to publish Shakespeare's plays divided into acts and scenes and with exits and entrances marked. Other important early editions include those of Alexander Pope (1725), Lewis Theobald (1733) and Samuel Johnson (1765).

Among Shakespeare's most important sources, Raphael Holinshed's *The Chronicles of England, Scotland and Ireland* (1587) is significant for the English history plays, although Shakespeare did not hesitate to transform a character when it suited him. As a reference work for his Roman tragedies he used Sir Thomas North's translation (1579) of Plutarch's *Lives*. He rewrote old plays and turned English prose romances into drama (*As You Like It* and *The Winter's Tale*). He also freely used the works of his contemporaries in Europe.

The following table shows how Shakespeare's plays are usually grouped:

Comedy	History	Tragedy
All's Well That Ends Well	King Edward III	Antony and Cleopatra
As You Like It	King Henry IV, Part I	Cardenio
The Comedy of Errors	King Henry IV, Part II	Coriolanus
Cymbeline	King Henry V	Hamlet, Prince of Denmark
Love's Labour's Lost	King Henry VI, Part I	Julius Caesar
Measure for Measure	King Henry VI, Part II	King Lear
The Merchant of Venice	King Henry VI, Part III	Macbeth
The Merry Wives of Windsor	King Henry VIII	Othello, Moor of Venice
A Midsummer Night's Dream	King John	Romeo and Juliet
Much Ado About Nothing	King Richard II	Timon of Athens
Pericles, Prince of Tyre	King Richard III	Titus Andronicus
The Taming of the Shrew	Sir Thomas More	
The Tempest		
Troilus and Cressida		
Twelfth Night		
The Two Gentlemen of Verona		
The Two Noble Kinsmen		
The Winter's Tale		

Shakespearean Comedy

What defines a Shakespearean comedy, broadly, is a light touch and
a happy ending, though these plays also contain farce and slapstick.

As he developed as a writer, Shakespeare seemed to deliberately shun
categorization, writing comedies that could be farcical, bitter, magical and
sometimes tragic all at the same time. To Shakespeare, comedy meant
that foolish humans were able to triumph over adversity, which implies
a positive reading of human experience. Comedy means looking to the
future, past the wedding that concludes the action onstage to the offstage

sexual union that ensures life goes on. The end of the comedy is an occasion for jokes, smiles and nudges with an elbow.

Yet the more complicated and sophisticated the comedy, the more likely that the triumphant ending will be undermined by melancholy. The paradox of including difficult characters in the comedies, such as Shylock or Malvolio, and the potentially tragic events that are averted at the eleventh hour, suggest to some scholars that Shakespeare was deliberately calling attention to the theatricality of the occasion.

Was *Romeo and Juliet* based on a true story?
Romeo and Juliet was based on the life of two lovers who lived in Verona, Italy, in 1303, and who died for each other. Both the Capulets and Montagues existed in Verona at this time, and Shakespeare is reckoned to have discovered this tragic love story in Arthur Brooke's 1562 poem entitled 'The Tragical Historye of Romeus and Juliet'.

He invites his audiences to enjoy a temporary perfection not found in the real world. Outside the magic circle of the theatre, lost children are not returned, wicked brothers rarely repent, statues do not come to life, and if we leave a Shakespearean comedy with tears in our eyes, it is only an acknowledgement that the enchantment of the theatre has staved off this 'mortal coil' for an hour or two, but we must now return to the bitterness that reality can bring us.

Shakespearean History

With the exceptions of *King John*, *Sir Thomas More* and *King Henry VIII* (co-authored with John Fletcher), the histories or historical plays cover the Wars of the Roses, a series of violent civil wars fought over the English crown. (*King John* stands as an odd man out, but it is a play more about character than plot.)

The Tudor Dynasty

The history of the Tudors starts with Edward III, whose army defeated the French at the Battle of Crécy in 1346, establishing England as a great military power, and picks up the story again in 1398, two years before Richard II is deposed. It then moves to 1485, when Henry Tudor defeated Richard III at the Battle of Bosworth and established the Tudor dynasty.

Henry VII was Elizabeth I's grandfather, and he went to considerable lengths to legitimize his right to the throne of England by force of arms. *Sir Thomas More* is an unfinished play about the main character's problems with King Henry VIII's divorce, and *King Henry VIII* itself is about the birth of his daughter Elizabeth as a result of that divorce.

The plays cleave quite rigidly to the Tudor party line. Shakespeare was certainly no fool and was not about to upset his patron, the Queen, by suggesingt that she was somehow not the legitimate heir to the throne, regardless of historical truth.

The Rise and Fall of the Lancaster Dynasty

The plays concerning the Wars of the Roses were not written in chronological order. The *King Henry VI* trilogy and *King Richard III* were written close together near the start of Shakespeare's career (around 1589–93). They cover the fall of the Lancaster dynasty – that is, events in English history between 1422 and 1485. Then, about three years later (around 1595–99) came *King Richard II*, and after another couple of years *King Henry IV, Parts I* and *II*, and then finally *King Henry V*. This second series, written at the height of Shakespeare's powers, moves back in time to examine the rise of the House of Lancaster, covering English history from 1398 to 1420.

Shakespeare's audiences would be somewhat familiar with the characters and events he was describing, but in a broad scope. Stories about the battles among rival houses and the rise and fall of kings were woven into the fabric of English culture, and have long been part of English patriotic legends and national mythology.

Sources of Historical Material

Shakespeare drew on a number of different sources in writing his history plays. His primary source for historical material, however, is generally agreed to be Raphael Holinshed's massive work, *The Chronicles of England, Scotland and Ireland*, published in 1586–7. Holinshed's account provides the chronology of events that Shakespeare reproduces, alters, compresses or conveniently avoids – whichever serves his dramatic purposes best. However, Holinshed's work was only one of an entire genre of historical chronicles that were popular during Shakespeare's time. He may well have used other sources. For *King Richard II*, for example, he may have used more than seven primary sources.

As he matured as a playwright, Shakespeare focused more on building character and less on plot or historical events. He realized that Falstaff, and the Boar's Head Tavern where he used to drink with Prince Hal, were worth more, dramatically, than a false recreation of a battle.

One of the principal beliefs that preoccupies the characters in the history plays is that of the divine right of kings. This linchpin philosophy of social order was not challenged until the overthrow of Charles I during the Civil War in 1642. If a king is divinely appointed, then his overthrow or murder will come back to haunt the usurper who gains the throne through such blasphemous means.

Such a ghost manifests itself in *Hamlet*, *Macbeth*, *Julius Caesar* and *King Richard III*, and it hovers over *King Richard II* and its sequels. The murder of the former King Richard II will haunt King Henry IV for the rest of his life, and only his son Henry V can redeem the curse.

When Shakespeare next returned to history, it was not to Holinshed's England, but to the Rome of Plutarch and Ovid for *Julius Caesar* and *Antony and Cleopatra*. Rightly, these are considered tragedies rather than histories because they focus firmly on character.

The Wars of the Roses

To best follow the eight Shakespeare plays that trace the Wars of the Roses, it's helpful to understand the historical events they recreate. For over 100 years, England's royal family was split into two struggling factions: the house of Lancaster, symbolized by a red rose, and the house of York, symbolized by a white rose.

The problems began in the late 14th century, with the death of King Edward III. Edward had seven sons, and the third and fourth became dynastic heads: John of Gaunt, Duke of Lancaster, and his younger brother Edmund, Duke of York.

Edward III was succeeded by Richard II, who was descended from Edward's oldest son, and was neither a Yorkist nor a Lancastrian. Richard ruled for several years before he was overthrown by his cousin, Henry Bolingbroke, the son of John of Gaunt. Bolingbroke became Henry IV and founded the Lancastrian dynasty. Henry IV was in turn succeeded by his son, Henry V, who was succeeded by his son, Henry VI.

In the late 15th century fighting broke out again, this time between Lancastrians and Yorkists. After a bloody struggle, the Yorkists Edward, Clarence and their younger brother Richard murdered Henry VI along with his son and destined heir, Edward, Prince of Wales.

The oldest of the York brothers took the throne as King Edward IV. After he died, his younger brother Richard III took the throne, and he remained there until he was defeated in battle by Henry, Duke of Richmond, who became Henry VII and established peace and the Tudor dynasty.

Shakespearean Tragedy

While Holinshed's history of England proved a source for many early plays, it's probably no exaggeration to say that North's translation of Plutarch's *Lives of Noble Greeks and Romans* exerted a greater influence over Shakespeare than anything else he read (with the possible exception of Aristotle on the essence of drama, which we can only conjecture he may have read as a schoolboy). For example, many scholars consider *Julius*

Caesar to be the play that bridges the history and tragedy genres, with Brutus the first of Shakespeare's tragic heroes.

Though there are others, the four most famous Shakespearean tragedies are *King Lear*, *Hamlet*, *Othello* and *Macbeth*. *Hamlet* is about an emotionally scarred young man trying to come to terms with his urge to avenge the murder of his father, the king, and his awareness of the resultant perdition should he follow that urge. Othello, a Moor and feted general in the army of Venice, is victimized as a result of his love for Desdemona, the daughter of a Venetian statesman. The villain of the play is Iago, Othello's trusted advisor, who plots revenge against Othello, Desdemona and Cassio because Othello has promoted Cassio to a position Iago feels should be his. Macbeth is a noble warrior driven by his ambition and that of his ruthless wife to murder to attain power. *King Lear* is a tragic story of hubris – of an old man who makes a foolish mistake and pays for it with a descent into madness as his children betray and abandon him and his world crumbles around him.

In Shakespeare's plays, the tragic hero is a nobleman who has enjoyed status and prosperity, but possesses a moral weakness or flaw that ultimately leads to his downfall. External circumstances such as fate can also play a part in the hero's fall, and evil agents can cause him to make wrong decisions.

Shakespeare's tragedies can be considered meditations on the spiritual conflict in the soul of man (and woman), and as such, heroes like Macbeth, Othello and Hamlet will always fail because their tragedy is that while they are great men capable of great deeds, they can never elude the consequences of the character flaw that guarantee their destruction. They are tragic heroes, doomed by the perilous impulses that are within their own hearts.

PART 2

The Plays in Alphabetical Order

1   A Midsummer Night's Dream

Main Characters

Theseus – Duke of Athens. He represents tradition, authority and wisdom. He is about to marry Hippolyta.

Hippolyta – An Amazon. Theseus won her as a bride by defeating her in a sword fight.

Egeus – Hermia's father.

Philostrate – Master of the Revels.

Hermia – Daughter of Egeus.

Lysander – A young man in love with Hermia.

Helena – Hermia's friend. In love with Demetrius.

Demetrius – Another young man in love with Hermia.

Oberon – King of the fairies.

Titania – Queen of the fairies.

Puck – Otherwise known as Robin Goodfellow.

Peaseblossom, Cobweb, Moth and Mustardseed – Fairy attendants to Titania.

Nick Bottom, Peter Quince, Francis Flute, Tom Snout, Snug and Robin Starveling – Athenian tradesmen.

Introduction

A Midsummer Night's Dream is one of Shakespeare's early comedies, probably composed in 1595 or 1596. Most scholars believe that Shakespeare wrote the play as a light entertainment for the marriage celebration of Elizabeth Carey, granddaughter of a patron of the Lord Chamberlain's Men, the theatrical troupe in which Shakespeare was a partner. Unlike the majority of his works, *A Midsummer Night's Dream* was not based on other primary source materials, making it one of the few original plays Shakespeare wrote.

The Play

Helena loves Demetrius. Demetrius once slept with Helena, but now loves her friend, Hermia. Hermia loves Lysander, and Lysander returns her love. Egeus, Hermia's father, gets Theseus, the Duke of Athens, to make Demetrius marry Hermia. According to Athenian law, Hermia has four days to choose between Demetrius, life in a nunnery or a death sentence. Hermia flees with Lysander into the surrounding forest.

Throughout the 20th century, *A Midsummer Night's Dream* proved to be one of Shakespeare's most popular plays, and many versions were staged and filmed.

In the forest, Oberon and Titania, King and Queen of the fairies, are arguing over a boy who Titania has adopted and Oberon wants as one of his retinue. Oberon instructs his servant Puck to sprinkle love drops in the Queen's eyes while she sleeps. On awakening, Titania will fall in love with the first creature she sees.

Helena and Demetrius chase after Lysander and Hermia. Oberon, overhearing Demetrius reject the lovesick Helena, takes pity upon her, and tells Puck to use the love drops on Demetrius as well, so that Demetrius will fall for Helena. Puck gets confused and puts the drops in Lysander's eyes instead. He wakes up to see Helena. Now Lysander wants Helena and rejects a stunned Hermia.

Ignorant of all these comings and goings, a group of Athenian craftsmen are rehearsing a production of a play, *Pyramus and Thisbe*, to be acted at the Duke's wedding. Puck casts a spell on Bottom, giving him the head of an ass, and then organizes things so that Bottom is the first creature Titania sees when she wakes up.

Bottom is unaware of his new head, but ends up being kept lavishly by the fairy queen. Oberon enjoys Titania's humiliation, but is not happy that Puck has botched the attempt to reunite Demetrius and Helena. Oberon himself puts the love potion in Demetrius's eyes and makes sure Helena is the first person he sees. Helena is unconvinced, and thinks both

Demetrius and Lysander are mocking her because they both now profess love for her.

Oberon decides it's time to sort things out. He puts the four lovers to sleep and gives Lysander the antidote for the love potion so that he will love Hermia again when they all wake up. Next, Oberon gives Titania the antidote, and the King and Queen are reconciled.

Theseus and Hippolyta discover Lysander, Hermia, Helena and Demetrius asleep in the forest. All return to Athens to make sense of what they think is a strange dream. Bottom, believing that he dreamt he had the head of an ass, returns to his players, and they perform *Pyramus and Thisbe* at the wedding feast, which becomes the wedding of three couples.

Various versions of the play, mostly abridged, were performed until 1840, when Madame Vestris (who also insisted on playing Oberon) restored the text. It was staged at Covent Garden in London, with music by Felix Mendelssohn that included the famous Wedding March, heard regularly all over the world as brides and grooms leave the church after being married.

Commentary

A Midsummer Night's Dream is full of paradoxes. The play is not only the poet's dream but also the audience's. It blends imaginative fancy with the stately traditions of Athenian aristocracy. The conflicts between youthful rebellion and authoritarianism and between the magical and the everyday lend the play a timeless quality, blurring the distinction between reality and imagination for both audience and characters.

The play has been an interesting reflector of the eras it has been produced in. Modern interpretations, for example, have cast the fairy world as a Freudian repository of repressions and erotic desires. It is a testament to Shakespeare's genius that the play can be reinvented in so many different ways; the universal concerns of the nature of love, reality, sexuality, imagination and of the status quo in the social order give the play a timeless appeal. It's worth recalling that, unlike other forms of literature, plays have live audiences – not passive readers – who are active participants in the theatrical experience.

Famous Lines

'For aught that I could ever read,
Could ever hear by tale or history,
The course of true love never did run smooth' (Act I, Scene I).

'Love looks not with the eyes, but with the mind;
And therefore is winged Cupid painted blind' (Act I, Scene II).

'That would hang us, every mother's son' (Act I, Scene II).

'I'll put a girdle round about the earth
In forty minutes' (Act II, Scene II).

'I know a bank where the wild thyme blows,
Where oxlips and the nodding violet grows,
Quite over-canopied with luscious woodbine,
With sweet musk-roses and with eglantine' (Act II, Scene II).

'Lord, what fools these mortals be!' (Act III, Scene II).

'I have had a dream, past the wit of man to say what dream it was' (Act IV, Scene I).

'The best in this kind are but shadows' (Act V, Scene I).

2 ♮ All's Well That Ends Well

Main Characters

Helena – The daughter of a great doctor, now the ward of the Countess of Rossillion. She loves the Countess's son, Bertram, though he does not return her affections.

Bertram – The Count of Rossillion. Handsome and well liked, he is an excellent soldier, but heartless in his relationship with Helena, whom he marries unwillingly and then abandons.

Countess of Rossillion – Bertram's mother and Helena's guardian.

King of France – Deathly ill when the play begins, he is miraculously cured by Helena, who uses one of her father's medicines. As a reward for saving his life, he makes Bertram marry Helena.

Parolles – A liar and a braggart.

Lafew – An old French nobleman.

Dumaine, First Lord – A genial French nobleman.

Dumaine, Second Lord – The First Lord Dumaine's brother.

Diana – A young Florentine who Bertram tries to seduce. She helps Helena trick Bertram.

Widow – Diana's mother.

Mariana – A woman of Florence.

Duke of Florence – The ruler of Florence.

Clown – An old servant of the Countess who serves as a messenger.

Steward – Another servant of the Countess.

Introduction

The earliest copy of *All's Well That Ends Well* appears in the Folio of 1623, seven years after Shakespeare died. Some critics date it from 1598 or earlier and associate it with a 'lost' play called *Love's Labour's Won*, which is listed in a 1598 catalogue of Shakespeare's plays. Others think that *All's Well That Ends Well* is a reworked version that Shakespeare published at a later date.

The most common dating puts it between 1601 and 1606, grouping it with *Troilus and Cressida* and *Measure for Measure* in what are typically referred to as Shakespeare's 'problem plays'. All three share a bitter humour and a cynical view of human relations that contrasts sharply with earlier, sunnier comedies such as *Twelfth Night* and *As You Like It*. In fact, the title of this play is almost cynical.

Throughout his career, Shakespeare explored the paradox of the evil in good people and goodness in bad people. The only truly unsympathetic figure in *All's Well That Ends Well* is Parolles, who is less a villain than a comically amoral rogue.

The source of the story is Boccaccio's *Decameron*, a classic of early Renaissance literature, written between 1348 and 1358. The *Decameron* (essentially a short story collection with a framework somewhat like *The Canterbury Tales* or *The Thousand and One Arabian Nights*) was translated into English in the mid-16th century by William Painter as *The Palace of Pleasure*, and it was this version that Shakespeare probably drew upon.

Shakespeare, of course, altered and reshaped the original story, adding characters such as Lafew, the Countess and Parolles, but kept the basic elements – the bed trick and the war in Florence.

The Play

When his father dies, Bertram becomes Count of Rosillion. Helena is the orphaned daughter of a great doctor and has lived in the Rosillion household under the guardianship of Bertram's mother, the Countess.

Helena follows Bertram to Paris, where the King of France has been taken deathly ill. Helena bears one of her father's prescriptions, and when she cures the King, in gratitude he tells her she can have her pick of the bachelors at his court. Over the years, Helena has developed a secret love for Bertram. Now she can act on this love.

She picks Bertram, who is distressed by the prospect, feeling that Helena is beneath him. Under protest, Bertram agrees to the marriage.

Helena returns to Rosillion and the Countess, at first assuming that her husband will be along directly. Bertram, however, slips off to fight in Tuscany with his cowardly friend, Parolles.

It becomes apparent that Bertram is not returning home, and then he sends word that Helena can't call him husband until she wears his ring (which he never takes off) and bears his child – not a simple task, given that Bertram is in Italy and has no intention of ever sleeping with her.

Helena now sets out for Florence. She finds herself lodging with a widow, whose daughter, Diana, ironically, is the object of Bertram's affections. With Diana's help, Helena designs a trap for Bertram.

Audiences and critics are almost always divided on how they feel about Helena ending up with Bertram. As a result, *All's Well That Ends Well* is not performed very often these days.

Diana makes Bertram give her his ring before they share a bed. Helena then takes Diana's place in the dark. She exchanges rings with him, giving him one that the King had given her to give to Bertram.

She next spreads a rumour that she has died, and Bertram believes that he is in the clear. However, back in France, the King recognizes the ring Bertram bears as the one he gave Helena. When Bertram is caught in a series of lies, the King has him arrested (supposing that Bertram has murdered her). Diana and her widowed mother arrive demanding justice, and when Helena finally turns up bearing Bertram's ring, carrying his child and revealing the truth to all, Bertram repents the error of his ways and swears his love for Helena.

Commentary

All's Well That Ends Well is often described as a problem play, distinguished from the earlier, more cheerful comedies by a sophisticated bitterness toward human relations. These plays' happy endings are really nothing of the sort. It's hard for a modern audience to imagine Bertram and Helena enjoying a happy marriage.

For a play about love, *All's Well That Ends Well* is remarkably cynical. Helena's low opinion of men seems well founded. The successful central deception is the bedroom switch that enables Helena to become pregnant by Bertram, who had earlier avoided consummating the marriage, and to trick him into accepting her as his wife. It works, Shakespeare suggests, because in the dark all women look alike to men.

For modern audiences, the idea of great women picking men who are unworthy of them is disquieting. It's particularly difficult with *All's Well That Ends Well*, because Bertram turns out to be such a nasty piece of work. He abandons Helena, tries to seduce an innocent woman and only repents because he has no choice. It's either marriage or jail.

Was Shakespeare commenting on what it meant to be a woman alone, with few prospects of earning a living in a male-dominated world? Given the cynicism of the story, one can't help but wonder if an undercurrent of desperation plays some small part in Helena's determination to nail Bertram.

The resourceful Helena, meanwhile, while loved by everyone (except Bertram), also gives us pause for thought. She seems to be a classic example of 'why good women make bad choices'. Why does she so relentlessly pursue a man who is so demonstrably unworthy of her? Nothing stands in Helena's way as she pursues her man. While we may admire her, by the time she's triumphant our opinion of her good taste is all but gone.

Famous Lines

'All the learned and authentic fellows' (Act II, Scene III).

'A young man married is a man that's marr'd' (Act II, Scene III).

'Praising what is lost makes the remembrance dear'
(Act V, Scene III).

3   Antony and Cleopatra

Main Characters

Mark Antony – Along with Octavius Caesar and Lepidus, he is a member of the triumvirate that rules the Roman Empire. Once a great general and powerful politician, Antony has abandoned Rome and his wife Fulvia in order to frolic in Egypt with Cleopatra.

Cleopatra – The Queen of Egypt and Antony's lover. She once seduced Julius Caesar.

Octavius Caesar – Julius Caesar's nephew and adopted son; one of the triumvirate of Rome.

Domitius Enobarbus – Antony's loyal supporter.

Marcus Aemilius Lepidus – The weakest member of the triumvirate. He tries to keep the peace between Octavius and Antony.

Sextus Pompeius – Son of a great general who was one of Julius Caesar's partners in power.

Octavia – Caesar's sister. She marries Antony in order to cement the alliance of the two triumvirs.

Charmian and Iras – Cleopatra's attendants.

The Soothsayer – An Egyptian fortuneteller.

Dolabella – One of Octavius Caesar's men.

Agrippa – One of Octavius Caesar's officers.

Canidius – Antony's general.

Ventidius – A Roman soldier under Antony's command.

Scarus – A brave soldier.

Proculeius – One of Caesar's soldiers.

Mardian, Alexas and Diomedes – Cleopatra's servants.

Thidias, Gallus and Maecenas – Caesar's men.

Demetrius and Philo – Antony's soldiers in Egypt.

Eros – An attendant, serving Antony.

Menas, Menecrates and Varrius – Soldiers under Pompey.

Seleucus – Cleopatra's treasurer.

Clown – An Egyptian who brings poisonous snakes (asps) to Cleopatra.

Decretas – One of Antony's soldiers.

Introduction

Antony and Cleopatra was written about 1606 and is considered Shakespeare's last great tragedy. It is an epic of the Roman Empire and a tragedy of global proportions.

Shakespeare's primary source for *Antony and Cleopatra* was the 'Life of Marcus Antonius' contained in Plutarch's *Lives of Noble Greeks and Romans*, which was translated into English by Sir Thomas North in 1579. Large sections of North's language found their way into the play with only a few changes.

This play greatly compresses a decade's worth of events. Antony is clearly much older than in *Julius Caesar*, and his political instincts seem to be waning. Octavius Caesar was a minor character in the earlier play, but now comes into his own as the man who will rise to become the first Roman emperor, Caesar Augustus.

The plot of the play also remains close to North's story, although characters such as Enobarbus and Cleopatra's attendants are largely Shakespearean creations. The action of the story takes place roughly two years after Shakespeare's earlier play, *Julius Caesar*.

Most of the events of the play are historically accurate. From the images we have of Cleopatra, it seems she was rather plain. Clearly, her seductive qualities must have come from her personality.

The Play

Octavius Caesar, Antony and Lepidus form the Roman triumvirate that rules the Western world. Lepidus decides to retire, leaving Caesar and Antony in charge. Antony, although married to Fulvia, lives in Egypt with his mistress, Cleopatra, the Queen of Egypt. Disgusted by Antony's lifestyle in Egypt and angry about wars caused by Antony's relatives, Caesar recalls Antony to Rome. Fulvia dies and Caesar and Antony try to make peace through Antony's marriage to Caesar's sister, Octavia.

Antony quickly returns to Cleopatra. Caesar vows to wrest Egypt from Antony and Cleopatra by force. As defeat seems near, Antony's best friend, Enobarbus, deserts him and joins Caesar's army, then, filled with guilt, kills himself near Caesar's headquarters. Facing certain defeat, Antony now kills himself by falling on his sword. Cleopatra, in grief over Antony's death and determined never to be taken in chains to Rome as a prisoner, commits suicide by allowing poisonous asps (snakes) to bite her.

Commentary

Antony and Cleopatra is an ambitious epic play with a vast cast and complex politics. The title characters are defined not by their intense interior life, as are Hamlet or Othello, but by their awareness of themselves as public figures. 'But what about me?' they seem to ask. 'When is my duty done? When does my personal happiness come?'

> Antony and Cleopatra may lose an empire to Octavius, but in the poetry of their final hours, as they realize their ambition to be together, if only briefly, we are led to feel that their suicides are a victory and they will be united beyond the grave.

The real struggle in the play is not between armies, but for Antony's soul, and Cleopatra's Egypt wins. Cleopatra is a complex character, deeply in love with Antony, yet willing to consider betraying him. She is a sexually mature seductress with a childlike understanding of war, and above all, a performer who is always 'on', playing herself for the benefit of those around her. While other Shakespearean tragic heroes, such as Hamlet or Macbeth, die in alienation and despair, Cleopatra and her lover achieve what she calls their 'immortal longings'.

Famous Lines

'There's beggary in the love that can be reckon'd' (Act I, Scene I).

'My salad days,
When I was green in judgment' (Act I, Scene V).

'The barge she sat in, like a burnish'd throne,
Burn'd on the water; the poop was beaten gold;
Purple the sails, and so perfumed that
The winds were lovesick with them; the oars were silver,
Which to the tune of flutes kept stroke, and made
The water which they beat to follow faster,
As amorous of their strokes. For her own person,
It beggar'd all description' (Act II, Scene II).

'Age cannot wither her, nor custom stale
Her infinite variety' (Act II, Scene II).

'He wears the rose
Of youth upon him' (Act III, Scene XIII).

'I am dying, Egypt, dying' (Act IV, Scene XV).

'I have
Immortal longings in me' (Act V, Scene II).

4   As You Like It

Main Characters

Duke Senior – Forced to live in exile in the Forest of Arden after his kingdom was usurped by his brother Duke Frederick. Father of Rosalind.

Rosalind (Ganymede) – Daughter of Duke Senior. Forced to flee to the forest of Arden disguised as a young man called Ganymede. In love with Orlando.

Lord Amiens – A faithful lord of Duke Senior in exile in the forest; an optimist.

Lord Jaques – A faithful lord of Duke Senior in exile in the forest; a pessimist.

Duke Frederick – Duke Senior's brother and usurper of Senior's throne. Celia's father.

Celia (Aliena) – Duke Frederick's daughter and Rosalind's best friend. She falls in love with Oliver at first sight.

Charles – A champion wrestler.

Touchstone – A court clown who accompanies Rosalind and Celia. He falls in love with Audrey, a goatherd.

Oliver – Eldest son of Sir Rowland De Bois, and Orlando's older brother. For some reason, unknown even to himself, Oliver hates Orlando.

Orlando – Younger brother of Oliver. Fearing for his life, he flees to the Forest of Arden. He's in love with Rosalind.

Adam – An old retainer of Sir Rowland De Bois.

Silvius – A young shepherd, in love with Phebe.

Phebe – A young shepherdess who falls in love with Ganymede (Rosalind).

Corin – A friend of Silvius.

Audrey – A goatherd, in love with Touchstone.

William – A young country boy in love with Audrey.

Introduction

As You Like It was most likely written between the years 1598 and 1600. It belongs to a literary tradition known as pastoral, which began in the literature of Ancient Greece, flourished through Roman times, most particularly in the work of Virgil, and continued into Shakespeare's time.

What is a pastoral?

Typically, a pastoral story involves exiles from urban life who arrive in the countryside and try to live as common folk. Their conversations are often about the benefits of 'country versus town'. In effect, the pastoral comedy became a useful forum for social commentary at a time when open criticism could be professionally problematic for a writer, not to mention dangerous on occasion.

The Play

As the play opens, Duke Senior has taken refuge in the Forest of Arden with a band of loyal followers, while his daughter, Rosalind, stays behind at the court of Duke Frederick, who has usurped his brother's throne.

We meet another set of brothers at odds with each other: Orlando and Oliver hate each other. Since their father's death, Oliver has mistreated his younger brother, Orlando. When Orlando enters a wrestling match sponsored by Duke Frederick, Oliver tells Orlando's opponent, Charles – a champion wrestler – to break Orlando's neck if he can. To everyone's surprise, Orlando wins the match and attracts Rosalind's attention.

Duke Frederick decides to banish Rosalind to Arden as he did her father, Duke Senior. Celia, Frederick's daughter and Rosalind's best friend, decides to travel with her. Rosalind disguises herself as a boy called Ganymede, and Celia becomes Ganymede's sister, Aliena. The clown Touchstone accompanies them.

Orlando wanders the forest leaving love poems on the branches of trees for Rosalind. She, meanwhile, sets out to lead a pastoral life. Before long, however, disguised as Ganymede, Rosalind promises to help

Orlando win his love's affection. Pretending to be Ganymede, she tells Orlando she will 'play' Rosalind and help him woo her.

Still disguised as Ganymede, Rosalind tries to make a match between Silvius and Phebe that goes awry; Phebe falls for Ganymede instead. Touchstone courts a country girl named Audrey, adding to the multiple romances.

Oliver enters the forest in pursuit of Orlando. But Orlando saves him from a lion, and the two brothers reconcile. Oliver then falls in love with Celia; Duke Senior promises to marry them the next day. Rosalind makes Phebe promise to marry Silvius if she can't have Ganymede, then tells Orlando that Rosalind will marry him that day as well.

When all have gathered for the weddings, Rosalind reveals herself as the erstwhile Ganymede. She and Orlando are happily reunited, and Phebe agrees to marry Silvius. Touchstone also marries Audrey. In a final resolution, we learn that Duke Frederick has seen the error of his ways and opted for a monastic life, restoring Duke Senior's throne.

Commentary

As You Like It is considered one of Shakespeare's best comedies. It pokes fun at the conventions of romantic love and explores the evils of primogeniture, a common English practice during Shakespeare's time in which the eldest son inherited everything, leaving younger siblings at their elder brother's mercy.

As You Like It delights in the ridiculousness of humans, constantly exposing flaws in the beliefs of one character through the analysis of other characters who are equally blind to the absurdity of their own value systems. This technique raises the play from simple entertainment to something that offers a social critique and emphasizes the complexity of being human, with its simultaneous pleasures and pains.

The play manipulates the typical conventions of a pastoral in order to explore other issues. For instance, it was common in a pastoral for people to wear disguises. In *As You Like It*, Rosalind dresses as a man in order to make her journey into exile less dangerous. But Shakespeare pushes the tradition by having Rosalind, in disguise, encounter Orlando, and then role-play herself (Rosalind) in order to teach Orlando how to woo her. In effect, the play raises questions about gender roles.

Famous Lines

'One out of suits with fortune' (Act I, Scene II).

'My pride fell with my fortunes' (Act I, Scene II).

'Beauty provoketh thieves sooner than gold' (Act I, Scene III).

'True is it that we have seen better days' (Act II, Scene VII).

'All the world's a stage,
And all the men and women merely players.
They have their exits and their entrances;
And one man in his time plays many parts,
His acts being seven ages. At first the infant,
Mewling and puking in the nurse's arms.
And then the whining school-boy, with his satchel
And shining morning face, creeping like snail
Unwillingly to school. And then the lover,
Sighing like furnace, with a woeful ballad
Made to his mistress' eyebrow. Then a soldier,
Full of strange oaths, and bearded like the pard;
Jealous in honour, sudden and quick in quarrel,
Seeking the bubble reputation
Even in the cannon's mouth. And then the justice,
In fair round belly with good capon lined,
With eyes severe and beard of formal cut,
Full of wise saws and modern instances;

And so he plays his part. The sixth age shifts
Into the lean and slipper'd pantaloon,
With spectacles on nose and pouch on side;
His youthful hose, well saved, a world too wide
For his shrunk shank; and his big manly voice,
Turning again toward childish treble, pipes
And whistles in his sound. Last scene of all,
That ends this strange eventful history,
Is second childishness and mere oblivion,
Sans teeth, sans eyes, sans taste, sans everything' (Act II, Scene VII).

'Blow, blow, thou winter wind!
Thou art not so unkind
As man's ingratitude' (Act II, Scene VII).

'He that wants money, means, and content is without three good
friends' (Act III, Scene II).

'With bag and baggage' (Act III, Scene II).

'Neither rhyme nor reason' (Act III, Scene II).

'I had rather have a fool to make me merry than experience to make
me sad' (Act IV, Scene I).

'Can one desire too much of a good thing?' (Act IV, Scene I).

'For ever and a day' (Act IV, Scene I).

'It is meat and drink to me' (Act V, Scene I).

'The fool doth think he is wise, but the wise man knows himself to be
a fool' (Act V, Scene I).

'How bitter a thing it is to look into happiness through another man's
eyes!' (Act V, Scene II).

'An ill-favoured thing, sir, but mine own' (Act V, Scene IV).

5 ❦ Cardenio

Main Characters

The Tyrant – Usurped the King's throne.
Govianus – The King. In love with the Lady.
The Lady – Govianus's love, and pursued by the Tyrant.
Helvetius – The Lady's father.
Memphonius, Sophonirus and Bellarius – Nobles of the court.
The Wife – The wife of Anselmus.
Anselmus – Brother-in-law of Govianus.
Votarius – Anselmus's best friend.
Leonella – The Wife's servant.

Introduction

Cardenio is considered by some scholars to be a lost play by William Shakespeare, probably co-authored with John Fletcher, and written around 1613. Little evidence of *Cardenio* appeared until 1728, when Lewis Theobald published a play called *Double Falsehood*, or *The Distressed Lovers*, based on the story of Cardenio and Lucinda in Cervantes's *Don Quixote*, which first appeared in English around 1612. Theobald said that he had revised the play and 'adapted [it] to the stage' from an old manuscript 'originally written by Fletcher and Shakespeare'. He did not include it in his edition of Shakespeare.

In fact, the most recent version of *The Norton Shakespeare* is the first edition of Shakespeare's works to include a separate description of it. We know that on 20 May 1613, John Heminges, who ran the King's Men, was presented a sum of money for performing six plays, one of which was entitled *Cardenio*, and another, *Cardenna*.

In 1653, the printer Humphrey Moseley entered in the Stationers' Register several plays, including 'The History of Cardenio, by Mr Fletcher and Mr Shakespeare'. In 1612, or thereabouts, an untitled, anonymous, handwritten final draft of a play was delivered to Sir George Buc, the

Master of the Revels to James I, as the final step prior to performance. Confused by the lack of a title, he referred to it as 'this *Second Mayden's Tragedy*', presumably for its resemblance to *The Maid's Tragedy* by Beaumont and Fletcher.

According to court diaries, the King's Men gave two performances at court of a play called '*Cardenno* [sic], by Mr Fletcher & Mr Shakespeare'. Scholars long assumed that the script for that play was lost. The original script that Sir George censored, however, still lacking a title page, floated around until it was purchased sometime after 1807 by the British Museum, where it still sits.

The script appears to have been a prompt book used by Shakespeare's company. Among other things, it has handwritten references to actors known to have been a part of the King's Men in 1611.

It is well known that John Fletcher was a great admirer of Cervantes, and he was probably able to read *Don Quixote* in its original Spanish. Could Shakespeare and Fletcher have written a play based on the Cardenio episodes in Volume I of *Don Quixote*?

The few scholars who examined the script concluded that it was the work of Thomas Middleton. In 1994, however, when historian Charles Hamilton published *Shakespeare with John Fletcher: Cardenio, or The Second Maiden's Tragedy*. The book included the script, along with 140 pages of testimony arguing that it is, in fact, the play *Cardenio* referred to in those old court diaries as co-authored by Shakespeare and Fletcher. If true, it would be the first play added to the Shakespearean canon, even if co-authored, since the publication of the Fourth Folio more than 350 years ago.

The Play

Cardenio has two distinct plots that are linked by the relationships of the main characters. One plays against the other in a scene-by-scene progression that neatly uses one plot to contrast with, and comment on, the other.

Act I opens in the midst of a coup, as Govianus, the rightful King, loses his throne to an obsessive Tyrant. Rubbing salt in an open wound (and recalling Richard III and Lady Anne), the Tyrant proceeds to woo Govianus's love, referred to in the play only as the Lady.

She remains steadfast in her devotion to Govianus, even in the face of her own father's appeals to make things easier for everyone by simply appeasing the Tyrant and giving him what he wants. Govianus and the Lady are imprisoned. Frustrated by the Lady, the Tyrant sends his soldiers to force her to submit to him. Rather than be 'borne with violence to the Tyrant's bed', she begs Govianus to kill her.

He can't bring himself to do this, so she kills herself instead. Undeterred, and angry that the Lady has managed to thwart him, the Tyrant steals her corpse from its tomb, intent on making her his Queen anyway. Govianus is released, finds his way to court, and avenges her death. Restored to the throne, Govianus returns her body to the tomb.

In the subplot, a jealous lord, Anselmus, brother-in-law to Govianus, persuades his best friend, Votarius, to seduce his wife as a test of her fidelity. Surprised by their unexpected passion for each other, Votarius and the Wife begin a clandestine affair. To divert her husband's suspicions, the Wife and Votarius plot to have Anselmus overhear a conversation in which the Wife will seemingly spurn Votarius' advances with a sword. The Wife's servant, however, has poisoned the sword's tip, and the Wife unwittingly kills her lover. As the various plots and deceptions are revealed, all are slain.

Commentary

For those who consider the play a lost Shakespeare piece, the evidence is seen in the characterizations, particularly of the women, such as the Lady herself, who seems to continue the lineage of the spiritually powerful princesses of *Cymbeline*, *The Winter's Tale* and *Pericles*. The language also seems to be that of Shakespeare, with its delight in new words and powerful imagery.

For each list of arguments that tries to link Shakespeare's and Fletcher's works to *The Second Maiden's Tragedy*, an equally persuasive list of comparisons can be made with the plays of Thomas Middleton.

However, proving a play's authorship is something of a detective game. Hamilton, for example, based part of his evidence on handwriting analysis. The manuscript contains stage directions, censor's cuts and slips of paper with textual corrections in the same hand as the body of the text, leading some scholars to conclude that the manuscript was handwritten by the playwright, while others believe it is a copy, prepared by a professional scribe. Particularly puzzling is that there is no character named Cardenio in *Cardenio, or The Second Maiden's Tragedy*.

Those who want to pursue the authorship question should start with Charles Hamilton's *Cardenio, or The Second Maiden's Tragedy*, Anne Lancashire's (ed.) *The Second Maiden's Tragedy*, and Harold L. Stenger, Jr.'s *The Second Maiden's Tragedy: A Modernized Edition with an Introduction*.

6 & Coriolanus

Main Characters

Caius Martius – A Roman general who is given the name Coriolanus after he defeats the Volscians. He is brave but arrogant.

Volumnia – Coriolanus's mother. She dominates her son.

Menenius – A friend of Coriolanus.

Brutus – A Roman tribune.

Sicinius – Brutus's ally in the plot against Coriolanus.

Tullus Aufidius – A Volscian general.

Cominius – A friend of Coriolanus.

Titus Lartius – An old Roman nobleman.

Virgilia – Coriolanus's wife.

Valeria – A friend of Virgilia and Volumnia.

Young Martius – Coriolanus and Virgilia's son.

Introduction

Coriolanus was probably written in 1607 or 1608 and first performed in 1609 at the Blackfriars Theatre in London, although these dates are uncertain. It is the penultimate tragedy written by Shakespeare, and follows *Othello*, *King Lear*, *Macbeth* and *Antony and Cleopatra*, all of which Shakespeare probably composed between 1604 and 1606.

The plot of *Coriolanus* probably came from *The Life of Caius Martius Coriolanus*, written in the first century by Plutarch and translated into English in 1579 by Sir Thomas North. (Another source may have been Livy's *History of Rome*.)

As with *Antony and Cleopatra*, it is a Roman play, but *Coriolanus* takes place early in Rome's history, when it was just one Italian city among many, fighting for survival. The action occurs just after the fall of Tarquin, the last Roman king, and highlights the period when Rome moved from being a monarchy to a republic.

English Renaissance scholars were fascinated with Roman history (no doubt in part because of North's rich translation). Poets, playwrights, politicians and philosophers consistently turned to Greece and Rome for inspiration, so Shakespeare's interest in the period makes a lot of sense.

However, one of the attractions of this play may have been the parallels between the events of the play and politics under the new king, James I. Jacobean London was plagued with radical thought, and there was a struggle brewing between James and Parliament as the middle classes demanded more say in the running of their lives. The struggle culminated in 1642 with the Civil War and the execution of James's son, Charles I, by the Parliamentarians under Oliver Cromwell. For a brief period, England became a republic before the restoration of the monarchy in 1660.

The Play

Caius Martius is a legendary Roman general who considers himself better than other men, though he prefers to be a power behind the throne. As plain Marcius, he defeats the Volscian defenders of the city of Corioli and nearly beats their general Aufidius in hand-to-hand combat. At the last moment Aufidius flees.

For his accomplishments Marcius is renamed Caius Martius Coriolanus. He returns to Rome, where the patricians want to make him a tribune of the common people (the plebeians). The tribunes Sicinius Velutus and Junius Brutus are afraid that Coriolanus may become too powerful. They persuade the plebians to condemn Coriolanus to death, and Coriolanus's arrogant attitude does nothing to help his cause.

Outraged, Coriolanus flees Rome, abandoning his wife Virgilia and mother Volumnia. Coriolanus heads to the city of Antium to help Aufidius and the Volscians defeat the Roman Empire and seize Rome. With Coriolanus's help, the Volscians plunder the outlying Roman towns and pause at the gates of Rome. Friends and relatives try to dissuade Coriolanus from attacking his own people. Volumnia persuades Coriolanus to make peace by using his son to play on Coriolanus's emotions.

Aufidius is infuriated that Coriolanus failed to sack Rome, and murders him in front of the lords of Corioli. Aufidius, though pleased that Coriolanus is dead, orders that he be given a noble memorial.

Commentary

Coriolanus is something of a potboiler, and is clearly not one of Shakespeare's best plays. It lacks depth, and its characters are somewhat two-dimensional. It is perhaps Shakespeare's most overtly political play.

While Coriolanus's skill in battle would seem to make him an ideal hero for the masses, his contempt for the mob allows him to be set up as an enemy of the people. While Coriolanus was in part responsible for the expulsion of Tarquin, the last Roman king, he himself is a kingly figure, born to command and unwilling to scheme his way to power. He clearly has no place in the republic that is taking command of his city.

Volumnia is not able to achieve power in her own right in male-dominated Roman society, so her ambition drives her son's. She alone is able to persuade Coriolanus to spare Rome, thus unwittingly sealing his doom.

While Coriolanus may be direct, he is surrounded by manipulative characters such as his friend, Menenius, and the two tribunes, Sicinius and Brutus. Their manipulation of the masses turns the people of Rome against Coriolanus and almost brings about the city's downfall.

The play has been adopted by both the political left and right with equal relish and, depending upon a director's philosophical inclinations, its ambiguities continue to fuel discussion.

Famous Lines

'Nature teaches beasts to know their friends' (Act II, Scene I).

'His nature is too noble for the world:
He would not flatter Neptune for his trident,
Or Jove for 's power to thunder' (Act III, Scene I).

7 ♪ Cymbeline

Main Characters

Cymbeline – The King of Britain, and Imogen's father.

Imogen – Cymbeline's daughter. She is in love with lowborn Posthumus rather than Cymbeline's stepson Cloten.

Posthumus – Cymbeline's protégé. He marries Imogen in secret, against her father's wishes.

Queen – Cymbeline's wife. A villainous woman.

Cloten – The Queen's son. An arrogant idiot.

Iachimo – A scheming Frenchman living in Italy.

Pisanio – Posthumus's loyal servant.

Belarius – A British nobleman, unjustly banished by Cymbeline. He kidnapped Cymbeline's infant sons to avenge himself on the King, and disguised as a shepherd, raised them as his own.

Guiderius – Cymbeline's eldest son, raised by Belarius as Polydore.

Arviragus – Cymbeline's younger son, raised by Belarius as Cadwal.

Philario – An Italian gentleman.

Caius Lucius – The Roman ambassador to Britain.

Cornelius – A doctor.

Soothsayer – A Roman seer.

Jupiter – The King of Olympus in Roman mythology.

Introduction

Cymbeline is one of Shakespeare's last plays and was written and performed around 1609–10, probably on the indoor Blackfriars stage rather than at the more famous Globe. It joins *Pericles*, *The Winter's Tale* and *The Tempest* in a list of problem plays that are considered tragicomedies. Death and despair, while never victorious in the end, loom as ever-present shadows.

The Play

Twenty years ago, Cymbeline, the King of Britain, lost his two boys Guiderius and Arviragus in a kidnapping, leaving his daughter Imogen as the only heir to the throne. Cymbeline remarries, gaining an arrogant idiot stepson Cloten. Cymbeline wants Imogen to marry her stepbrother, but Imogen is in love with her childhood friend Posthumus Leonatus and secretly marries him. When he finds out, Cymbeline banishes Posthumus and confines Imogen to the castle grounds.

Posthumus goes to Rome to stay with his friend, Philario. Iachimo, a mutual acquaintance, bets Posthumus that Iachimo can seduce Imogen. In Britain, Iachimo finds that Imogen is no pushover, so he sneaks into her bedroom, peers at her while she is sleeping, steals her bracelet, and returns to Rome to successfully convince Posthumus that he has succeeded in his aim.

Cymbeline seems to be an original play. Though the Iachimo plot, in which a seduction is attempted on a virtuous wife, may have its roots in Boccaccio's *Decameron*, and the scenes in the Welsh wilderness recall fairy tales like Snow White, most of the plot and characters probably came directly from Shakespeare's imagination.

Posthumus is distraught that Imogen has cuckolded him, and orders his servant Pisanio to kill her. Pisanio can't bring himself to do the deed. Instead, he makes it look as if Imogen is dead, then takes her to Milford Haven, where she disguises herself as a man named Fidele.

In Milford Haven, Imogen (as Fidele) meets her kidnapped brothers, though she doesn't know who they really are, of course. (Belarius kidnapped the boys as revenge for Cymbeline's unfairly banishing him.)

Cloten, wearing Posthumus's clothes, follows Imogen to Milford Haven in the hope of tricking her. He gets into a fight with Guiderius, and Guiderius cuts off Cloten's head.

Meanwhile, the Queen tries to trick Pisanio by giving him medicine (which she thinks is poison), hoping he will give it to Imogen or Posthumus as a gift. The Queen calculates that if Imogen is dead her son becomes Cymbeline's only heir, and if Posthumus dies, Imogen will be widowed and thus forced to marry Cloten.

In Milford Haven, Imogen falls sick and takes the medicine Pisanio gave her as a present. It is not poison, as the Queen believed. The medicine puts Imogen into a deep sleep, and Belarius and the sons, believing her dead, lay her beside Cloten's body. When Imogen recovers, she sees the headless body dressed in Posthumus's clothes and thinks that he is dead.

Meanwhile, Caius Lucius demands that Britain pay tribute to Rome and Augustus Caesar. Cymbeline refuses, and Lucius declares war on Britain. The Queen falls ill, and on her deathbed admits her crimes and sins, including hating Cymbeline. Caius Lucius's army invades Britain, and he comes across Imogen and rescues her from the wild. In the only battle of the war, Cymbeline is captured by the Romans, then rescued by Belarius, Guiderius and Arviragus, with help from Posthumus on the inside. The Britons then capture Posthumus, thinking he is Roman, and take him to Cymbeline. Posthumus has a vision where he is visited by the god Jupiter.

In the last scene of the play, Imogen returns to her father, Iachimo confesses he tricked everyone, Cornelius explains the Queen's 'poison', Cloten's death is explained, Belarius admits to kidnapping the princes, Cymbeline allows Imogen and Posthumus to stay married, a soothsayer explains a prophecy in a book left in Posthumus's lap by the god Jupiter, and peace is made with the Romans. Cymbeline does not punish Iachimo or Belarius.

Commentary

Cymbeline is Shakespeare's attempt to tell a fairy tale using the elements of tragedy, and it really doesn't work that well. The language, while rich, is often clumsy, and the mediocrity of certain scenes (notably the appearance of Jupiter) have led a number of critics to suggest that

Shakespeare may well have collaborated with a less talented playwright. While the play includes the wonderful Imogen and the entertaining Iachimo, the title character, Cymbeline, is rather two-dimensional, as is a lot of the supporting cast.

Like Helena and Portia, Imogen is a woman whose man does not really deserve her. Posthumus disappears from the action for long periods of time, and the various subplots make the play hard to follow.

The ageing Shakespeare seems to have revisited elements of his earlier plays, albeit in a less impressive form. *Cymbeline* feels like a pastiche, as if Hollywood were to make a film that takes the best bits of several successful movies and stitches them together in another framework.

The Imogen–Cymbeline relationship suggests Cordelia and Lear in *King Lear*, though Cymbeline is a failure compared to Lear, while Iachimo reminds one of Iago in *Othello*, though he hardly reaches the depths of Iago's villainy, and Posthumus is a poor revisiting of Othello. The sleeping potion and Imogen awakening next to her 'husband's' dead body remind us of *Romeo and Juliet*, while Imogen's cross-dressing recalls *As You Like It*, but none of these elements combine into a coherent whole. *Cymbeline* may seem a tragedy, yet disaster never really strikes. Only the wicked characters die, and by the end everyone is reconciled.

The final scene, in which all the tangled strands of plot are tied together, is cleverly constructed, with everyone getting their just deserts. The villains die, Imogen and Posthumus are reunited, and King Cymbeline's abducted sons are restored to him; as Cymbeline declares, 'Pardon's the word to all.'

Famous Lines

'Hath his bellyful of fighting' (Act II, Scene I).

'As chaste as unsunn'd snow' (Act II, Scene V).

'Some griefs are medicinable' (Act III, Scene II).

'The game is up' (Act III, Scene III).

'I have not slept one wink' (Act III, Scene IV).

8   Hamlet, Prince of Denmark

Main Characters

Hamlet – The Prince of Denmark. The son of the late King Hamlet, and the nephew of the present King Claudius.

Claudius – The King of Denmark. Hamlet's uncle who murdered Hamlet's father to obtain the throne.

Gertrude – The Queen of Denmark. Hamlet's mother. After the death of her husband (Hamlet's father), Gertrude married her brother-in-law, Claudius.

Polonius – The Lord Chamberlain and father to Laertes and Ophelia.

Horatio – Hamlet's friend.

Ophelia – Polonius's daughter.

Laertes – Polonius's son.

Fortinbras – The Prince of Norway. His father was killed by Hamlet's father. He intends to attack Denmark to avenge his father's death.

The Ghost – Hamlet's recently murdered father.

Rosencrantz and Guildenstern – Former friends of Hamlet from Wittenberg.

Osric, Voltemand and Cornelius – Courtiers.

Marcellus and Barnardo – The officers of the watch who report seeing the Ghost.

Francisco – A soldier.

Reynaldo – Polonius's servant.

Introduction

Hamlet may well be the most famous play ever written in the English language. Composed during the first part of the 17th century, at the close of Elizabeth I's reign, *Hamlet* was probably first performed in July 1602. It was first published in 1603 and appeared in a longer edition in 1604.

Hamlet is the story of a Danish prince whose uncle murders his father and marries his mother. Shakespeare probably knew the story from an earlier German play, *Hystorie of Hamblet,* an English translation of a French prose work (François de Belleforest's *Histoires Tragiques)*, and from an ancient history of Denmark that was written by Saxo Grammaticus in the 13th century.

The revenge tragedy was a staple of the Elizabethan theatre, and it may seem that *Hamlet* falls into this genre; however, it is clearly much more. It is a rumination on life and death and the reason for existence.

What Shakespeare did with this raw material may well have been informed by the death of his young son, Hamnet, several years before the play was written. Critics speculate that Shakespeare's continuing grief for his son is echoed in Hamlet's grief for his father.

The Play

Hamlet, Prince of Denmark, has a lot to be depressed about: the ghost of his father haunts Elsinore, claiming he was murdered by his brother, Claudius; Claudius, meanwhile, has married Queen Gertrude, Hamlet's mother, and assumed the throne; and Fortinbras of Norway threatens to invade Denmark.

The Gghost demands that Hamlet exact revenge for his murder. In order to carry this out, Hamlet feigns madness. As part of his insanity, he scorns the affections of Ophelia, whom he has previously been courting.

Polonius grows concerned over Hamlet's growing insanity and discusses his concern with the King and Queen. Meanwhile, Hamlet tries to come to terms with the idea that his uncle may have murdered his father, and in an effort to 'catch the conscience of the king', Hamlet persuades a travelling troupe of actors to perform a play whose action closely parallels the murder of his father. Claudius reacts badly at the murder scene, convincing Hamlet that the Ghost told him the truth. Still, he can't bring himself to slay his uncle, because he feels it is a sin.

Hamlet starts to torment his mother, Gertrude, by insisting she is sleeping with her husband's killer. Polonius, who hides behind a tapestry in the Queen's chamber to eavesdrop, panics and cries for help. Hamlet stabs him, thinking it is his uncle, Claudius.

Claudius sends Hamlet to England with Rosencrantz and Guildenstern, two of Hamlet's childhood friends. He gets Hamlet to carry a letter to the King of England in which Claudius asks England to kill Hamlet (the bearer of the letter). Hamlet turns the tables on his friends, and they are put to death instead.

Is *Hamlet* Shakespeare's greatest play?

Whether *Hamlet* is Shakespeare's greatest play is debatable. It is certainly his most famous. *Hamlet* has been analysed exhaustively for its aesthetic, moral, political, psychological, historical, allegorical, logical, religious and philosophical meanings. There are thousands of words devoted to the play, and while there may be wrong ways to understand the tragedy, there is no single right way.

Driven to madness herself by Hamlet's condition and the death of her father, Polonius, Ophelia drowns herself. Her brother, Laertes, returns from his studies and vows his vengeance upon Hamlet for what the Pprince has done to his family. Claudius plots with Laertes to kill Hamlet. At Ophelia's funeral Laertes and Hamlet confront one another and Laertes challenges Hamlet to a duel.

Claudius tells Laertes to select a sharp blade instead of a dull one for the duel, and to poison the tip so that a wound will kill the Prince. Claudius also decides to keep some poisoned wine for Hamlet to drink. But everything goes wrong.

Laertes is unable to wound Hamlet during the first pass of the duel. Between passes, Gertrude drinks from the poisoned wine before Claudius can stop her. In the heat of the fray, Laertes wounds Hamlet but loses the poisoned rapier to him, and Laertes is poisoned as well. Gertrude collapses. Laertes reveals the plot against Hamlet before he dies, telling him he has 'not a half-hour's life' in him. Hamlet stabs Claudius with the poisoned foil, then forces him to drink from the poisoned wine that killed his mother.

Hamlet now collapses and dies in Horatio's arms as Fortinbras enters the castle. Fortinbras is left to rule, as the entire Danish royal family is dead. He tells his men to give Hamlet and the rest proper funerals.

Commentary

Hamlet is one of the most complex and compelling characters of English literature. His actions and thoughts have been analysed over and over, and it is this seemingly bottomless well of possibilities that accounts for *Hamlet*'s enduring appeal.

Hamlet is concerned with the profound truths of human nature and our place in the universe, and it is not possible to responsibly reduce the play to a set of simple themes. Things to consider, however, include Shakespeare's questioning of the whole revenge play genre, and the nature of revenge itself and how it affects us. Hamlet's struggle over whether or not to murder Claudius, echoed by the Fortinbras and Laertes subplots, forms a base from which Shakespeare explores the relationship between thought and action. It is human instinct to want revenge when wronged, but is it right to act on that instinct?

Hamlet is not a man of action by nature, but a scholar, a man of thought and consideration and learning, and many critics feel that the imbalance between his active and passive natures is a tragic flaw that makes his wretched fate inevitable.

Hamlet is a kind of everyman, and his dilemmas echo those that we all face in some form. We can come to any number of reasonable conclusions about Hamlet, but arriving at a definitive one is very difficult.

Other important themes explored in *Hamlet* include the line between sanity and madness, the nature of political power, the connection between the well-being of the state and the moral condition of its leaders, and the moral questions of how to live a good life and the consequences of committing suicide. Hamlet's ghostly father is in agony in purgatory, having died unconfessed and with his sins still heavy on his shoulders. Hamlet considers killing himself, but fears God's wrath in the afterlife. Ophelia, clearly an innocent, in a fit of madness does kill herself, but will she still suffer in the afterlife because of it? Other themes are the relationship between sons and fathers (Hamlet and the Ghost, Laertes and Polonius, Fortinbras and the dead King of Norway), the nature of the family, the inevitability of death and, against that inevitability, the question of what gives life meaning.

Hamlet's love of learning and reason is pulverized by a growing nihilism, as every truth that is supposed to comfort him (religion, society, philosophy, love) either fails him or proves false. Just how insane Hamlet actually was and how much he faked it is one of the most hotly contested controversies surrounding the play. The probable answer is that he decided to feign madness as a strategic way of covering his deep distress at what the Ghost reveals to him, without putting himself in danger. Yet there is little doubt that his mind is so troubled, confused and desperate that his pretence assumes the intensity of real madness for a while as he deals with the enormity of what has happened.

Famous Lines

'For this relief much thanks: 't is bitter cold,
And I am sick at heart' (Act I, Scene I).

'A little more than kin, and less than kind' (Act I, Scene II).

'All that live must die,
Passing through nature to eternity' (Act I, Scene II).

'But I have that within which passeth show;
These but the trappings and the suits of woe' (Act I, Scene II).

'He was a man, take him for all in all,
I shall not look upon his like again' (Act I, Scene II).

'Give thy thoughts no tongue' (Act I, Scene III).

'Neither a borrower nor a lender be;
For loan oft loses both itself and friend,
And borrowing dulls the edge of husbandry.
This above all: to thine own self be true,
And it must follow, as the night the day,
Thou canst not then be false to any man' (Act I, Scene III).

'But to my mind, though I am native here
And to the manner born, it is a custom
More honoured in the breach than the observance' (Act I, Scene IV).

'Something is rotten in the state of Denmark' (Act I, Scene IV).

'There are more things in heaven and earth, Horatio,
Than are dreamt of in your philosophy' (Act I, Scene V).

'Brevity is the soul of wit' (Act II, Scene II).

'Doubt thou the stars are fire;
Doubt that the sun doth move;
Doubt truth to be a liar;
But never doubt I love' (Act II, Scene II).

'Though this be madness, yet there is method in 't' (Act II, Scene II).

'There is nothing either good or bad, but thinking makes it so' (Act II, Scene II).

'A dream itself is but a shadow' (Act II, Scene II).

'What a piece of work is a man! how noble in reason! how infinite in faculty! in form and moving how express and admirable! in action how like an angel! in apprehension how like a god!' (Act II, Scene II).

'The devil hath power
To assume a pleasing shape' (Act II, Scene II).

'To be, or not to be: that is the question:

Whether 't is nobler in the mind to suffer
The slings and arrows of outrageous fortune,
Or to take arms against a sea of troubles,
And by opposing end them? To die: to sleep:
No more; and by a sleep to say we end
The heartache and the thousand natural shocks
That flesh is heir to,—'t is a consummation
Devoutly to be wish'd. To die, to sleep;
To sleep: perchance to dream: ay, there's the rub:
For in that sleep of death what dreams may come,
When we have shuffled off this mortal coil,
Must give us pause: there's the respect
That makes calamity of so long life;
For who would bear the whips and scorns of time,
The oppressor's wrong, the proud man's contumely,
The pangs of despised love, the law's delay,
The insolence of office and the spurns
That patient merit of the unworthy takes,
When he himself might his quietus make
With a bare bodkin? who would fardels bear,
To grunt and sweat under a weary life,
But that the dread of something after death,
The undiscover'd country from whose bourn
No traveller returns, puzzles the will
And makes us rather bear those ills we have
Than fly to others that we know not of?
Thus conscience does make cowards of us all;
And thus the native hue of resolution
Is sicklied o'er with the pale cast of thought,
And enterprises of great pith and moment
With this regard their currents turn awry,
And lose the name of action' (Act III, Scene I).

'Be thou as chaste as ice, as pure as snow, thou shalt not escape
     calumny. Get thee to a nunnery, go' (Act III, Scene I).

'Suit the action to the word, the word to the action; with this special observance, that you o'erstep not the modesty of nature' (Act III, Scene II).

'I must be cruel, only to be kind:
Thus bad begins, and worse remains behind' (Act III, Scene IV).

'When sorrows come, they come not single spies,
But in battalions' (Act IV, Scene V).

'Alas, poor Yorick! I knew him, Horatio: a fellow of infinite jest, of most excellent fancy. He hath borne me on his back a thousand times; and now, how abhorred in my imagination it is! my gorge rises at it. Here hung those lips that I have kissed I know not how oft. Where be your gibes now; your gambols, your songs? your flashes of merriment, that were wont to set the table on a roar? Not one now, to mock your own grinning? Quite chap-fallen? Now get you to my lady's chamber, and tell her, let her paint an inch thick, to this favour she must come' (Act V, Scene I).

'The rest is silence' (Act V, Scene II).

9   Julius Caesar

Main Characters

Julius Caesar – A great Roman general and senator.

Brutus – The tragic hero of the play. A Roman senator.

Mark Antony – Caesar's friend.

Cassius – Conspirator against Caesar.

Octavius – Caesar's adopted son and appointed successor.

Calphurnia – Caesar's wife.

Portia – Brutus's wife.

Flavius and Murellus – Civil servants.

Decius – A member of the conspiracy.

Cicero – A famous Roman orator.

Cinna – One of the conspirators.

Cinna the Poet – An innocent man killed by the mob because he has the same name as Cinna the conspirator.

Casca, Metellus, Trebonius and Ligarius – Conspirators against Caesar.

Lepidus – The third member of the triumvirate with Antony and Octavius.

Artemidorus – He tries to warn Caesar of the conspiracy.

Soothsayer – He warns Caesar about the ides of March, but Caesar ignores him.

Lucilius, Titinius, Pindarus and Messala – Soldiers in Brutus's army.

Varrus and Claudio – Brutus's attendants.

Introduction

Julius Caesar is Shakespeare's shortest play. It was written around 1599 and performed at the Globe Theatre, a playhouse owned by Shakespeare's increasingly successful company, the Lord Chamberlain's Men. However, the only authoritative text of the play is the 1623 First Folio edition. The stage directions suggest this text is based on the theatre company's prompt book, rather than Shakespeare's manuscript.

Julius Caesar is the earliest of Shakespeare's three Roman plays. As are *Antony and Cleopatra* (which is a sort of sequel) and *Coriolanus, Julius Caesar* is a history in that it dramatizes real events. The play is clearly a tragedy because of the tragic character of Brutus, the noble Roman whose involvement in the conspiracy to save the state plunges both him and his country into chaos.

Shakespeare drew on North's popular translation of Plutarch's *Lives of the Noble Greeks and Romans.* Plutarch saw the role of the biographer and historian as bound together, saying that history was the result of the achievements of great men. Shakespeare was clearly influenced by this philosophy. In this regard *Julius Caesar* is unlike *Coriolanus,* which dramatizes the conflicts between the classes.

Rome was sharply divided into the patrician citizens, the senators and the growing but under-represented plebeians, or common folk. Citizens who favoured republican democratic rule were afraid that Julius Caesar's power would lead to their enslavement. So a group of conspirators assassinated Caesar, but the civil war they hoped to avoid erupted anyway. The play follows events leading up to Caesar's death and the beginning of the civil war.

Elizabethans would have been quick to pick up on the parallels between Ancient Rome becoming an imperial power, and Elizabeth's ability to consolidate the powers of the monarchy.

By 1599, Elizabeth I had been Queen for close to 40 years and had enlarged her powers at the expense of the aristocracy and the House of Commons. At 66, particularly old for the time, and with no heirs or named successor, many feared her death would plunge England into the kind of chaos suffered during the 15th century. The story of Caesar's downfall provided a perspective on what might happen when accepted methods of distributing power were disrupted.

The Play

Julius Caesar enters as a hero, having defeated the Gauls, then Pompey's army. Mark Antony attempts three times to crown Caesar king; however, some senators take this as a threat to Rome. Cassius, in particular, has serious misgivings about Caesar's ambition and is clearly jealous of his achievements. To offset Caesar's popular support, Cassius approaches Marcus Brutus, a nobleman known for his integrity. If Brutus were to support a coup, it would be more acceptable to the citizens of Rome, and, equally important, Brutus is also a close friend of Caesar.

Brutus clearly emerges as the play's most complex character and its tragic hero. He is a powerful public figure, but is also a loving husband and dignified military leader. His rigid idealism becomes both his greatest virtue and his tragic flaw.

During a great storm, Brutus considers his options, realizing that the conspirators may well have to assassinate Caesar. Caesar, already warned by a soothsayer and Calphurnia, his wife, ignores all advice to the contrary and pays a visit to the Senate. There he is stabbed to death by Brutus, Cassius and the rest of the conspirators.

Brutus dissuades the conspirators from slaying Antony with Caesar, and after the assassination Antony asks to accompany Caesar's body and speak at his funeral. Brutus agrees, and at the funeral delivers a stirring oration that explains the reasoning for the assassination. Antony follows with his famous 'Friends, Romans, countrymen' speech, and through his masterful use of irony stirs the crowd to the point where they call for the blood of Cassius, Brutus and anyone else associated with Caesar's death.

Antony then joins Octavius (Caesar's nephew) and Lepidus to wrest control of Rome by force of arms. Brutus and Cassius raise armies against them. In a final battle, with many of his co-conspirators now dead, Cassius kills himself when facing defeat, and is quickly followed by

Brutus, who takes his own life rather than be taken captive. Upon discovering the body, Antony laments the tragic fall of Brutus.

Commentary

In a world of self-serving ambition, Brutus is truly 'the noblest Roman of them all', but his commitment to principle repeatedly causes him to miscalculate. He ignores Cassius's suggestion to kill Antony as well as Caesar, and, again against Cassius's advice, he allows Antony to speak a funeral oration over Caesar's body, plunging the city into chaos.

Antony, however, is strong where Brutus is weak. He is impulsive and quick witted, and is able to save himself by first convincing the conspirators that he is on their side, then in enraging the mob against the conspirators. Brutus is noble, to be sure, but Antony proves himself the consummate politician.

Shakespeare explores several themes in *Julius Caesar*. The play raises questions about what in our lives is determined by fate and how much free will we have. Cassius says 'The fault, dear Brutus, is not in our stars, But in ourselves, that we are underlings'. On the other hand, Caesar tells his wife, 'death, a necessary end, will come when it will come'. The text explores public versus private self and inflexibility versus compromise.

Brutus interprets his defeat as the work of Caesar's ghost – empowered by the people's devotion to Caesar – and the legacy of a man who somehow transcended fate. Both Brutus and Caesar are stubborn men who ultimately suffer fatally for it. It is the adaptable people, the ones who will compromise, who survive.

Famous Lines

'The live-long day' (Act I, Scene I).

'Beware the ides of March' (Act I, Scene II).

'Let me have men about me that are fat,
Sleek-headed men, and such as sleep o' nights:
Yond Cassius has a lean and hungry look;
He thinks too much: such men are dangerous' (Act I, Scene II).

'A dish fit for the gods' (Act II, Scene I).

'Cowards die many times before their deaths;
The valiant never taste of death but once.
Of all the wonders that I yet have heard,
It seems to me most strange that men should fear;
Seeing that death, a necessary end,
Will come when it will come' (Act II, Scene II).

'Et tu, Brute!' (Act III, Scene I).

'O, pardon me, thou bleeding piece of earth,
That I am meek and gentle with these butchers!
Thou art the ruins of the noblest man
That ever lived in the tide of times' (Act III, Scene I).

'Cry "Havoc", and let slip the dogs of war' (Act III, Scene I).

'Friends, Romans, countrymen, lend me your ears;
I come to bury Caesar, not to praise him.
The evil that men do lives after them;
The good is oft interred with their bones' (Act III, Scene II).

'If you have tears, prepare to shed them now' (Act III, Scene II).

'This was the most unkindest cut of all' (Act III, Scene II).

'Great Caesar fell.
O, what a fall was there, my countrymen!
Then I, and you, and all of us fell down,
Whilst bloody treason flourish'd over us' (Act III, Scene II).

'There is a tide in the affairs of men
Which taken at the flood, leads on to fortune;
Omitted, all the voyage of their life
Is bound in shallows and in miseries' (Act IV, Scene III).

'His life was gentle, and the elements
So mix'd in him, that Nature might stand up
And say to all the world, "This was a man!"' (Act V, Scene V).

10 § King Edward III

Main Characters

King Edward III	King John II (the Good)
Queen Philippa (de Hainault)	Prince Charles (of Normandy)
Prince Edward (Prince of Wales)	Prince Philip
Earl of Salisbury	Duke of Lorraine
Countess of Salisbury	Lord Villiers
Earl of Warwick	French captain (at Calais)
Sir William Montague	Another captain
Earl of Derby	A mariner
Lord Audley	King of Bohemia
Lord Percy	Polonian captain
John Copland	The Scots
Lodowick	King David II of Scotland
Robert of Artois	Douglas
Lord Montfort	Scottish messenger
Gobin Agace	

Introduction

For over 400 years everyone but a handful of renegade critics classified *King Edward III* as an anonymous play. First printed in 1596 by the London bookseller and publisher, Cuthbert Burby, the play's title page told Elizabethan readers that 'it hath bin sundrie times plaied about the Citie of London', but Burby credited no author. The play was successful at the time, for Burby published another edition in 1599, again without naming an author. Capell re-edited the play in his *Prolusions* (1760) and first put forward the claim that Shakespeare wrote the play.

Although Capell's assertions received some support in the 19th century, most significantly from the poet Tennyson, critics remained unconvinced and *King Edward III* seemed doomed to remain part of the

Shakespeare apocrypha – that is, material reputed to be written by Shakespeare but unproven to be so.

However, over the last few years critics have reassessed the play's merits and are beginning to argue that 'hollow and insincere' passages are not reason enough to deny that Shakespeare had a hand in writing the drama. The writing in *King Edward III* measures up to Shakespeare's early work in the *King Henry VI* trilogy and *King John*.

In 1998, the Arden Shakespeare series (the leading publisher of William Shakespeare's works), the Cambridge University Press and American Riverside Press included the play in their collected Shakespeare editions (the Oxford University Press scholars are holding out). Computer analysis of the play's text and language was used to verify its main source of authorship. *King Edward III* is a major addition to the Shakespearean canon, and while no one claims Shakespeare is the sole author, he is considered the author of a significant part of the play.

The question remains: why, if Shakespeare wrote *King Edward III*, did it become a forgotten play and omitted from the First Folio? What follows is pure speculation, of course, but as it is considered an early play, possibly even his first, it's possible that Shakespeare shelved the work because he was unhappy with it, and decided to use parts of it for other plays. As a result it did not become part of the repertoire that Shakespeare revised and revived, and Heminges and Condell therefore did not know that the play was his.

King Edward III tells the story of the first campaigns of the Hundred Years' War. Written in verse, the play opens with a scene similar to the first scene of *King Henry V*, but the preparations for King Edward's campaign in

France quickly give way to the other plot, dealing with the romance of the King and the Countess of Salisbury.

The Play

King Edward opens the play by rejecting his political obligations to the French King and claiming the French crown. The King instructs Prince Edward to prepare to invade France, while he himself repulses the Scots besieging Roxborough Castle in the north. The Prince is eager to do the job properly, and his youthful idealism is in contrast to his father's political opportunism.

Distracted by a Woman

Edward's campaign against the Scots is put on hold when he meets the Countess of Salisbury. He knows she is the wife of one of his loyal lords, but he nevertheless becomes besotted with her. Edward never confronts the Scottish King, forsaking war for lustful adultery. He commissions a poem from Lodowick, the court secretary, who seems to deliberately misunderstand the situation. Edward tries wooing her, but the Countess says she realizes he is only testing her honour.

> The dramatic tension of *King Edward III* is built on the contrast between King Edward and his son, Prince Edward, the Black Prince. The King is a somewhat passive, less-than-honourable father, while the Prince is a genuinely honourable warrior son.

Edward extracted a thoughtless oath of loyalty from the Countess's father, the Earl of Warwick, and now asks him to win over the Countess to his adulterous desires. Warwick is reluctant to break his oath and discusses the matter with his daughter who, to his relief, rejects the King's proposition.

While Edward has been besieging the Countess, the Prince has assembled an army to invade France. However, receiving a message that the Countess is against war with France, Edward decides that the invasion would be a sin worse than adultery. The Countess demands that both her husband Salisbury and the Queen be put to death. Edward says he can't do this because what she wants is 'beyond our law', and the Countess tartly replies, 'So is your desire [for me].'

Edward reluctantly agrees, and the Countess pulls out two daggers, gives one to the King, and proposes that they kill their spouses by killing themselves, since they both carry the images of their spouses in their hearts. The Countess now adds that if he doesn't leave her alone, she'll kill herself immediately. Edward realizes that the Countess's suicide would certainly embarrass him politically, and that the war in France is a much better bet. He claims she has shamed him awake, and leaves her alone and goes off to battle the French.

Returning to War

In France, Prince Edward becomes his father's steward in the battle. At one point the Prince is surrounded and in trouble, but the King refuses to help him. If the Prince can 'redeem' himself he will 'win a world of honour'. If not, the King says, 'we have more sons than one, to comfort our declining age'. Happily, the Prince enters in triumph. The French King, however, escapes to Poitiers. King Edward sends the Prince to pursue him and, meanwhile, decides to wait at Calais.

In Poitiers, Prince Edward is surrounded by the French and is in danger of being killed. King Edward, meanwhile, captures Calais and demands that the six richest men in the city throw themselves on his mercy. How Edward will treat these merchants is a mystery, but things do not look good.

The old knight Audley tells the Prince they are surrounded by four French armies. The Prince, characteristically optimistic, replies: not so, we have one army; they have one army: 'One to one is fair equality'.

Against great odds, the Prince faces almost certain death bravely. But the Battle of Poitiers ends in defeat for France's John II, whose army is cut to ribbons by the English under Prince Edward. Edward, a badly wounded Audley and their captives set out for King Edward at Calais.

King Edward, meanwhile, tells his men to put all to the sword 'and make the spoil your own'. The six wealthy men of Calais beg for peace and mercy. Edward decides to take possession of the city in peace, but also to drag the six men around the city walls, 'and after feel the stroke of quartering steel'.

Edward's Queen, Philippa, who has just arrived at Calais, talks him into being merciful. The King agrees, claiming, somewhat ironically, 'that we as well can master our affections as conquer others by the dint of sword'.

At this point Copeland enters with the Scottish King David as his captive. Salisbury enters to announce that the Prince has (apparently) fallen at Poitiers. But then the Prince enters triumphant, with the French King and his son in tow.

Commentary

King Edward goes north to relieve the siege of Roxborough, only to become the passive besieger of the Countess of Salisbury and Calais. His son becomes the active warrior who wrests great victories from daunting odds at Crécy and Poitiers. The King acts for political gain; the Prince acts for honour and national pride, and without the Prince there would be, in this play, no conquest of France.

No sooner are the preparations for the invasion put underway than King Edward's romantic besieging of the Countess of Salisbury begins. Finally, when the King conquers his adulterous passion, the military conquest takes place, with the honourable Prince of Wales as its hero.

11 ✺ King Henry IV, Part I

Main Characters

King Henry IV – The King of England. He feels guilty about his involvement in the murder of Richard II. He's also irritated by the irresponsible antics of his eldest son, Prince Hal.

Prince Hal, the Prince of Wales – He will become King Henry V. He is sometimes called Harry or Harry Monmouth. He is the heir to the throne of England, but spends all his time hanging around the unsavoury side of London, wasting his time with highwaymen, robbers and whores.

Hotspur – The son and heir of the Earl of Northumberland. His real name is Henry Percy.

Sir John Falstaff – A fat old knight; a rogue and Prince Hal's closest friend.

Earl of Westmoreland – Allied with King Henry.

Prince John of Lancaster – One of King Henry's younger sons.

Sir Walter Blunt – Serves as a messenger of King Henry.

Thomas Percy – The Earl of Worcester. The mastermind behind the Percy rebellion.

Henry Percy – The Earl of Northumberland. Hotspur's father.

Edmund Mortimer – The Earl of March.

Owen Glendower – The leader of the Welsh rebels.

Archibald, Earl of Douglas – Usually called 'The Douglas' (a traditional way of referring to a Scottish clan chief). The leader of the large army of Scots allied with the Percys.

Sir Richard Vernon – Allied with the Percys.

Richard Scroop – The Archbishop of York.

Ned Poins, Peto, Bardolph and Gadshill – Criminals and highwaymen who drink with Falstaff and Prince Hal in the Boar's Head Tavern.

Mistress Quickly – Hostess of the Boar's Head Tavern, a seedy dive in Eastcheap, London.

Introduction

King Henry IV, Part I is the second part of a four-part series that deals with the rise of the house of Lancaster. The play was probably composed during 1596–97. Set around the years 1400–03, the action of *King Henry IV, Part I* takes place two centuries before Shakespeare's own time.

In general, it follows real events and onvolves historical people, although Shakespeare significantly alters or invents history as it suits him. For instance, the real Hotspur was not the same age as Prince Hal, and Shakespeare's Mortimer is a conflation of two historical people.

The Play

King Henry IV is tormented by guilt over the murder of Richard II, and beside himself at the antics of his eldest son Prince Hal, the heir to the throne. Hal spends most of his time in taverns in the seedy part of London, hanging around with highwaymen, prostitutes and vagrants. His closest friend is a worldly, fat old knight named Falstaff, a substitute father figure, who steals and lies for a living, surviving on his wits with great gusto.

tips

Falstaff, Prince Hal's fat, aged and criminally degenerate mentor and friend, is one of Shakespeare's most famous creations. Falstaff has many historical precedents, such as the figures of Vice and Gluttony from the medieval morality plays, but he has become second only to Hamlet as an object of critical interest.

A discontented family of noblemen, the Percys feel they have not been adequately rewarded for helping the King come to power, so they plan a rebellion. Harry Percy, known as Hotspur, leads the Percy forces. Hotspur is about Prince Hal's age, and as much as Hal is scorned and despised for his idle tavern life, Hotspur is widely respected for his bravery in battle.

The Percys gather a formidable army of rebels from Scotland and Wales, and from amongst English nobles and clergymen who have grievances against King Henry. The King has no choice but to go to war. Prince Hal decides it is time to reform, and plans to defeat Hotspur in battle in order to reclaim his good name. Drafting his tavern friends to fight in the King's army, Hal accompanies his father to the battlefront.

At the Battle of Shrewsbury, Prince Hal saves his father's life, thus winning his approval and affection. Hal also defeats Hotspur in single combat. The King's forces win, and most of the leaders of the Percy family are put to death. Falstaff manages to survive the battle by avoiding any actual fighting. Powerful rebel forces remain in Britain, however, so by the play's end the ultimate outcome of the war has not yet been resolved.

Commentary

King Henry IV, Part I has been called Shakespeare's greatest history play. Its three-dimensional characters and overt politics have been the subjects of many books and critical essays. It is an epic play, paralleling two worlds – the world of King Henry IV and his advisers, and that of the lower-class reprobates who spend their days at the inn in Eastcheap. Bridging these worlds is Prince Hal, who is actually involved in an unorthodox plan to prepare for the throne by getting to know the people he will eventually rule.

King Henry IV, Part I refers to its 'prequel', *King Richard II*. Its source was Raphael Holinshed's *The Chronicles of England, Scotland and Ireland*.

The play mixes history and comedy, moving from the realm of kings and political intrigue, to the world of rogues who become cannon fodder in the battles and spend their days in taverns or thieving. The play is concerned with the nature of kingship, honour and loyalty.

Although the play is named after Henry IV, he is really a minor character. King Henry is politically shrewd, unlike his predecessor, Richard II. But because he came to the throne as a usurper responsible for the death of God's anointed king, Richard, Henry's ability to rule is diminished, and the country is inevitably plunged into chaos.

Shakespeare explores honour through the characters of Hotspur, Falstaff and Prince Hal. Prince Hal must balance the two extremes of honour   Hotspur's obsession with the principle and Falstaff's apparent lack of it altogether – in order to distil his own concept so that he may become an honourable king.

Famous Lines

'He will give the devil his due' (Act I, Scene II).

'I know a trick worth two of that' (Act II, Scene I).

'Out of this nettle, danger, we pluck this flower, safety'
     (Act II, Scene III).

'O, monstrous! but one half-pennyworth of bread to this intolerable
     deal of sack!' (Act II, Scene IV).

'Exceedingly well read' (Act III, Scene I).

'Two stars keep not their motion in one sphere' (Act V, Scene IV).

'The better part of valour is discretion' (Act V, Scene IV).

12 ❧ King Henry IV, Part II

Main Characters

King Henry IV – The King of England.

Prince Hal – Also called Prince Henry, Harry, Prince Harry, Harry Monmouth, the Prince of Wales and, after his father's death, King Henry V.

Princes John, Duke of Lancaster, Humphrey, Duke of Gloucester, and Thomas, Duke of Clarence – Prince Hal's younger brothers.

The Lord Chief Justice – The most powerful law official in England.

Earl of Warwick, Earl of Surrey, Earl of Westmoreland, Gower, Harcourt and Sir John Blunt – King Henry IV's allies and advisors.

Sir John Falstaff – Sometimes called Jack. Prince Hal's mentor and close friend.

Page – A boy who serves Falstaff.

Poins, Peto and Bardolph – Friends of Falstaff and Prince Hal.

Ancient Pistol – A soldier (ancient meant 'ensign' in Elizabethan times).

Mouldy, Shadow, Wart, Feeble and Bullcalf – Army recruits.

Archbishop of York – A powerful clergyman who leads the rebellion against King Henry IV.

Mowbray and Hastings – Two lords who conspire with the Archbishop of York.

Henry Percy, Earl of Northumberland – Brother of Worcester and father to Hotspur, who have recently been killed in battle against King Henry IV.

Travers – Northumberland's servant.

Hotspur – Northumberland's son and a leader of the rebellion against the King.

Lord Bardolph – An ally of Northumberland (not to be confused with Falstaff's friend Bardolph).

Owen Glendower – A Welsh rebel leader.

Mistress Quickly (the Hostess) – Proprietor of the seedy Boar's Head Tavern in Eastcheap, London.

Doll Tearsheet – Falstaff's favourite prostitute and a good friend of Mistress Quickly.

Fang and Snare – Incompetent policemen.

Justice Shallow and Justice Silence – Justices of the Peace (minor judges).

Davy – Justice Shallow's servant.

Introduction

King Henry IV, Part II is the third part of Shakespeare's four-part series dealing with the rise of the royal house of Lancaster. (It is preceded by *King Richard II* and *King Henry IV, Part I*, and followed by *King Henry V*.) The play was probably written in about 1598.

There are no good film versions of either of the Henry IV plays, but people who have read them might like to take a look at *My Own Private Idaho*, a 1992 film by Gus Van Sant based loosely on the plays.

The Play

The Earl of Northumberland (Henry Percy) learns that his son Hotspur has been killed in battle and that Richard Scroop, the Archbishop of York, is continuing the rebellion against Henry IV.

Back in London, the Lord Chief Justice criticizes Falstaff for his wicked ways and tells the old knight that King Henry IV has decided to separate Falstaff from Prince Hal by sending Falstaff with Prince John of Lancaster (Hal's brother) to fight Scroop and Northumberland. Prince Hal returns from fighting the Welsh and meets with some of his friends to discuss his father's sickness and a pompous letter Falstaff has written to Hal, complaining about being abandoned by his friend.

Northumberland's wife and his daughter-in-law persuade him to flee to Scotland. The Earl of Warwick (with the Earl of Surrey and Sir Walter Blunt) assure the King that Northumberland will be defeated, though Henry repeats Richard II's prediction that Northumberland, who helped Henry IV to the throne, would eventually revolt and defeat Henry.

On his way to battle, Sir John Falstaff arrives at Justice Shallow's home seeking old friends to be soldiers. Falstaff conscripts Mouldy, Shadow, Wart, Feeble and Bullcalf, though Bullcalf and Mouldy bribe Bardolph (Falstaff's friend) to avoid having to fight.

At the battlefield, Scroop, Mowbray and Hastings learn that Northumberland will not help them. Prince John yields to Scroop's demands, granting protection to the rebelling nobles, who quickly tell their armies to disperse. Westmoreland and Prince John now betray Hastings, Scroop and Mowbray and arrest them for treason. Falstaff stumbles on Sir John Coleville of the Dale (a rebel) and captures him without a fight.

Hal arrives while Henry IV is asleep and tries on his father's crown. Henry wakes and rebukes Hal for wishing him dead and taking the crown. Hal claims he thought his father was dead and wanted to protect the crown.

Back in London, Henry IV vows to go on a crusade to the Holy Land if the rebellion is suppressed. When it is, he is distressed that Hal is still associating with criminals. Henry IV advises Hal to wage foreign wars when he is king, to occupy Britain's time and to increase Hal's popularity. Henry IV then dies. Hal becomes King Henry V and swears to be kind to all, even the Chief Justice who once jailed Prince Hal.

Falstaff returns to London, hoping to receive favours from King Henry V, his alehouse friend. However, during a coronation march Falstaff and his gang are banned from approaching Henry V within ten miles, after which Falstaff is arrested for his crimes.

Commentary

In contrast with *King Henry IV, Part 1*, this sequel is concerned with justice, sickness and betrayal. The play is sometimes described as the dramatization of a battle between vice and virtue for the soul of a king, and although Hal banishes Falstaff, the knight's philosophy offers an alternative view to the serious and the rational.

The play captures the entire English national life, from the country to the town, and from lowly drinking houses to the anguish and responsibilities of kings. It reflects Shakespeare's own experience – the country boy who came from Stratford, lived in the taverns of London and then made a success of his life by writing plays that were presented to kings, queens and nobility.

Famous Lines

'I do now remember the poor creature, small beer' (Act II, Scene II).

'Uneasy lies the head that wears a crown' (Act III, Scene I).

'We have heard the chimes at midnight' (Act III, Scene II).

'A man can die but once' (Act III, Scene II).

13 ❦ King Henry V

Main Characters

King Henry V – The young, recently crowned King of England.

Exeter, Westmoreland, Salisbury and Warwick – Advisors to the king.

Clarence, Bedford and Gloucester – Henry's younger brothers.

The Archbishop of Canterbury and the Bishop of Ely – Wealthy and powerful clergymen.

Cambridge, Scroop and Grey – Three conspirators against King Henry.

York and Suffolk – Cousins who die at the Battle of Agincourt.

Charles VI – The King of France.

Isabel – The Queen of France.

The Dauphin – The son of the King of France and heir to the throne.

Katherine – The King of France's daughter.

The Constable of France, the Duke of Orleans, the Duke of Britain, the Duke of Bourbon, the Earl of Grandpre, Lord Rambures, the Duke of Burgundy and the Governor of Harfleur – French noblemen and military leaders.

Sir Thomas Erpingham – A veteran soldier.

Fluellen, Macmorris, Jamy and Captain Gower – Captains of Henry's troops.

Pistol, Bardolph, and Nym – Commoners from London who serve with King Henry's army.

Boy – Formerly in the service of Falstaff, the nameless Boy leaves London after his master's death and goes with Pistol, Nym and Bardolph to the war in France.

Michael Williams, John Bates and Alexander Court – Common soldiers with whom King Henry argues while in disguise the night before the Battle of Agincourt.

Mistress Quickly – The keeper of the Boar's Head Tavern in London; she is married to Pistol.

Alice – Princess Katherine's maid.

Montjoy – The French herald.

Monsieur le Fer – A French soldier.
Chorus – The character who narrates the play.

Introduction

King Henry V is the last part of the four-part series that deals with the historical rise of the royal house of Lancaster. *King Henry V* was probably composed in 1599 and is one of the most popular of Shakespeare's history plays. It is rife with colourful characters, noble speeches, battles and a young king (Henry) who seems to be brave, modest and fiercely focused, yet with a sense of humour.

This is a stirring play, and when you watch it, it's useful to keep the paradoxes of morality and character in mind. The brilliance of Henry's speeches and his wit make him a John F. Kennedy-esque young and inspiring leader.

The Play

Worried by impending legislation that would effectively rob the Church of England of its power and wealth, the Archbishop of Canterbury persuades Henry V to focus, instead, on laying claim to France. When he does so, however, the Dauphin sends an insulting response, balls – a gift of tennis balls – that convinces Henry that the French want war. He puts together an army to invade France. But before he can leave, he must sort out the last of the rebels against his father and his house.

Lords Cambridge, Scroop and Grey conspire to assassinate Henry (they are paid by the French). The plot is discovered, and Henry arrests them personally and oversees their public execution. The army then lays siege to Harfleur, France, capturing it after heavy losses.

The night before a battle where the English face overwhelming odds, Henry disguises himself as a commoner to mingle with his troops. He talks candidly with his men and discovers that they may be unsure of their King, but are steadfast in their willingness to do battle with the French.

On the morning of the Battle of Agincourt, St Crispin's Day, Henry makes a stirring speech, knowing his army is outnumbered five to one. His expert archers help Henry rout the French, who are forced to ask for peace, which Henry grants on his own terms, of course. He signs the Treaty of Troyes, marries Princess Katherine of France, and insists he is named heir to the French throne, thus uniting England and France in peace.

Commentary

The play is harder to analyse than it first appears. Henry seems a model hero, but for all his patriotism – or, alternatively, land lust – he invades a non-aggressive country and slaughters thousands. He sentences former friends and prisoners of war to death, paying lip service to mercy; and he never accepts any responsibility for the bloodshed he has initiated.

King Henry V concludes the saga begun in *King Henry IV, Part I* – the making of a king. At the end of *Part I*, Hal seems to have evolved from profligate prince to mature heir to the throne. Yet in *Part II*, while Prince Hal has become Prince Harry, he still appears to shun the responsibilities of his father's court in favour of Falstaff's clearly defined and 'honestly' declared licentiousness. Prince Harry, caught trying on the crown while his father lies dying, intuitively understands (and fights against) the knowledge that 'uneasy lies the head that wears the crown'. Falstaff's anarchic, irresponsible world is hard to resist, particularly when the alternative is a kingdom embraced by vicious politics and feuding strife.

It is only at his father's deathbed that Prince Harry resolves the doubts that have plagued him. He recognizes that the crown, though blemished while on his father's head because it was illegally wrested from Richard II, will sit comfortably on his own, because he will inherit it lawfully.

Prince Harry becomes King Henry V, transforming himself finally into the great king who will defeat the French at Agincourt and win for England her lost dominions. But before making the last leg of this great journey, he must reject the disreputable and dishonourable anarchy of Falstaff's world, which he does with a chilling firmness: 'I know thee not, old man. Fall to thy prayers.'

Famous Lines

'Turn him to any cause of policy,
The Gordian knot of it he will unloose,
Familiar as his garter: that when he speaks,
The air, a chartered libertine, is still' (Act I, Scene I).

'Even at the turning o' the tide' (Act II, Scene III).

'Once more unto the breach, dear friends, once more,
Or close the wall up with our English dead!
In peace there's nothing so becomes a man
As modest stillness and humility;
But when the blast of war blows in our ears,
Then imitate the action of the tiger:
Stiffen the sinews, summon up the blood' (Act III, Scene I).

'I would give all my fame for a pot of ale and safety' (Act III, Scene II).

'Men of few words are the best men' (Act III, Scene II).

'This day is called the feast of Crispian:
He that outlives this day and comes safe home,
Will stand a tip-toe when this day is named,
And rouse him at the name of Crispian' (Act IV, Scene III).

'We few, we happy few, we band of brothers' (Act IV, Scene III).

14 ✶ King Henry VI, Part I

Main Characters

King Henry VI – King of England and various regions in France. The son of Henry V.

Charles – The Dauphin of France.

Gloucester – Regent until Henry is old enough to rule. He and Winchester are in a feud.

Winchester – Head of the English church; Gloucester's nemesis.

Richard Plantagenet – Later known as York. His father once had a claim to the throne of England before Henry IV killed him.

Talbot – English general of the troops in France. Talbot is so feared by the French that when he is captured, archers guard him while he sleeps.

Joan – Also known as Joan of Arc.

Somerset – An English lord who argues with Richard Plantagenet.

Suffolk – An English lord.

Mortimer – Richard Plantagenet's uncle.

Burgundy – A French lord.

Bedford – An English general.

Alençon – A French lord.

René – A French lord.

Bastard of Orléans – A French lord.

Exeter – An English lord. Exeter becomes a kind of chorus, remarking on the problems caused by internal dissension and strife in England and abroad.

Warwick – An English lord.

Salisbury – An English soldier.

Gargrave – An English soldier.

Glansdale – An English soldier.

Vernon – One of Somerset's men.

Basset – One of York's men.

Sir William Lucy – A messenger.

John – Talbot's son.
Margaret of Anjou – René's daughter, captured by Suffolk.
Margaret, Countess of Auvergne – A French noblewoman.
Sir John Fastolf – A cowardly English soldier (not the same as Falstaff).
Woodville – The Warden of the Tower of London.
The Lord Mayor – The Lord Mayor of London.
Master Gunner – A French soldier.
Boy – The Master Gunner's son.
Governor – The Governor of Paris.
General – The General of Bordeaux.
Shepherd – Joan's father.

Introduction

King Henry VI, Part I was probably written in 1592 and is one of Shakespeare's earliest plays. It picks up events some seven years after the Battle of Agincourt. Henry V has just died. This play covers the origins of the Wars of the Roses and the loss of Britain's territories in France.

Some scholars have theorized that Thomas Nashe wrote parts of *King Henry VI, Part I*; some believe Shakespeare wrote only the scene in the Temple Garden and the battle scenes in which Talbot and his son meet their deaths. Other scholars believe Shakespeare wrote the whole play, adding that the playwright was unlikely to have collaborated with other authors so early in his career.

Shakespeare wrote two more plays about Henry VI, *King Henry VI, Parts II* and *III* – the second two were published first, and some believe them to have been written first as well, though no one knows whether the order of publication of Shakespeare's works reflects their order of composition.

The *King Henry VI* plays are among Shakespeare's first attempts at history plays. They were followed by others that traced the years after Henry VI's death and the ensuing civil wars over the succession. Only later in his career did Shakespeare look back to the events prior to Henry VI's kingship, including that of his father, Henry V.

The history play held a particular fascination for the Elizabethan public and helped create a sense of a collective national memory. Patriotic sentiment was no doubt still running high after the defeat of the invading Spanish Armada in 1588. The history play drew upon such sentiments. *King Henry VI, Part I* in particular appears to refer to the specific incident of the English campaign in France, led by Elizabeth's charismatic favourite Essex. The play's depiction of 15th-century noblemen attacking the city of Rouen would certainly have reminded audiences of Essex's 1592 efforts at Rouen to aid the French in quashing a Protestant uprising.

Shakespeare probably used chronicles of the 15th century about the struggles during those years between the houses of York and Lancaster in the Wars of the Roses. His primary source was probably Raphael Holinshed's *The Chronicles of England, Scotland and Ireland*.

The Play

Henry V, King of England and parts of France, has died, and his young son, Henry VI, is on the throne. Charles, the Dauphin of France, is nurturing a rebellion across the Channel, and rifts among the nobles in England are festering, notably between the houses of York and Lancaster. Emboldened by the exploits of Joan of Arc, the French attack Talbot at Orléans. Henry VI manages to retake Orléans by night in a surprise attack.

In England, Richard Plantagenet and the Duke of Somerset have a disagreement concerning the letter of a law. The two men ask others to show their support for their respective positions: those supporting Richard pick a white rose, and those supporting Somerset pick a red one. After talking with his uncle, Edmund Mortimer, Richard is convinced that the throne more rightfully belongs to the house of York than young King Henry. Meanwhile, Winchester and Gloucester, guardians of the young King, continue a feud of their own.

Back in France, Joan drives the English from Rouen, but an English counterattack gets it back. Joan now persuades the Duke of Burgundy to switch to the French side. Talbot marches against him, and Henry orders Richard Plantagenet and the Duke of Somerset to reinforce Talbot in the battle. Somerset and Richard continue to feud, however, and while Talbot fights valiantly, he is slain in the combat when reinforcements don't arrive.

As with many public depictions of women, Joan's identity slips between the two biblical polarities of Mary the virgin and Mary the whore. Queen Elizabeth I also provoked reverence with her title 'The Virgin Queen', as well as malicious rumours of infertility or a sexual defect. Both Joan of Arc and Elizabeth could therefore be regarded as exceptional people or as perversions of nature.

Richard and Somerset set aside their differences long enough to capture Joan of Arc and burn her as a witch. In the meantime, Gloucester tries to set up a match between Henry and Margaret, Countess of Auvergne, in order to force a peace between France and England. The Earl of Suffolk, however, introduces Henry to Margaret of Anjou in an attempt to get him to marry her, which he does. Suffolk hopes to use her to control Henry, which leads to the action of *King Henry VI, Part II*.

Commentary

King Henry VI, Part I depicts England's struggle to retain its military and political control over French territories gained by Henry V. The play compresses events of the early reign of Henry VI, including the feuding of English lords and the eventual loss of half the French lands.

Nowadays, Shakespeare's histories are not as popular as his tragedies and comedies. Many people assume they are tedious textbook reconstructions. But while Shakespeare drew on historical records, he condensed dates and events, reordering things to create drama. For example, Henry VI was actually only nine months old when he became

King, while in the play he is a teenager. What's more, one of the play's most striking scenes, in the Temple Garden, in which the followers of Richard Plantagenet and Somerset pick white and red roses as emblems of their opposing views, is complete fabrication. It does, however, explain the reasons for the Wars of the Roses, an affair whose actual origins are banal and complicated.

Shakespeare gives equal voice to two predominant theories of the cause of 15th-century British turmoil: (1) history is the result of human choices and actions, and (2) the violence of the 15th century was some sort of divine punishment for the murder of King Richard II.

The warrior culture of *King Henry V* is changing around Henry VI. After Henry V's death, lords abandon a unity for the sake of King and country, and return to plotting their own advancement. War loses its chivalrous quality. The death of Talbot and his son signals the death of 'romantic' chivalry.

While *King Henry V* (which was written later) portrays a man who claims his birthright and lives up to the full potential of his masculinity, *King Henry VI, Part I* acknowledges the potential weaknesses of men. Sometimes, as in the case of Queen Elizabeth, a woman must step up and take charge, even if it means usurping a traditional male role.

Thomas Nashe wrote a pamphlet on the importance of history plays as a genre, stating that they helped to preserve the memories of glorious English heroes, such as the chivalrous Lord Talbot. Nashe added that the history play creates a collective memory of the nation's past for the masses, celebrating the realm's heroes and particularly patriotic moments in English history.

Famous Lines

'Halcyon days' (Act I, Scene II).

'She's beautiful, and therefore to be wooed;
She is a woman, therefore to be won' (Act V, Scene III).

15 ❦ King Henry VI, Part II

Main Characters

Henry VI – King of England.

Gloucester – Regent until Henry was old enough to rule.

Somerset – Somerset stands for the red rose, against York and those who wear the white rose.

Buckingham – A lord who joins Somerset, Suffolk, Beaufort and Margaret to plot against Gloucester.

Beaufort – Head of the English church. In *King Henry VI, Part I* he was called Winchester.

York – Called Richard in the earlier play. He is heir to Edward III's third son, while Henry is heir to Edward III's fourth son.

Suffolk – A lord of the court.

Salisbury – A lord of the court. Salisbury supports York.

Warwick – A lord of the court. Warwick supports York.

Margaret – King Henry's wife, captured during the French wars by Suffolk.

Duchess – Wife of Gloucester.

Hume – A procurer of conjurers and witches.

Peter – A working man.

Horner – Accused by Peter of treason.

Witch – Hired by the Duchess, the Witch helps raise a spirit.

Bolingbroke – A conjurer.

Simpcox – A poor man who pretends he has been blind since birth.

Jack Cade – Hired by York to cause trouble in England while York is away.

Captain – In charge of the ship that captures Suffolk at sea.

Whitmore – One of the Captain's men. Whitmore kills Suffolk.

Rebels – Common people led by Jack Cade.

Butcher – One of Jack Cade's men.

Weaver – Another of Jack Cade's men.

The Staffords – Two nobles of the court who challenge Jack Cade. Stafford and his brother die, and their bodies are dragged behind Cade's horse to London.

Lord Saye – Sought and killed by Jack Cade.

Sergeant – Husband of the woman the Butcher rapes.

Clifford – A lord of the court. Clifford persuades Jack Cade's troops to surrender.

Alexander Iden – A noble who kills Cade.

Edward – York's son. Edward will be the next king of England.

Richard – York's son. Richard will become Richard III.

Introduction

Some editors think *King Henry VI, Part II* was written before *King Henry VI, Part I*, probably in 1591, making it one of Shakespeare's earliest plays. It takes place after the French wars, when the English lost and regained most of the lands originally won by Henry V. During the wars depicted in *King Henry VI, Part I*, disagreements between Somerset and York led to the creation of two factions, those who supported the red rose and those who supported the white, setting the stage for the civil wars known as the Wars of the Roses.

Shakespeare probably used Raphael Holinshed's *The Chronicles of England, Scotland and Ireland* for details of Cade's rebellion, modelling it on the uprising led by Wat Tyler in the Peasants' Revolt of 1381, during the reign of Richard II.

King Henry VI, Part II concerns the continued power struggles between Gloucester and Beaufort, and York and Somerset. This infighting and the popular uprising by Jack Cade show what happens when a king is too weak to rule. The play charts the rise and fall of many lords and lesser figures within the kingdom.

A version of the play was first published in 1594, then a longer one appeared in the First Folio in 1623. The relationship between these two texts has been a long-debated point in Shakespeare scholarship.

Some scholars suggest that the shorter version was a reconstruction of the play prepared by actors, who remembered as much of the play as they could for publication. Others think the 1594 version may have been an early draft, and the later published play a more polished version. Most editors agree that actors, scribes, publishers and censors all had a hand in altering the play as it moved onto the stage. The editors of the Oxford series decided to use the later, longer version of the play, but incorporated lengthy stage directions and lines from the earlier version.

The Play

The action picks up from the end of *King Henry VI, Part I*. Humphrey, Duke of Gloucester, is unhappy with Margaret's lack of dowry and with Henry's giving up territory in France. Suffolk, who introduced Margaret to Henry in the hope of controlling her, and thus the King, sets plots in motion against Gloucester. He arranges for Gloucester's wife to be arrested for witchcraft. Meanwhile, York bides his time, convinced of the legitimacy of his claim to the throne.

Gloucester is eventually arrested on trumped-up charges. During Gloucester's trial, York is sent to Ireland to put down a revolt. While in Ireland, York encourages Jack Cade to muster support among the common folk for York to depose Henry. If Cade succeeds, York has an army at his back to use against Henry when he returns from Ireland.

Gloucester is murdered at Suffolk's behest. Henry banishes Suffolk. En route to France, Suffolk is captured by pirates and is summarily put to death.

Cade's rebellion gathers support, and he marches on London, leaving brutality and havoc in his wake, with Henry retreating before him. Buckingham confronts his force with an army and extends pardons to all who abandon Cade. After a five-day flight without food, Cade is killed while foraging in a private garden. In the wake of Cade's failed uprising, York returns from Ireland and demands that the King arrest Somerset before York's men lay down their arms.

The King does so, but Margaret, now Queen but also Suffolk's lover, frees him almost immediately. York declares war on King Henry, determined to take the crown by force if necessary. At the Battle of St Albans, Richard, son of York, slays Somerset. The Yorkists then set out in pursuit of the fleeing Henry and Margaret.

Commentary

It is Henry's weakness as a king and leader that is the focus of the play. If Henry were stronger, he would not have agreed to the imprisonment of an innocent man. Yet Henry seems powerless to resist his nobles and his wife. Suffolk arrests Gloucester, Beaufort orders him taken away, and the others all accuse him. And though the nobles agree that they have no real proof of wrongdoing, they agree he should be killed immediately, without a trial. Similar to Cade's rampage through the countryside, the nobles play out their own version of mob rule, removing their enemies from office and killing them without reason.

16 § King Henry VI, Part III

Main Characters

York – Richard, Duke of York.

Henry VI – King of England.

Edward – York's eldest son, soon to be Edward IV.

George – Also known as Clarence. Edward's younger brother.

Richard – Soon to be Richard III. A younger brother of Edward and George. Most noted for his physical deformities, including a hunchback, lame leg and shrivelled arm.

Warwick – One of York's allies, who switches his allegiance to Henry.

Margaret – Henry's French wife.

Prince Edward – Son of Margaret and Henry.

Rutland – York's youngest son, killed by Clifford.

Clifford – He kills York's son, Rutland, then York himself.

Montague – One of Warwick's relatives.

Westmoreland – One of Henry's supporters.

Exeter – One of Henry's supporters.

Norfolk – One of Henry's supporters.

Somerset – One of Edward's supporters.

Northumberland – One of Henry's supporters.

Lady Bona – Sister of Louis, King of France.

Lady Grey – Edward propositions her, but she refuses. Then she agrees to become Queen.

Louis – King of France.

Oxford – One of Henry's supporters.

Rivers – One of Edward's supporters, brother of Lady Gray.

Hastings – One of Edward's supporters.

Montgomery – One of Edward's supporters.

Richmond – Henry, Earl of Richmond (soon to be Henry VII).

Introduction

King Henry VI, Part III has attracted attention for its boldness in adapting a complex historical narrative to the requirements of the theatre, and is considered one of Shakespeare's earliest plays. It was first published in 1595 in an octavo volume under the title *The True Tragedy of Richard Duke of York and the Good King Henry the Sixth*.

Some scholars believe that the first version was an early draft of the later folio edition. Others believe that the octavo version was reconstructed from memory by actors and audience members, which explains its shorter length. It is thought the folio version is based on Shakespeare's own manuscript before he gave it to his players, while the octavo version may have been based on a prompt book for the actual production. Most editors use the longer folio version, with occasional additions from the octavo.

Shakespeare again probably referred to 15th-century histories as well as Raphael Holinshed's *The Chronicles of England, Scotland and Ireland* and Edward Hall's *Union of the Two Noble and Illustre Families of Lancaster and York* (1548) when researching the play.

King Henry VI, Part III is a continuation of the depiction of the Wars of the Roses, begun in *King Henry VI, Parts I* and *II*, which traces the struggles between the Lancastrian (red rose) and Yorkist (white rose) descendants of Edward III. The third part depicts some of the many significant battles fought during that civil war.

The Play

Part III picks up from the end of *Part II*. Following his victory at St Albans, York is now set to take the crown of England. Henry VI presents York with an offer: Henry will rule England until his death, and then the crown will pass to the house of York.

York agrees, but Queen Margaret is irate because her son, the Prince of Wales, should be the next King. Margaret fights a battle that kills the Duke of York and his youngest son, Rutland. The Yorkists rally, however, and Margaret and Henry have to flee the country. Edward, eldest son of York, now becomes King.

Henry secretly returns to England, but is captured by Edward and put in the Tower of London. Margaret petitions the King of France for help. However, Warwick tries to outmanoeuvre her by attempting to broker a marriage between Edward and the French King's sister-in-law, Bona. This plan falls apart when word comes that Edward has married Lady Grey.

Back in England, Warwick manages to capture Edward, temporarily restoring Henry to the throne. Richard, now Duke of Gloucester, rescues Edward. Edward and the Yorkists then defeat and kill Warwick at the Battle of Tewkesbury. Margaret and the Prince of Wales are captured, and while the Prince is killed, Edward grants Margaret mercy.

Richard pays a visit to the Tower of London to see Henry, who is a prisoner. When Henry foretells Richard's bloody future, Richard kills him. Edward now holds the throne as King Edward IV, but his brother Richard plots to usurp the crown for himself. The story continues in *King Richard III*.

Commentary

Some critics have seen *King Henry VI, Part III* as a flawed play, perhaps showing Shakespeare's weariness with the dramatization of the Wars of the Roses, or the difficulty of getting so much historical matter on the stage. Yet contemporary productions have been successful, particularly in depicting the ruthless Margaret and the increasingly alienated and enraged Richard, who emerges as the play's antihero.

Famous Lines

'The smallest worm will turn, being trodden on' (Act II, Scene II).

'Didst thou never hear
That things ill got had ever bad success?
And happy always was it for that son
Whose father for his hoarding went to hell?' (Act II, Scene II).

17 & King Henry VIII

Main Characters

King Henry VIII – King of England.

Cardinal Wolsey – The King's right-hand man.

Queen Katharine – Married to Henry's brother before marrying Henry.

Buckingham – A lord of the court. He is accused of plotting to gain the throne.

Anne Boleyn – Spelt 'Anne Bullen' in the play. Henry's future wife. She dies giving birth to the child Elizabeth.

Cranmer – Archbishop of Canterbury.

Cardinal Campeius – An emissary from the Pope.

Norfolk – A lord of the court. At first he doesn't believe Buckingham's criticism of Cardinal Wolsey and urges Buckingham to hold his tongue.

Suffolk – A lord of the court.

Lord Chamberlain – A lord of the court.

Lord Chancellor – A lord of the court.

Cromwell – Friend of Cardinal Wolsey. Cromwell is devastated by Wolsey's demise. Yet Wolsey encourages him to go back to the King and continue serving the state.

Sands – A lord of the court.

Lovell – A lord of the court.

Gardiner – Cardinal Wolsey's former secretary.

Guildford – A lord of the court.

Vaux – A lord of the court.

Surrey – Buckingham's son-in-law.

Abergavenny – Buckingham's friend.

Brandon – Sergeant-at-arms.

Denny – A lord of the court.

Butts – The King's doctor.

Surveyor – Surveyor to Buckingham.

Old Lady – Anne Boleyn's attendant.

Griffith – Queen Katharine's attendant.
Capucius – An ambassador from the King of Spain.
The Child – Christened Elizabeth, she will later become Queen.
Prologue – A character who introduces the play to the audience.
Epilogue – A character who ends the play for the audience.
Gentlemen – People in the streets.

Introduction

King Henry VIII was written in 1613 and combines the genres of history play with tragicomic romance, a form gaining new popularity in the early 17th century. The play focuses on the instabilities of the royal court from roughly 1530 to 1533, when Elizabeth is born. When Shakespeare wrote the play, the King of England was James I (James VI of Scotland), who was the son of Mary, Queen of Scots, the daughter of Henry VIII's sister who married a Scottish king. James, though a Stuart, was a direct descendent of the Tudors. The play centres on Henry VIII's break with Rome and the Catholic Church.

King Henry VIII was performed on 29 June 1613, the day the Globe Theatre burned to the ground. Eyewitness accounts of the fire disagree about the point in the play when it happened, but several small sound-effect cannon were fired during certain scenes, which ignited the thatch roof of the theatre and led to the fire. No one was hurt, though a man's clothes caught fire. The theatre was destroyed.

In 1531, disappointed that his wife Catherine of Aragon (spelt 'Katharine' in this play) had not given him a male heir, Henry decided to divorce her. His advisers argued that because she had been his brother's widow the marriage was invalid, but the Pope did not agree.

Henry nevertheless went forward with the divorce and married Anne Boleyn ('Anne Bullen' in the play) in 1533. The Pope excommunicated Henry, who promptly declared himself the head of the Church of England, and dissolved the monasteries and seized their wealth.

The rest of Henry's reign was plagued with rebellions by groups who either wanted to restore Catholicism or were supporters of various religious reformation groups. The actual break with the Pope is not dramatized in the play, although we see Henry's advisers discuss ways to negotiate a legal divorce. We even see Cardinal Wolsey urge the Pope to refuse the divorce. But the excommunication itself is only alluded to.

The years following Henry's death were racked with religious disagreement and rebellions. When Elizabeth finally came to the throne, she returned England to Protestant rule, but the religious unrest continued. The frequent public executions that took place following Henry's break with Rome, and during the reigns of Mary and Elizabeth, are foreshadowed by the execution of Buckingham.

No one believed that Henry's reason for wanting to divorce Katharine resulted from a pricking of his conscience about the legality of his marriage. Everyone knew he wanted to marry Anne because he believed she could give him a son and heir. Despite a compliment to James I at the end of the play, criticism of Henry as an inattentive ruler was probably also aimed at James, who was known to neglect affairs of state.

The Play

Cardinal Wolsey, a close adviser to King Henry VII, has arranged the arrest of the Duke of Buckingham on charges of treason. Henry's wife, Queen Katharine, pleads on Buckingham's behalf with no success. Buckingham is tried and executed.

At a party hosted by Wolsey, Henry meets and is smitten with Anne Bullen, a lady-in-waiting to Queen Katharine. Henry decides he needs a new wife and seeks Wolsey's advice. Henry's argument is that Katharine is the widow of his brother, which makes the marriage one step removed from incest – ignoring the fact that Henry and Katharine have been wed for almost 20 years.

Wolsey has become despised for taxes he has levied in Henry's name, as well as for his role in Buckingham's death. He is now further despised because Henry wishes a divorce. Wolsey agrees to ask the to Pope send a representative to render a decision on the matter. Katharine, however, views her marriage as sacred.

King Henry VIII recounts the fall of the three main figures of King Henry VIII's early court, and the near fall of a fourth. The traditional Renaissance idea of a wheel of fortune is at work here: what rises must inevitably fall.

A series of political stumblings present Wolsey in an unflattering light to King Henry. Most damning is Wolsey's meddling in the King's divorce. Wolsey is disgraced, and Henry divorces Katharine and marries Anne in secret, regardless of the Pope's opinion. Wolsey dies soon after, and Katharine (who is in poor health) follows him to the grave.

The new Archbishop of Canterbury, Cranmer, becomes the focus of a plot by Gardiner, Wolsey's secretary. Cranmer is brought to trial in much the same manner as Buckingham, but enjoys the King's protection. Henry exonerates the Archbishop and has him christen his and Anne Bullen's new daughter, Elizabeth. At the christening, Cranmer prophesies a noble reign for Elizabeth and glory for England in her time.

Commentary

The merging of romance and history suggests that fate somehow helped shape English history, and the most important of these fateful events is the birth of Elizabeth, future Queen of England, who had died by the time the play was produced. In order for the birth to take place, a complex set of events must be put into motion, and anyone who stands in the way must be removed.

Unlike other histories that dramatized the fate of kings, this play deals with the rise and fall of lesser court figures such as Buckingham, Katharine, Wolsey and Cranmer. Each downfall or near-downfall is played out in scenes of pageantry.

With the exception of Cranmer, each character must go because he or she prevents Elizabeth being born. Buckingham believes he has a claim to

Henry's throne; Katharine is Queen and can't give Henry a male heir; and Wolsey opposes Henry's marriage to Anne. If Elizabeth's birth is ensured, then so is the legitimacy of the succession of the King who was on the throne when Shakespeare wrote the play: James I, chosen by Elizabeth as her successor.

It's a mystery why Cranmer survives his trial. He suffers from the same kind of negative rumour mill that brings down the other characters, yet the King clearly wants to save him. We can conjecture that the cycle of lords blaming each other had to stop somewhere, or it threatened to spin out of control and into civil conflict. But history reveals that Cranmer was later executed anyway.

Famous Lines

'Heat not a furnace for your foe so hot
That it do singe yourself' (Act I, Scene I).

'Press not a falling man too far!' (Act III, Scene II).

'Had I but served my God with half the zeal
I served my king, he would not in mine age
Have left me naked to mine enemies' (Act III, Scene II).

'To dance attendance on their lordships' pleasures' (Act V, Scene II).

18 ♪ King John

Main Characters

King John – The King of England, the third son of Henry II. His older brother, Richard the Lionheart, was King before him.

Eleanor – John's mother.

Philip – The King of France. Arthur's champion.

Arthur – Son of Geoffrey, John's elder brother.

The Bastard – Philip, the illegitimate son of Richard the Lionheart, and a chorus for the play.

Louis – Philip's son.

Pandulph – A messenger from the Pope.

Hubert – One of John's men.

Constance – Arthur's mother.

Pembroke – One of John's followers.

Salisbury – One of John's followers.

Austria – One of Philip's men, killed by the Bastard.

Blanch – John's niece. She marries Louis, thus cementing a bond between John and Philip.

Essex – One of John's followers.

Bigot – One of John's followers.

Melun – One of Louis's men.

Faulconbridge – The Bastard's younger (legitimate) brother.

Lady Faulconbridge – The Bastard's mother.

Chatillon – A messenger from France.

Prince Henry – John's son. He becomes King Henry III at John's death.

Introduction

King John was written in about 1596 or earlier, and stands as the odd play out in the early histories that trace the Wars of the Roses. It was published in the First Folio of 1623. Chronologically, it is the earliest of the history plays, covering the period of John's reign from 1199 to 1216.

While parallels oversimplify the facts, they nevertheless capture the themes Shakespeare wanted to emphasize in this play. John's claim to the throne is based on the will of his older brother, Richard the Lionheart. Elizabeth's father, Henry VIII, made Elizabeth his heir by will, despite disputes about the legality of appointing successors. Also, the Pope excommunicated both John and Elizabeth for disobedience.

Some critics believe an earlier anonymous play, *The Troublesome Reign of John, King of England* (1591), was a primary source for *King John*. Both plays relied on Raphael Holinshed's *The Chronicles of England, Scotland and Ireland*.

John's rival to the throne was Arthur, the son of Geoffrey, John's elder brother, in much the same way that Elizabeth's rival, Mary, was the daughter of Henry VIII's older sister, who married into the Scottish line of kings. (Her son, James VI of Scotland, became James I of England on Elizabeth's death.) Because succession traditionally passed to the son of the oldest child, both John's and Elizabeth's claims to the throne were weak. Arthur's cause was championed by King Philip of France, while Mary's claims were supported by Philip II of Spain.

John brings about Arthur's death, regrets his decision, and tries to distance himself from it, just as Elizabeth ordered Mary's execution and then distanced herself from it. Arthur's death provided an excuse for a French invasion; Mary's death provoked Philip II to launch the Spanish Armada. What's more, the invasion against John is frustrated by a storm that shipwrecks the French reinforcements, while a storm also saved England from the brunt of the Spanish Armada in 1588.

The Play

King John's nephew, Arthur, believes he is the rightful heir to the throne of England, and is backed by Philip of France in a rebellion. Refusing the King of France's demand that he surrender his throne, John sends an army to

France under the command of Philip Faulconbridge (also known as Philip the Bastard), illegitimate son of Richard I and Arthur's half-brother.

The English army clashes with the French at Angiers, but neither can claim a decisive victory. John proposes peace, ceding Philip some English territory in France and arranging for the Dauphin (the French King's son) to wed his niece, Blanch.

The Pope excommunicates John over a dispute concerning the appointment of the Archbishop of Canterbury. Pandulph, the Pope's legate, orders the French to resume their war with King John. John's army beats back the French and captures Arthur. John wishes him executed. His Chamberlain, Hubert, disobeys the order, but Arthur later plunges to his death while trying to escape. Ironically, the nobles suspect John of murder, his original intent, and desert him for the French. Meanwhile, John arranges peace with Pandulph, to whom he gives the crown of England. He receives it back, thus becoming a vassal of the Catholic church once more.

Now that John is back in the fold, Pandulph tries to stop the war. The French won't accede to this, and the armies clash at St Edmundsbury. During the battle, a French noble named Melun warns the turncoat English noblemen that the King of France will have them executed as soon as John has been conquered. The nobles, seeing the winds of fortune shift, return their allegiance to John.

Without his allies, the French King comes to terms with Pandulph and John, who is hardly able to enjoy his victory. While staying at Swinstead Abbey, he is poisoned by one of the monks. His son will ascend the throne as King Henry III.

Commentary

King John focuses on historical events, but these events seem repeatedly to get in the way of intention and outcome – the characters are continually thwarted by historical accident and adversity. It is almost the antithesis of Cassius's famous speech in *Julius Caesar*: 'The fault, dear Brutus, is not in our stars, But in ourselves, that we are underlings'. In other words, we control what happens to us, but in *King John*, it seems, we are not in full control of things.

King John treats history as an unpredictable unfolding of events. Decisive moments seem insignificant episodes in a haphazard universe. Elizabethan audiences would have picked up on *King John*'s comment on the contemporary debate about Elizabeth I's legitimacy to the throne, as opposed to that of Mary, Queen of Scots.

John thinks he can secure his hold on the throne by killing Arthur, but his lords turn against him, proving him wrong. Arthur is actually spared, only to ruin everything by panicking and killing himself by accident. John is again foiled by fate.

Famous Lines

'I would that I were low laid in my grave:
I am not worth this coil that's made for me' (Act II, Scene I).

'Talks as familiarly of roaring lions
As maids of thirteen do of puppy-dogs!' (Act II, Scene I).

'Grief fills the room up of my absent child,
Lies in his bed, walks up and down with me,
Puts on his pretty looks, repeats his words,
Remembers me of all his gracious parts,
Stuffs out his vacant garments with his form' (Act III, Scene IV).

'Life is as tedious as a twice-told tale
Vexing the dull ear of a drowsy man' (Act III, Scene IV).

'Make haste; the better foot before' (Act IV, Scene II).

19 ☙ King Lear

Main Characters

King Lear – The ageing King of Britain.

Goneril – King Lear's ruthless eldest daughter. Married to the Duke of Albany.

Regan – King Lear's second daughter, as ruthless as Goneril. Married to the Duke of Cornwall.

Cordelia – King Lear's youngest daughter.

Gloucester – Father of Edgar and Edmund.

Edgar – Gloucester's eldest son. He disguises himself as a crazy beggar called Poor Tom.

Edmund – Gloucester's younger, illegitimate son.

Kent – A nobleman loyal to King Lear.

Fool – Lear's fool. He mysteriously disappears during Act III.

Albany – Goneril's husband.

Cornwall – Regan's husband.

Oswald – Goneril's steward.

Introduction

King Lear is one of Shakespeare's most famous tragedies, and along with *Hamlet,* one of his most challenging. Written about 1605, between *Othello* and *Macbeth,* it rivals *Hamlet* as Shakespeare's greatest play.

King Lear is not performed that often, partly because it explores madness, despair, chaos, ageing and death. It is a difficult and disturbing play whose dark psychology and symbolic ambiguity seem relentlessly nihilistic. The scenes in which the mad Lear rages – naked, on a stormy heath – against his deceitful daughters and nature itself, are considered by many scholars to be the finest examples of tragic poetry in English.

If the philosophical questioning of *Hamlet* (written around 1601) arose in part because of the death of Shakespeare's young son some four years earlier, one wonders what dark personal event was in the forefront of the Bard's thoughts when he composed *Lear*. The cynicism and bitterness that pervade his later works seem to find their zenith in *Lear*.

The actual text of *King Lear* also presents special problems. The play exists in two very different editions – an early one printed in 1608, and a revised version printed in 1623. Today, editions of *King Lear* vary, depending on which version they are based on. Most often, the two editions of the play are woven together.

The Play

King Lear, the ageing King of Britain, decides to split his kingdom among his three daughters, Goneril, Regan and Cordelia. Goneril and Regan pour flattery on him, protesting their love for their father, while Cordelia, sincere in her love for her father, simply says she loves him the way a daughter should. Lear is upset by her response and disinherits her. The King of France says that he will marry her anyway. When Kent, one of Lear's nobles, tries to reason with him, Lear banishes him as well.

Shakespeare adapted a folk tale based on older oral stories for the play's storyline. Shakespeare's was the first version of the tale where the king goes mad, his good daughter dies and there is no happy ending.

Meanwhile, Edmund, Gloucester's bastard son, decides to gain his father's inheritance by tricking him into thinking that Edgar, his legitimate son, is plotting to murder Gloucester. Edgar flees for his life and, disguised as a madman, goes into hiding.

The King's Fall

Lear soon discovers how much Goneril and Regan actually love him. Both daughters belittle him and try to take away from him the little dignity and power he has kept for himself. Lear is transformed from a powerful king to an impotent old man with only Kent – who has disguised himself and disobeyed Lear's decree of banishment – and his Fool for company.

In the middle of the play, Lear is driven mad by grief at his foolishness and the betrayal of his children. On a lonely heath he rages, naked, at a storm. They meet Edgar, who is disguised as Poor Tom. Gloucester provides them with shelter and guides them to Dover to meet Cordelia and the French King, who has landed an army in England to come to Lear's aid. For pitying Lear, Gloucester is betrayed by Edmund, and Cornwall puts out Gloucester's eyes. However, a servant is so distressed by the scene that he fatally stabs Cornwall before Regan kills him in turn.

Now blind, Gloucester meets up with Edgar disguised as Poor Tom. Edgar does not reveal himself, but leads his father towards Dover. Meanwhile, Goneril's husband, Albany, has begun to speak up for Lear and Gloucester. Both sisters independently start affairs with Edmund.

Father and Daughter United in Death

The English and French armies battle, and the English win. Lear and Cordelia are taken prisoner, and Edmund orders them hanged. Edgar tracks down his brother, and in a duel stabs Edmund fatally. Goneril poisons Regan to win Edmund from her, then kills herself when she learns of Edmund's fate. Realizing he is about to die, Edmund repents his sins and reveals his plots, including the imminent deaths of Lear and Cordelia.

It is all too late: Lear enters carrying Cordelia's body. Overcome by grief and exhaustion, Lear collapses, and dies a broken old man beside the only daughter who loved him. Gloucester dies after being reconciled with Edgar. Kent and Edgar retire, leaving Albany to rule Britain.

King Lear is a tragedy of such power that audiences are left emotionally drained at its conclusion. We can only wonder at the meaninglessness of life after the physical and moral horrors at the play's end. Kent, on seeing Lear reduced to a mad, pathetic creature with the murdered Cordelia in his arms, murmurs, 'Is this the promis'd end?'

Commentary

While traditional critics of *King Lear* find a heroic pattern in the story, modern audiences see a nihilistic play about the frailty and futility of the human condition. Even the most powerful are humbled before the forces of fate and nature.

One of the important questions about Lear is whether he learns from his mistakes and becomes more personally aware. Do his humiliation and insanity strip away the hubris that caused his downfall? It seems that while he never completely regains his sanity, his values do change for the better by the end of the play. As he is made to realize his insignificance by the awesome natural forces that are unleashed on him, he becomes a humbled yet caring man, finally appreciating Cordelia for the jewel she is, though too late to save either himself or her.

Edmund's change of heart is rare among Shakespeare's villains, and can make us wonder if *Lear* is not in some ways a play about the power of love amid carnage. Goneril and Regan, for example, totally lack love until they meet Edmund. How is it possible that they are sisters to Cordelia?

The depth of Cordelia's love for Lear is a counterpoint to the height of the King's arrogance. By banishing her, he abandons his soul and plunges his kingdom into chaos and brutal anarchy. As we watch Goneril and Regan torment and plot against their father, deliberately pushing Lear toward madness, we pray that Cordelia will come back and rescue him from himself and his dreadful fate.

When at last they find each other, their reunion marks the restoration of peace and order in the kingdom, and the triumph of love and forgiveness over hatred and spite. This fleeting moment of redemption makes the devastating finale of *King Lear* that much more cruel, as Cordelia, the personification of kindness and virtue, is sacrificed for nothing, depriving Lear's world of the meaning he thought he had found at last.

Famous Lines

'Although our last, not least' (Act I, Scene I).

'Nothing will come of nothing' (Act I, Scene, I).

'How sharper than a serpent's tooth it is
To have a thankless child!' (Act I, Scene IV).

'Striving to better, oft we mar what's well' (Act I, Scene IV).

'Blow, winds, and crack your cheeks! rage! blow!' (Act III, Scene II).

'A poor, infirm, weak, and despised old man' (Act III, Scene II).

'I am a man
More sinn'd against than sinning' (Act III, Scene II).

'O, that way madness lies; let me shun that' (Act III, Scene IV).

'The worst is not
So long as we can say, "This is the worst." ' (Act IV, Scene I).

'Pray you now, forget and forgive' (Act IV, Scene VII).

'Her voice was ever soft,
Gentle, and low, – an excellent thing in woman' (Act V, Scene III).

20 ✆ King Richard II

Main Characters

King Richard II – The King of England.

Henry Bolingbroke – Duke of Hertford. Occasionally referred to by his nickname, Harry. King Richard's cousin and the son of Richard's uncle, John of Gaunt.

John of Gaunt – Duke of Lancaster. Called either Gaunt or Lancaster.

Edmund of Langley – Duke of York. Called York. Richard's uncle, and a brother of John of Gaunt.

Duke of Aumerle – Earl of Rutland. Also called Rutland.

Thomas Mowbray – Duke of Norfolk. Called Norfolk.

Bushy, Bagot and Greene – Richard's friends and supporters.

Henry Percy, Earl of Northumberland, Lord Ross and Lord Willoughby – Noblemen who join Bolingbroke's rebel army to fight against King Richard.

Duchess of York – The wife of the Duke of York and mother of the Duke of Aumerle.

Duchess of Gloucester – Sister-in-law of John of Gaunt and the Duke of York.

Queen Isabel – King Richard's wife.

Lord Berkeley – The ruler of Berkeley Castle in Gloucestershire.

Lord Salisbury – A lord loyal to Richard.

Bishop of Carlisle – A clergyman loyal to Richard.

Sir Stephen Scroop – A nobleman loyal to Richard.

Abbot of Westminster – A clergyman loyal to Richard.

Sir Piers Exton – A nobleman who assassinates Richard.

Introduction

King Richard II was probably composed around 1595, and certainly no later than 1597. It is set around the year 1398, and documents the fall of the last Plantagenet king, Richard II, and the rise of the first Lancastrian king, Henry IV.

Richard came to the throne as a young man. He chose his counsellors unwisely and was detached from the people, wasting too much time spending money on his close friends and raising taxes to fund his pet wars in Ireland and elsewhere.

King Richard II is chronologically the first play in Shakespeare's second history quartet, a series of four plays that dramatizes the Wars of the Roses, the civil war between the houses of Lancaster and York that lasted for nearly a hundred years. (Its sequels, although written earlier, are *King Henry IV, Parts I* and *II,* and *King Henry V.*)

He rented pieces of English land to wealthy noblemen, and seized the lands and money of the Duke of Lancaster (the father of Henry Bolingbroke, who was to take the throne from Richard on his death) in order to raise funds for a war, which upset both commoners and nobles alike. Bolingbroke, in particular, was incensed to learn that Richard had stolen his inheritance.

The Play

Henry Bolingbroke and the Duke of Norfolk prepare to settle an argument through trial by combat. Bolingbroke believes that Norfolk is responsible for the murder of Richard's uncle, the Duke of Gloucester. However, at the last moment King Richard decrees that both men are to be banished. Soon after, Bolingbroke's father, the Duke of Lancaster, dies. Richard seizes the estates to fund an army for a campaign in Ireland.

Bolingbroke returns to find that the Earl of Northumberland has joined other disaffected nobles against the Duke of York, Richard's regent while the King is in Ireland. When Richard returns, he discovers that Bolingbroke has not only reclaimed the lands stolen from him, but also dispersed Richard's army and executed two of Richard's favourites.

Richard flees to Flint Castle for his own protection. Bolingbroke overtakes him and brings him back to London as a prisoner. Richard is made to confess crimes against the state and abdicate the crown to Bolingbroke, who becomes King Henry IV.

The Duke of York's son, Aumerle, loyal to Richard, conspires against King Henry. Aumerle is granted clemency, but Richard is imprisoned in Pomfret Castle. Sir Pierce of Exton murders Richard because he thinks Henry wants him dead. Henry disavows the deed when he hears of it; however, he promises a crusade to atone for Richard's death.

Commentary

Richard's poetic and metaphysical musings on the nature of kingship and identity mark a new direction for Shakespeare and his histories. Some scholars feel that *King Richard II* reads like a dry run for the later, more mature *Hamlet*.

King Richard II is stylized and in sharp contrast to the 'Henry' plays that follow it chronologically (although they were written before), and it contains virtually no prose. The play is replete with grand metaphors, such as the famous comparison of England to a garden, and of its reigning king to a lion or to the sun.

Famous Lines

'In rage deaf as the sea, hasty as fire' (Act I, Scene I).

'The tongues of dying men
Enforce attention like deep harmony' (Act II, Scene I).

'This royal throne of kings, this scepter'd isle,
This earth of majesty, this seat of Mars,
This other Eden, demi-paradise,
This fortress built by Nature for herself
Against infection and the hand of war,
This happy breed of men, this little world,

This precious stone set in the silver sea,
Which serves it in the office of a wall,
Or as a moat defensive to a house,
Against the envy of less happier lands,—
This blessed plot, this earth, this realm, this England'
    (Act II, Scene I).

'The ripest fruit first falls' (Act II, Scene I).

'Let's talk of graves, of worms, and epitaphs' (Act III, Scene II).

'And nothing can we call our own but death
And that small model of the barren earth
Which serves as paste and cover to our bones.
For God's sake, let us sit upon the ground,
And tell sad stories of the death of kings' (Act III, Scene II).

'Comes at the last, and with a little pin
Bores through his castle-wall – and farewell king!' (Act III, Scene II).

'As in a theatre, the eyes of men,
After a well-graced actor leaves the stage,
Are idly bent on him that enters next,
Thinking his prattle to be tedious' (Act V, Scene II).

21 § King Richard III

Main Characters

Richard – The Duke of Gloucester.

Buckingham – The Duke of Buckingham. Richard's right-hand man.

Ratcliff and Catesby – Two of Richard's supporters.

Tyrrel – A murderer whom Richard hires.

King Edward IV – Older brother of Richard and Clarence.

Clarence – The trusting middle brother of Edward and Richard.

Queen Elizabeth – The wife of King Edward IV.

Dorset, Rivers and Grey – Kinsmen and allies of Elizabeth.

Lady Anne – The young widow of Prince Edward, son of the former King, Henry VI.

Duchess of York – Widowed mother of Richard, Clarence and Edward IV. Not to be confused with Margaret.

Margaret – Widow of the dead Henry VI. Mother of the slain Prince Edward.

The Princes (in the Tower) – The two young sons of Edward IV, Prince Edward and the young Duke of York.

Elizabeth – Daughter of the former Queen Elizabeth, who was married to Edward IV.

Richmond – Challenges Richard for the throne and becomes Henry VII.

Hastings – A lord who supports the Yorkist cause.

Stanley – Lord Stanley, Earl of Derby. Stepfather of Richmond.

Lord Mayor of London – A gullible and suggestible fellow.

Vaughan – A friend of Elizabeth, Dorset, Rivers and Grey.

Introduction

King Richard III is the last of the four plays in Shakespeare's first quartet of history plays. It concludes a dramatic chronicle started in *King Henry VI, Part I* and then moving through *King Henry VI, Part II* and *King Henry VI,*

Part III. The entire four-play saga was composed early in Shakespeare's career, and most scholars date *King Richard III* to about 1591 or 1592.

King Richard III is a dramatization of historical events that concluded in 1485 with the defeat of King Richard III at the Battle of Bosworth, when the Tudors replaced the Plantagenet family as rulers of England. Shakespeare often plays fast and loose with the facts, however, stretching and altering the timeline. The events of this civil war – including the murders of King Henry and Prince Edward by the York brothers, and the earlier killing of Rutland by Henry's family – are an important background to *King Richard III*.

Elizabethan audiences were certainly familiar with these events and were particularly fascinated with Richard III. Shakespeare's audiences could readily identify the various political factions and complex family relationships depicted in the play. In Shakespeare's version, both Henry and Edward leave widows: Margaret and Lady Anne. Although Anne mourns Prince Edward's death, she nevertheless becomes Richard's wife.

Richard III is a fascinating figure, in the same way that we are entranced by the charismatic malevolence of a Hannibal Lecter, and for generations audiences have found themselves seduced by Richard's eloquence and cunning emotional manipulation, even as they are repelled by his evil.

When *King Richard III* begins, Edward IV is growing old. His malicious and deformed younger brother, Richard, is plotting to get his hands on the throne. But a great many people stand between him and the kingship. When Edward dies, he leaves behind two sons who are in line for the crown before Richard. They are still children, though, and Richard has them murdered while they live in captivity in the Tower of London. Their young sister, Elizabeth, becomes an important pawn in bringing peace to the realm.

Richard's ambition is also blocked by his older brother, Clarence, and his two children, all of whom Richard must get rid of in order to seize the crown. Once on the throne, however, Richard soon finds himself besieged by his second cousin, Henry, the Earl of Richmond, who has been gathering strength overseas. Henry believes he has a rightful claim to the throne, and in preparing to challenge Richard sets up the final conflict of the Wars of Roses.

The Play

The play picks up from the end of *King Henry VI, Part III*. Richard's brother is now King Edward IV. In order to gain the crown himself and eliminate his brothers, Richard pits his older brother George, Duke of Clarence, against Edward. He convinces Edward that George is guilty of treason and has him arrested. He also brazenly woos Anne, widow of the murdered Prince of Wales, in the midst of her husband's funeral procession.

Shakespearean audiences would have thought of the 'wicked Italian' Machiavelli when watching this play, because Richard is the epitome of the amoral, power-hungry courtier made famous in the book *The Prince* (1532) by the Renaissance Italian writer Niccolo Machiavelli.

Edward IV, who is deathly ill at the beginning of the play, dies. Richard has already arranged for his brother George to be murdered while in prison, and now he becomes regent until Edward's son, the Prince of Wales (also named Edward) comes of age.

In order to 'protect' the Prince of Wales and his younger brother, Richard puts them in the Tower of London. He then executes Edward's loyalist lords Vaughan, Rivers, Hastings and Grey. With the aid of Buckingham, Richard has Edward's sons declared illegitimate. Buckingham 'offers' the throne of England to Richard, who pretends to be reluctant to accept. Few are fooled by his false modesty. Even his mother curses him as a bloody tyrant.

Richard hires a murderer to kill the Princes in the Tower because Buckingham has refused to help him. Having married Anne, who conveniently dies, Richard proposes marriage to Princess Elizabeth, King

Edward's daughter. Her mother Elizabeth (Edward's widow) pretends to go along with the match, but actually arranges for her daughter to marry the Earl of Richmond instead.

Richmond raises an army in France to fight Richard. Buckingham, out of favour with Richard because he refused to go along with the murder of the young Princes, gives his allegiance to Richmond. Buckingham is captured, and Richard has him executed.

Richmond finally lands with his army and marches for London. The French and English armies get ready to fight near Bosworth Field. The night before the battle, Richard is visited by the ghosts of the people he has killed, and all prophesy his death.

During the battle Richard is thrown from his horse ('A horse! a horse! my kingdom for a horse!'). He and Richmond fight to the death, with Richmond prevailing. Richmond is crowned King Henry VII. The Battle of Bosworth is the final engagement of the Wars of the Roses and marks the founding of the Tudor dynasty of kings and queens.

Commentary

King Richard III is a chronicle of bloody deeds and atrocities, and modern audiences can find it difficult to follow the complex political intrigue, family relationships and personal vendettas. The play is as much melodrama as history, and Richard is a self-professed villain of monstrous proportions comparable only to Iago in *Othello*, or to a lesser extent Edmund in *King Lear*. Richard's ambition makes Macbeth look like an amateur by comparison. He is a totally Machiavellian creature, able to splinter and nearly destroy the forces opposing him, until he is finally defeated by Richmond.

Richard is obviously ambitious and sadistic, but no clear reason for his motivations or his hatred is given. It is as if he decides early on in life that he will be as twisted inside as he is out, because that is the only pleasure he can ever really expect to have. Like the character the Devil from medieval morality pageants, who represented evil, Richard does not even try to justify what he does.

Richard was probably no more murderous than the kings who came before or after him. He had more the right to be King of England when he died in battle than did Richmond. History is written by the victors, however, and at the time Shakespeare was writing England was ruled by Queen Elizabeth – granddaughter of Henry VII, the man who defeated Richard. The official party line was that Richard had been a monster who was not the legitimate King of England. To suggest anything else would have been thoroughly dangerous for Shakespeare.

Modern historians are split on whether the real Richard murdered the young princes, or whether he even had a hunchback. However, Richard came to be known as Humpty, and historians say the nursery rhyme 'Humpty Dumpty' is about Richard's defeat at the Battle of Bosworth.

Famous Lines

'Now is the winter of our discontent
Made glorious summer by this sun of York,
And all the clouds that loured upon our house
In the deep bosom of the ocean buried.
Now are our brows bound with victorious wreaths,
Our bruised arms hung up for monuments,
Our stern alarums changed to merry meetings,
Our dreadful marches to delightful measures.
Grim-visaged war hath smoothed his wrinkled front;
And now, instead of mounting barbed steeds
To fright the souls of fearful adversaries,
He capers nimbly in a lady's chamber
To the lascivious pleasing of a lute.
But I, that am not shaped for sportive tricks,
Nor made to court an amorous looking-glass;
I, that am rudely stamped, and want love's majesty
To strut before a wanton ambling nymph;

I, that am curtailed of this fair proportion,
Cheated of feature by dissembling nature,
Deformed, unfinished, sent before my time
Into this breathing world, scarce half made up,
And that so lamely and unfashionable
That dogs bark at me as I halt by them, –
Why, I, in this weak piping time of peace,
Have no delight to pass away the time,
Unless to spy my shadow in the sun' (Act I, Scene I).

'O, I have passed a miserable night,
So full of fearful dreams, of ugly sights,
That, as I am a Christian faithful man,
I would not spend another such a night,
Though 'twere to buy a world of happy days' (Act I, Scene IV).

'Lord, Lord! methought, what pain it was to drown!
What dreadful noise of waters in mine ears!
What ugly sights of death within mine eyes!
Methought I saw a thousand fearful wracks,
Ten thousand men that fishes gnawed upon,
Wedges of gold, great anchors, heaps of pearl,
Inestimable stones, unvalued jewels,
All scattered in the bottom of the sea:
Some lay in dead men's skulls; and, in those holes
Where eyes did once inhabit, there were crept,
As 'twere in scorn of eyes, reflecting gems' (Act I, Scene IV).

'Off with his head!' (Act III, Scene IV).

'An honest tale speeds best being plainly told' (Act IV, Scene IV).

'I have set my life upon a cast,
And I will stand the hazard of the die:
I think there be six Richmonds in the field' (Act V, Scene IV).

'A horse! a horse! my kingdom for a horse!' (Act V, Scene IV).

22 ✤ Love's Labour's Lost

Main Characters

Ferdinand – King of Navarre, a scholar.

Berowne, Longaville and Dumaine – Three lords who have joined the King in his oath of scholarship. They fall in love with Rosaline, Maria and Katherine, respectively.

Princess of France – A visitor to the King.

Rosaline, Maria and Katherine – Three ladies attending the Princess who catch the fancy of the King's lords.

Boyet – A lord attending the Princess.

Don Armado – Described as 'a fantastical Spaniard'. He catches Costard and Jaquenetta in the forest and falls in love with Jaquenetta.

Moth – Don Armado's page.

Costard – A clown.

Jaquenetta – A country girl.

Sir Nathaniel – A curate.

Holofernes – A schoolmaster.

Dull – A constable.

Introduction

Love's Labour's Lost is an early play, published in 1598 and probably written about 1595. It was included as a comedy in Shakespeare's First Folio and is a meditation on love, though without a marriage at the end, which is untypical of a Shakespearean comedy. This is one of the few plays whose source is unknown, though some scholars guess it may have come from *L'Académie Françoise* (1577) by Pierre de la Primaudaye, which is about a society of scholars.

Love's Labour's Lost was probably first performed in December 1597, most probably as a Christmas entertainment for Elizabeth I, and was repeated at about the same time of year for James I in 1604.

The Play

Ferdinand, King of Navarre, declares that for a year his court will, in effect, become a school, and to keep distractions to a minimum, no women will be allowed to be present during that time. His nobles, Berowne, Longaville and Dumaine, agree to cloister themselves with the King, although Berowne has his reservations about how successful they will be. Berowne also points out that the King has forgotten that the Princess of France is arriving that very day with an embassy. Rather than receive her at court, the Navarrese set out to meet the Princess. Meanwhile, Costard, the King's fool, is about to be punished for dallying with a country girl, Jaquenetta.

The Princess and her entourage are not happy when Ferdinand denies them entrance. In protest, they camp in front of the court, and the Princess and her ladies make plans to get even with Ferdinand and his courtiers.

Armado, who is in love with Jaquenetta, tells Costard he can go free if Costard delivers a letter to Jaquenetta. Next, Berowne asks him to take a letter to Rosaline. Totally confused, Costard delivers the letter intended for Jaquenetta to the Princess of France, and gives Rosaline's letter to Jaquenetta.

Ferdinand and his men eavesdrop on one another and overhear each other professing love for the Princess and her gentlewomen. When the lords pay a visit in disguise to the ladies, however, the women are forewarned, disguise themselves and make fun of the men. The men return as themselves, but the women continue to bait them, delighting in the men's confusion.

When things are finally being sorted out, and they are to be entertained by a play performed by some amateur actors, the Princess learns that her father has died, and she must leave immediately. She tells Ferdinand that if he spends a year cloistered in a remote hermitage to atone for breaking his oath, she will marry him. Each of her ladies-in-waiting extracts a similar promise from the King's lords, vowing that they will return to Navarre the following year and marry if their loves have proven true.

Commentary

The play examines the idea that despite efforts to avoid emotions, as human beings we can't get away from them. At the end, we are reminded of this truth when, in the middle of blossoming love, the pain of loss intrudes. Shakespeare also seems to be suggesting that we often don't treasure what we have until we no longer have it, sounding a warning to lovers to appreciate the happiness that may be right in front of them.

Shakespeare is famous for his puns, and this play has over 200 of them. It is something of a send-up of Elizabethan manners and personality types, and so it tends to go over the heads of modern audiences. However, while the play might seem a dour, dreary affair, in the right hands it can actually be pretty funny.

Famous Lines

'Light, seeking light, doth light of light beguile' (Act I, Scene I).

'Affliction may one day smile again; and till then, sit thee down, sorrow!' (Act I, Scene I).

'To sell a bargain well is as cunning as fast and loose' (Act III, Scene I).

'They have been at a great feast of languages, and stolen the scraps' (Act V, Scene I).

'A jest's prosperity lies in the ear
Of him that hears it, never in the tongue
Of him that makes it' (Act V, Scene II).

23 🜁 Macbeth

Main Characters

Macbeth – An ambitious Scottish general.
Lady Macbeth – Macbeth's wife. A deeply ambitious woman.
Banquo – A brave general.
King Duncan – The King of Scotland whom Macbeth murders.
Malcolm – A Scottish prince, the son of Duncan.
Macduff – A Scottish nobleman.
The Three Witches   Seers who prophesy Macbeth's fate.
Hecate – The goddess of witchcraft.
Fleance – Banquo's son.
Lennox – A Scottish nobleman.
Ross – A Scottish nobleman.
Siward – An English general.
The Murderers – Assassins hired by Macbeth to kill Banquo and his children.

Introduction

With the possible exception of *Titus Andronicus*, which is considered a lesser play, *Macbeth* is Shakespeare's bloodiest tragedy. It traces the disintegration of a powerful man who longs for more power and will stoop to anything, even murder, to get it.

Macbeth was probably composed in late 1606 or early 1607, and is the last of Shakespeare's four great tragedies, the others being *Hamlet, King Lear* and *Othello*. *Macbeth*'s supernatural element suggests that fate dominates our lives. Macbeth chooses to walk the bloody path of ambition in order to attain the glory promised to him by the witches.

Macbeth is loosely based on a real king of the same name who lived from 1005 to 1057. He launched a civil war in order to seize the throne from his cousin, Duncan. There is no evidence that the real Macbeth was ever incited by his wife, Gruoch, or that his actions led to the kind of turmoil dramatized in the play. The real Macbeth, in fact, reigned peacefully for 15 years.

In theatre lore, no actor ever actually calls *Macbeth* by its given name. It is called 'The Scottish Play', instead, because it has been associated with bad luck over the centuries. The curse began, it is said, with the first performance of the play, when the boy actor playing Lady Macbeth collapsed, apparently from a fever, and died before the play had finished.

A crucial element in this examination of the nature of ambition is the play's most memorable character, Lady Macbeth. Unlike her husband, who is enticed by supernatural evil (in the form of Hecate and the witches) into pursuing his bloody desires, Lady Macbeth's lust for power is innate, and leads her into the realm of hallucinations and madness.

The Play

During a thunderstorm on a Scottish moor in the midst of a battle between the Scots and the Norwegians, Macbeth kills the traitorous Scot, Macdonald, Thane [Earl] of Cawdor. The King hears of the death and promises to make Macbeth Thane of Cawdor as soon as he sees him.

On the heath near the battlefield, Macbeth and Banquo come upon three witches. They hail Macbeth as Thane of Cawdor, baffling him, as he has not yet learned of his promotion. They also say he will be king one day. They then call Banquo 'lesser than Macbeth, and greater', and 'not so happy, yet much happier'. They tell him that he will never be king, but that his children will sit upon the throne.

When Macbeth and Banquo reunite with King Duncan, Macbeth learns that he has been promoted to Thane of Cawdor in place of the man he killed in battle. Part one of the witches' prophecy has come to pass. Macbeth begins to consider the possibility that he might be King one day. However, Duncan announces Malcolm as his heir. Publicly, Macbeth declares his joy, but in private he admits his disappointment. Macbeth invites Duncan to dine at his castle that evening, to which Duncan agrees.

Lady Macbeth

At the castle Lady Macbeth reads a letter from her husband, announcing his promotion and detailing the promises of the witches. Lady Macbeth fears he is too full of 'the milk of human kindness' to do what it takes to become king. If only she were a man, she would do the deeds herself, she says. She tells her husband she has a plan.

Duncan and his retinue arrive. Macbeth ponders his decision to assassinate Duncan. On the one hand, he considers murder morally wrong and admires the King; on the other hand is his driving ambition. He tells Lady Macbeth he no longer intends to kill Duncan, who has been kind to him. Outraged, she calls him a coward and unmanly, and persuades him to reconsider.

That night Lady Macbeth puts her plan into action. A tolling bell is the signal that the King's servants are asleep. Macbeth emerges from Duncan's chamber steeped in gore. He is badly shaken and says that as he killed the King he thought he heard a voice cry out that Macbeth would never sleep again.

Lady Macbeth tries to steady him, but is angry when she notices he has forgotten to leave the daggers with the servants to frame them for the killing. Macbeth refuses to go back into the room. Lady Macbeth takes them herself, calling him a coward once again. When she returns she tells Macbeth a little water will clear them both of the murder.

Macduff and Lennox arrive, asking for the King. Lennox describes storms that have raged during the night. He says no one can remember anything like it. Macduff goes to wake the King and returns horrified, crying murder. Chaos reigns. Macbeth goes in to see and returns lamenting, declaring that in a grief-stricken rage he killed the servants who had murdered Duncan.

Descent into Murder and Madness

Later that evening Macduff meets with Ross outside the castle and tells him that Macbeth has been made King. Macduff adds that, although the servants seem the most likely murderers, suspicion has now also fallen on the King's sons, the Princes, because they have fled the scene.

The witches lurk as the personification of evil; yet their mischief is due mainly to their ability to exploit the weaknesses of their victims. They play upon Macbeth's ambition like puppeteers, while Banquo resists them.

Banquo takes time to think about Macbeth's coronation, and the prophecy of the witches who foretold not only that Macbeth would be king, but also that Banquo's sons would sit on the throne. Macbeth, elsewhere, is pondering the same topic. His old friend Banquo is the only man in Scotland he now fears. According to the witches' prophecy, Duncan's murder has simply cleared the way for Banquo's sons to become kings. Two murderers now enter. Macbeth asks them if they have the stomach to kill Banquo and his children. The assassins hide in a wooded park outside the palace and ambush Banquo and his son Fleance as they ride in and dismount. Banquo is killed, but Fleance escapes.

At the coronation feast the murderers quietly tell Macbeth what has happened. As Macbeth walks among his guests and goes to sit at the head of the table, he finds Banquo's ghost sitting in his chair. Horror-struck, Macbeth speaks to the ghost, which is invisible to the rest of the company. Lady Macbeth makes excuses for her husband, saying that he occasionally has such 'visions', and that the guests should simply ignore his behaviour. Macbeth cannot control his 'fits', and in the end she has to send the guests away.

Lennox walks with another lord, and both confess that they suspect Macbeth of involvent in the murders of Duncan and Banquo. The lord tells Lennox that Malcolm and Macduff have fled to England to ask King Edward for aid. Their success has prompted Macbeth to begin preparing for war. Lennox and the lord quietly wish luck to Malcolm and Macduff.

Macbeth tells Lady Macbeth that he will visit the witches again in the hope of learning more. Entering a dark cavern, Macbeth asks the witches to reveal more details of their prophecy to him. They summon horrible apparitions: a floating head tells him to beware Macduff; a bloody child tells him that 'none of woman born' can harm him; and a crowned child holding a tree tells him that he is safe until 'Great Birnam Wood to high Dunsinane Hill shall come against him'. Then a procession of eight crowned kings walks through, the last carrying a mirror. Banquo's ghost is at the end of the line. Macbeth demands to know the meaning of this final vision, but the witches cackle with glee and vanish.

Death to the Macbeths

At night, in the King's palace at Dunsinane, Lady Macbeth enters in a trance, bemoaning the deaths of Lady Macduff and Banquo. She continually sees blood on her hands, even though she has tried desperately to wash it off. She leaves, and the doctor and gentlewoman who are looking after her marvel at her descent into madness. Outside the castle, a group of Scottish lords discuss the military situation: the Scottish army will engage Malcolm's English army near Birnam Wood.

Macbeth boasts that he has nothing to fear from the English army or from Malcolm, since 'none of woman born' can harm him. Malcolm and the English general, Siward, decide that each soldier should cut down a bough of the forest and carry it in front of him as they march to the castle, thereby disguising their numbers.

While organizing defences Macbeth is told that the Queen has killed herself. A messenger now enters with the astonishing news that the trees of Birnam Wood are advancing toward Dunsinane. The witches' prophecy is coming true. The battle commences. On the battlefield, Macbeth slaughters with vigour, convinced that 'none of woman born' can harm him. Macduff fights his way toward him. They meet at last. As the fight gets underway Macduff tells Macbeth that he was not of woman born, but rather he was 'from my mother's womb untimely ripp'd' (that is, he was born by Caesarian section). He kills Macbeth.

Malcolm and Siward capture the castle. Macduff emerges with Macbeth's head in his hand and proclaims Malcolm King of Scotland.

Malcolm declares that all his thanes will be made earls, as is the English custom. They will be the first such lords in Scottish history. Cursing Macbeth and his 'fiend-like' queen, he invites all to see him crowned at Scone.

Commentary

Macbeth is often interpreted as an examination of what happens when ambition goes unchecked by moral constraints. Macbeth is a brave soldier who is tempted by the devil (Hecate) into becoming King of Scotland. The bloodbath that results from trying to realize this destiny propels Macbeth and Lady Macbeth into a swift descent into arrogance, madness and death.

It is not a particularly complicated play, but it is powerful, and is possibly Shakespeare's most emotionally intense. *Hamlet* and *Othello* explore the intellectual complications of their subjects, and *King Lear* deals with the inner chaos of a deranged mind, but *Macbeth* is like a scythe unerringly mowing down anything in its way, leaving corpse after corpse in its wake from the moment the witches appear. The play is a sharp, jagged sketch of theme and character, and as such it has shocked and fascinated audiences of stage and screen for nearly 400 years.

Macbeth is a powerful critique of political power, as it ponders exactly what qualities make a good ruler, and the values or dangers of manliness. Whenever a discussion of manhood takes place during the play, it is swiftly followed by violence and death.

Macbeth starts the play as a noble, courageous warrior; he kills Duncan somewhat against his better judgement, but ends the play in a ferment of frantic, boastful madness. Lady Macbeth, one of Shakespeare's most compelling female characters, mercilessly drives on her husband's butchery without being able to imagine the awful price her ambition will cost both her and her husband.

Famous Lines

'When shall we three meet again
In thunder, lightning, or in rain?
When the hurlyburly's done,
When the battle's lost and won' (Act I, Scene I).

'What are these
So wither'd and so wild in their attire,
That look not like the inhabitants o' the earth,
And yet are on 't?' (Act I, Scene III).

'If you can look into the seeds of time,
And say which grain will grow, and which will not' (Act I, Scene III).

'Nothing is
But what is not' (Act I, Scene III).

'Yet do I fear thy nature;
It is too full o' the milk of human kindness' (Act I, Scene V).

'I dare do all that may become a man;
Who dares do more is none' (Act I, Scene VII).

'Is this a dagger which I see before me,
The handle toward my hand? Come, let me clutch thee.
I have thee not, and yet I see thee still.
Art thou not, fatal vision, sensible
To feeling as to sight? or art thou but
A dagger of the mind, a false creation,
Proceeding from the heat-oppressed brain?' (Act II, Scene I).

'There's daggers in men's smiles' (Act II, Scene III).

'Stand not upon the order of your going,
But go at once' (Act III, Scene IV).

'Double, double toil and trouble;
Fire burn, and cauldron bubble' (Act IV, Scene I).

'By the pricking of my thumbs,

Something wicked this way comes.
Open, locks,
Whoever knocks!' (Act IV, Scene I).

'Out, damned spot! out, I say!' (Act V, Scene I).

'Fie, my lord, fie! a soldier, and afeard?' (Act V, Scene I).

'Yet who would have thought the old man to have had so much blood
in him?' (Act V, Scene I).

'To-morrow, and to-morrow, and to-morrow,
Creeps in this petty pace from day to day
To the last syllable of recorded time,
And all our yesterdays have lighted fools
The way to dusty death. Out, out, brief candle!
Life's but a walking shadow, a poor player
That struts and frets his hour upon the stage
And then is heard no more: it is a tale
Told by an idiot, full of sound and fury,
Signifying nothing' (Act V, Scene V).

24 ✒ Measure for Measure

Main Characters

Isabella – A virtuous young woman, sister to Claudio.

Vincentio – The Duke of Vienna. He spends most of his time disguised as a friar.

Claudio – Isabella's brother. Sentenced to death for impregnating an unmarried woman.

Lord Angelo – A hypocrite who rules strictly and without mercy.

Escalus – A wise lord who advises Angelo.

Lucio – A flamboyant bachelor.

Mariana – Angelo's fiancée.

Mistress Overdone – A madam.

Pompey – A clown who works for Mistress Overdone.

Provost – The jailer.

Elbow – A dimwitted constable.

Barnadine – A prisoner in the jail.

Juliet – Claudio's lover.

Introduction

Measure for Measure takes the idea for its title from the Gospel of St Matthew: 'with what measure ye mete, it shall be measured to you again' (Matthew 7:2). This is a passage from the Sermon on the Mount, one of Christ's most famous sermons.

While some documents indicate it was first performed at court at Whitehall on St Stephen's Night (26 December) 1604, others suggest that it was written and first performed earlier that year. Lucio's allusion to a hoped-for peace may well refer to James I's attempts in 1604 to negotiate a peace agreement with Spain; the proclamation to tear down the brothels may refer to James's edict in 1603 to so deal with houses affected by the plague (the plague and venereal disease were often related in Renaissance literature). A number of critics have noted similarities between the Duke and James's dislike of crowds, his use of disguise, and his particular aversion to slander.

Cinthio, an Italian writer and philosopher, first wrote this story as a 1565 novella called *Hecatommithi*, then as a play called *Epita* in 1583. Another dramatist, George Whetstone, wrote the story as a play called *Promos and Cassandra* in 1578, and in 1581 Thomas Lupton wrote a play called *Too Good To Be True*.

The earliest, and thus most authoritative, text for the play is the First Folio, which was printed in 1623. The lack of stage directions suggests it is a prompt copy. Shakespeare took the source of the play from a real case in Italy. In 1547, a judge promised a murderer he would not be sentenced to death if the murderer's wife had sex with the judge. After he had enjoyed himself, the judge went back on his word and executed the man anyway.

The Play

In order to find out why he is not a better ruler, Vincentio, Duke of Vienna, decides to take a sabbatical, appointing his deputy, Angelo, to rule in his place. The Duke wants to enforce morality laws, and he appoints Angelo to do so, mainly because he doesn't want to seem a bad ruler, but also because someone has to accept the unpopular task of being more strict. Because Angelo is a zealot, the Duke considers him perfect for the job. Meanwhile, the Duke decides to keep an eye on things by remaining in Vienna disguised as a monk.

Claudio's Death Sentence

Angelo's harshness upsets a lot of people, particularly when Claudio is arrested for making his fiancée, Juliet, pregnant before they are married. Angelo condemns him to death. While agreeing with his moral stance, Claudio's sister, Isabella, nevertheless pleads with Angelo for her brother's life.

Angelo won't budge at first. Gradually, Isabella's beauty and chaste virtue excite him. He propositions her: he will pardon Claudio if she sleeps with him. Isabella turns him down, vowing that her chastity and honour are her life.

When she tells Claudio what happened, he at first agrees with her, but soon tries to talk his sister into trading her virtue for his life. The Duke (in disguise) overhears their conversation and sets in motion a plot to save both Claudio and Isabella from their predicament.

The Duke Steps In

The Duke knows Angelo was once engaged to Mariana, who still loves him. He persuades Isabella to feign acceptance of Angelo's offer, and when the moment comes, Mariana will switch places in the dark with Isabella (the bed trick of *All's Well That Ends Well*). Mariana agrees, and events go as planned, except that after getting his way, Angelo orders Claudio's execution anyway.

Luckily, the Duke hears about this and persuades the jailer to substitute another condemned man for Claudio, and to carry out the execution 'as planned'. Isabella is led to believe that Claudio has died; Angelo has betrayed her, and she should seek justice from the Duke, who is expected to return soon.

Isabel and Mariana make their accusations against Angelo to the Duke, who appears as himself. Angelo first says Isabella is lying and blames the 'monk' for putting her up to this. When the Duke reveals himself as the monk, Angelo is forced to throw himself on the mercy of the Duke and Isabella. Claudio is revealed to be alive, Mariana pleads for Angelo's life, and the Duke orders that Angelo should marry Mariana and Claudio should marry Juliet. The Duke makes his own arrangements to be married to Isabella.

Commentary

Measure for Measure has been criticized for having an unsatisfying resolution and obvious gaps in plotting. For example, why does Isabella agree to the Duke's plan? After all, the bed switch still makes Mariana commit the same crime that Claudio is condemned for, and Isabella is vocal in condemning her brother's actions. The fact is that she agrees with Angelo, but disagrees on the punishment he intends to mete out.

At the beginning of the play Isabella was about to become a nun. At no time during the play does she profess love for the Duke, or he for her. He's disguised as a monk for most of it, anyway. Yet we are left with the distinct impression she will become his bride.

Measure for Measure's themes of sexual harassment and women's rights had hardly been explored at the time the play was first performed, and they have made it a popular play, since it touches on issues of sexuality, independence and the objectification of women, and does so without one strong female character. In fact, the female characters in *Measure for Measure* are unusually weak for Shakespeare. They simply go along with what the men decide. Despite this, the play is considered a comedy, and the story is filled with amusing minor characters as well as broad sociological questions.

The play certainly raises important moral issues. Its structure revolves around secret identities: the Duke disguises himself as a monk, and most of the problems are resolved when he reveals his identity. The Duke solves Claudio and Isabella's problem with a plan involving mistaken identity. Mariana takes Isabella's place, and the head of a dead pirate is used to deceive Angelo.

The Duke, in effect, functions as a kind of ringmaster. He may have placed a proxy ruler in power during his absence, but he is still pulling the puppet strings. He is an interesting paradox: a character who is wise but unable to maintain order.

Measure for Measure is also a problem play because it does not follow through with the moral questions it raises. No one reconsiders his or her beliefs about freedom, justice, sexual relationships or morality, and Isabella in particular never really has to deal with the consequences of having to commit a sin in order to save her brother.

Famous Lines

'Our doubts are traitors,
And make us lose the good we oft might win
By fearing to attempt' (Act I, Scene IV).

'Some rise by sin, and some by virtue fall' (Act II, Scene I).

'Condemn the fault, and not the actor of it?' (Act II, Scene II).

'O, it is excellent
To have a giant's strength; but it is tyrannous
To use it like a giant' (Act II, Scene II).

'The miserable have no other medicine,
But only hope' (Act III, Scene I).

'O, what may man within him hide,
Though angel on the outward side!' (Act III, Scene II).

'They say, best men are moulded out of faults,
And, for the most, become much more the better
For being a little bad' (Act V, Scene I).

'What's mine is yours, and what is yours is mine' (Act V, Scene I).

25 ∮ Much Ado About Nothing

Main Characters

Leonato – The father of Hero and the uncle of Beatrice.

Don Pedro – Sometimes called 'the Prince'. A long-time friend of Leonato.

Don John – Sometimes called 'the Bastard'. The illegitimate brother of Don Pedro.

Claudio – A young soldier who falls in love with Hero.

Hero – The beautiful young daughter of Leonato, and the cousin of Beatrice.

Benedick – A friend and soldier of Don Pedro.

Beatrice – Leonato's niece and Hero's cousin.

Margaret – Hero's maid.

Ursula – One of Hero's servingwomen.

Borachio – Don John's servant and Margaret's lover.

Conrade – One of Don John's servants.

Dogberry – The Constable of Messina.

Verges – Dogberry's assistant.

Antonio – Leonato's older brother and uncle to Hero and Beatrice.

Friar Francis – A monk.

Introduction

Much Ado About Nothing is generally considered one of Shakespeare's best comedies. It was probably written around 1598–99, as Shakespeare was approaching the middle of his career. Like *A Midsummer Night's Dream*, *As You Like It*, and *Twelfth Night* it has few dark elements and provides a happy ending with no deaths.

The verbal sparring between Beatrice and Benedick may have been inspired by the fictional debates between a man and a woman created by the Italian writer Baldassare Castiglione in *The Book of the Courtier* (1528). Critics think the Hero–Claudio plot is based on *Orlando Furioso* (1532), a poem by the Italian Ludovico Ariosto. Shakespeare may have read a translation by Sir John Harrington, published in 1591. The character of Dogberry, the comic policeman or constable, is reminiscent of Constable Dull in *Love's Labour's Lost*, and is an original creation by Shakespeare.

The play has been popular since it was first staged, and is a contemporary favourite. In 1862, Hector Berlioz used it as the basis for his opera *Beatrice and Benedict. What To Do About Nothing*, a 1998 play by Judy Sheehan, retells the story, using gossip and eavesdropping as key elements, and setting it against the backdrop of the McCarthy 'red scare' in the America of the early 1950s.

The Play

Don Pedro, the Prince of Arragon, and two of his officers, Benedick and Claudio, visit Don Pedro's old friend Leonato, the Governor of Messina. Claudio quickly falls in love with Leonato's daughter, Hero. Benedick continues a battle of wits with Beatrice, the Governor's niece.

Don Pedro, with Leonato, Claudio and Hero's help, decides it's time Benedick and Beatrice stopped tormenting each other verbally and admitted they were in love. To that end, both Benedick and Beatrice are made to think the other has secretly professed a great love for them.

Don John, who seems to be reconciled with his brother, Don Pedro, despises Claudio, and when he learns about his impending marriage to Hero, decides to ruin it. He tells Claudio that Pedro wants Hero for himself. Then he gets his servant, Borachio, and Hero's maid, Margaret, to stage an episode that will make it seem as though Hero is a loose woman.

Claudio is so upset, he denounces Hero at the altar. Friar Francis hides her away, and with Beatrice's help announces that Hero has died of grief. Borachio drunkenly boasts of his part in the plan – and the 1000 ducats Don John paid him – and is arrested by Dogberry and the watch.

Hero is exonerated and Claudio is grief-stricken at what he has done, thinking Hero still dead. Leonato demands a public apology from

Claudio, then tells him that he must marry one of his nieces in Hero's place. The niece turns out to be Hero, of course, miraculously brought back to life. Claudio and Hero are reunited, and Benedick and Beatrice, realizing they love each other, get married at the same time. Don John is apprehended and will be brought to justice for his mischief-making.

Commentary

Although *Much Ado About Nothing* is a light comedy, some critics are troubled by the anger, betrayal, hatred, grief and despair that are at the centre of the play. Like other Shakespearean comedies, for part of the time *Much Ado About Nothing* threatens to become a tragedy. The plot is an elaborate network of schemes and tricks, and it shares elements with *Romeo and Juliet*, *The Taming of the Shrew* and even *Othello*, reminding us that comedy and tragedy are opposite ends of the same spectrum.

Beatrice and Benedick's mature love affair can be compared in some ways to Antony and Cleopatra's, but it is much happier and healthier. They are one of Shakespeare's most mature and subtle couples.

While Hero and Claudio are the engine of the plot, it is actually the courtship of the older and wiser Benedick and Beatrice that makes this play such fun. Their journey from an emotional defensiveness and withdrawal, resulting from their ages, which they defend with great wit, to deep affection, is developed with rich humour and compassion.

Famous Lines

'He wears his faith but as the fashion of his hat' (Act I, Scene I).

'What, my dear Lady Disdain! are you yet living?' (Act I, Scene I).

'Shall I never see a bachelor of threescore again?' (Act I, Scene I).

'As merry as the day is long' (Act II, Scene I).

'Speak low, if you speak love' (Act II, Scene I).

'Friendship is constant in all other things
Save in the office and affairs of love:
Therefore all hearts in love use their own tongues;
Let every eye negotiate for itself
And trust no agent' (Act II, Scene I).

'Some Cupid kills with arrows, some with traps' (Act III, Scene I).

'Every one can master a grief but he that has it' (Act III, Scene II).

'Are you good men and true?' (Act III, Scene III).

'O, what men dare do! what men may do! what men daily do, not
    knowing what they do!' (Act IV, Scene I).

'For it so falls out
That what we have we prize not to the worth
Whiles we enjoy it, but being lack'd and lost,
Why, then we rack the value; then we find
The virtue that possession would not show us
Whiles it was ours' (Act IV, Scene I).

'Condemned into everlasting redemption' (Act IV, Scene II).

'For there was never yet philosopher
That could endure the toothache patiently' (Act V, Scene I).

'Done to death by slanderous tongues' (Act V, Scene III).

26 ✿ Othello

Main Characters

Othello – A Moor commanding the armies of Venice.

Desdemona – The daughter of a Venetian senator, and Othello's bride.

Iago – Othello's ensign. Perhaps Shakespeare's greatest villain.

Cassio – Othello's lieutenant, promoted in place of Iago.

Emilia – Iago's wife and Desdemona's attendant.

Roderigo – A jealous suitor of Desdemona.

Bianca – A courtesan in Cyprus, and Cassio's mistress.

Brabantio – Desdemona's father, and a senator in Venice.

Lodovico – Brabantio and Desdemona's kinsman.

Gratiano – Brabantio's brother.

Clown – Othello's servant.

Montano – The Governor of Cyprus before Othello.

The Duke of Venice – The official authority in Venice.

Introduction

Othello was probably written in early 1604, and first performed in front of James I on 1 November of that year. The great Richard Burbage played Othello. In 1660 Margaret Hughes played Desdemona and became the first woman allowed to perform on the English stage.

Othello is set against the backdrop of the wars between Venice and Turkey that raged in the latter part of the 16th century. Cyprus, which is the setting for most of the action, was a Venetian outpost attacked by the Ottoman Turks in 1570 and conquered by them in the following year. Shakespeare's information probably comes from *The History of the Turks* by Richard Knolles, which was published in England in autumn of 1603.

Shakespeare's choice of a black African as a hero was strikingly original. Blackness in Elizabethan England was a colour associated with moral evil and death, and Moors in the theatre, like Jews, were usually stereotyped as villains, such as Aaron the Moor in *Titus Andronicus*, an early play. Othello is a noble, towering figure whose good nature is the cause of his downfall, making the play that much more tragic.

Ira Aldridge (who died around 1867) was born a slave in the United States and moved to Europe, becoming an acclaimed Shakespearean actor. He is thought to be the first black actor to play Othello.

Some scholars believe *Othello* is derived from an Italian prose tale written in 1565 by Giraldi Cinthio in his collection *Hecatommithi*, although there seems to have been no English translation at the time Shakespeare wrote *Othello* (prompting the thought that he may well have been able to read some Italian). The original story concerns a Moorish general who is deceived by his ensign into believing his wife is unfaithful.

The Play

Othello, a celebrated Moorish general of Venice, has promoted Cassio as his lieutenant instead of Iago. Iago is incensed, and plots against Cassio and Othello to get his due. Othello and Desdemona, the beautiful daughter of Brabantio, fall in love, elope and marry. Brabantio is deeply upset by the deceit and the marriage. When Othello is posted to Cyprus by the Duke of Venice, Iago escorts Desdemona.

Framing Cassio

Arriving in Cyprus, Iago immediately begins plotting. He tricks Cassio into getting drunk, then persuades Roderigo, a former suitor of Desdemona who is upset at her marriage, to pick a fight with Cassio. Cassio ends up being arrested, and is subsequently demoted. Iago then encourages Cassio to call on Desdemona, saying that if she speaks up for him with her husband, Othello may reinstate him.

Iago now goes to Othello and, as they watch Desdemona and Cassio talk, recalling her father's accusations of her betrayal of trust, Iago plants the seeds of jealousy in Othello. Iago suggests that Cassio and Desdemona are having an affair.

By chance, because his wife Emilia is Desdemona's maid, Iago gets hold of a handkerchief Othello gave Desdemona as a token of his love for her. Iago plants the handkerchief in Cassio's room, and then tells Othello that he saw Cassio with it. When Othello asks Desdemona about the handkerchief, she tells him that it was lost. Cassio, meanwhile, gives it to a courtesan with whom he is intimate. Iago then gets Othello to overhear a conversation whereby Othello thinks they are discussing Desdemona, when in fact they are talking about Bianca, the courtesan.

Iago's evil is the antithesis of the love that Othello and Desdemona share. The purity of their passion is perhaps one of the strongest portrayals of romantic affection in any tragedy, including *Romeo and Juliet*. It is this deep love that Iago hates so much, because he is incapable of it, and his awareness of his own weakness provides him with the key to destroying Othello.

Based on this misinformation, Othello reacts. He tells Iago to kill Cassio, and then angrily confronts Desdemona. Despite Desdemona's protests of innocence and Emilia's vouching for her, Othello is now convinced she is sleeping with Cassio.

The Scheme Unravels

Iago gets Roderigo to murder Cassio. However, Roderigo only wounds him, and Iago kills Roderigo so Roderigo can't betray his machinations. Othello hears the commotion in the street, and thinks Iago has kept his part of their bargain. Now it is time to strangle Desdemona in her bed.

When Emilia discovers the crime, Desdemona, with her dying breath, refuses to accuse her husband. Emilia becomes distraught and accuses the Moor of being a murderous villain, refusing to believe that Iago has so evilly manipulated Othello. However, Iago's appearance and subsequent answers make Emilia realize her husband is responsible for this tragedy.

Letters found on Roderigo's body confirm Iago's villainy. Faced with the shame of having murdered an innocent Desdemona, Othello stabs himself and dies on Desdemona's bed beside her.

Commentary

Othello is an intense, fast-paced play with most of the action compressed into a 24-hour period. Scenes begin in mid-conversation, and subplots are pretty inconsequential. Everything plays to the domestic tragedy, centring on the three principal characters manipulated by Iago. Indeed, in no other tragedy does a single figure have so much control over events.

The horror of the play is its inevitability. We know what Iago is planning, and we are forced to watch it unfold. The audience shares in the fate of Desdemona and Othello – caught in Iago's trap.

We suffer with Iago's victims because he manages to use the purity of Othello and Desdemona's love against them. They, and we, are helpless against the chaos that Iago represents. Indeed, Othello says of Desdemona, 'When I love thee not, Chaos is come again.' And chaos, embodied in 'honest Iago', seems to win the day.

The swiftness with which Iago manages to destroy Othello is stunning. He needs only two conversations and a missing handkerchief to convince the Moor that Desdemona has been unfaithful. Iago's 'evidence' reminds Othello of her father's parting words: 'Look to her, Moor, if thou hast eyes to see. She has deceived her father, and may thee.'

Once Othello snaps, Shakespeare delays Desdemona's murder, and we can hope that she may be saved at the last moment. Instead, Iago tries to make Othello suffer even more. Once his plan has borne its bitter fruit, the play is ended.

Famous Lines

'We cannot all be masters, nor all masters
Cannot be truly follow'd' (Act I, Scene I).

'I will wear my heart upon my sleeve
For daws to peck at' (Act I, Scene I).

'Reputation, reputation, reputation! Oh, I have lost my reputation! I
have lost the immortal part of myself, and what remains is bestial'
(Act II, Scene III).

'O God, that men should put an enemy in their mouths to steal away
their brains!' (Act II, Scene III).

'How poor are they that have not patience!' (Act II, Scene III).

'Good name in man and woman, dear my lord,
Is the immediate jewel of their souls:
Who steals my purse steals trash; 'tis something, nothing;
'Twas mine, 'tis his, and has been slave to thousands;
But he that filches from me my good name
Robs me of that which not enriches him
And makes me poor indeed' (Act III, Scene III).

'O, beware, my lord, of jealousy!
It is the green-eyed monster, which doth mock
The meat it feeds on' (Act III, Scene III).

'Trifles light as air
Are to the jealous confirmations strong
As proofs of holy writ' (Act III, Scene III).

'He that is robb'd, not wanting what is stolen,
Let him not know 't, and he's not robb'd at all' (Act III, Scene III).

'Take note, take note, O world,
To be direct and honest is not safe' (Act III, Scene III).

'Tis neither here nor there' (Act IV, Scene III).

'Put out the light, and then put out the light:
If I quench thee, thou flaming minister,
I can again thy former light restore
Should I repent me; but once put out thy light,
Thou cunning'st pattern of excelling nature,
I know not where is that Promethean heat
That can thy light relume' (Act V, Scene II).

'So sweet was ne'er so fatal' (Act V, Scene II).

'Then, must you speak
Of one that loved not wisely, but too well;
Of one not easily jealous, but, being wrought
Perplex'd in the extreme; of one whose hand,
Like the base Indian, threw a pearl away
Richer than all his tribe; of one whose subdued eyes,
Albeit unused to the melting mood,
Drop tears as fast as the Arabian trees
Their medicinal gum' (Act V, Scene II).

27   Pericles, Prince of Tyre

Main Characters

John Gower – A chorus.
Antiochus – King of Antioch.
The Daughter of Antiochus
Thaliart – A villain hired by Antiochus to kill Pericles.
Pericles – Husband of Thaisa and father of Marina.
Helicanus – One of Pericles's advisors in Tyre.
Escanes – Another of Pericles's advisors.
Cleon – Governor of Tarsus, a city beset by famine.
Dionyza – Wife of Cleon.
Simonides – King of Pentapolis, father of Thaisa.
Thaisa – Daughter of Simonides, mother of Marina.
Marina – Daughter of Pericles and Thaisa.
Leonine – Murderer hired by Dionyza to kill Marina.
Lychorida – Thaisa's nurse, later Marina's nurse.
Cerimon – A kindly physician in Ephesus.
Philemon – Cerimon's assistant.
Lysimachus – Governor of Mytilene.
Pander – A brothel-keeper.
Bawd – A madam in charge of prostitutes, probably Pander's wife.
Master – The master of the fishermen; he takes Pericles to the jousting competition on Pentapolis.
Knights – Suitors for Thaisa's hand at the jousting competition in Pentapolis.
Boult – Servant to Pander and Bawd.
Diana – Goddess of chastity.
Shipmaster – Captain of the ship on which Thaisa supposedly dies.

Introduction

Pericles, Prince of Tyre was probably written in around 1607, late in Shakespeare's career. As in most of Shakespeare's plays (and those of his contemporaries), Shakespeare drew on earlier authors and common stories as source material for the play. The 14th-century poet John Gower, who appears in the play as a chorus, wrote the most important direct source for *Pericles,* a story about Apollonius of Tyre in his *Confessio Amantis*. The story probably dates back to fifth- or sixth-century Latin texts, and before that perhaps even to a Greek romance influenced by Homer's *Odyssey,* which it superficially resembles.

Authorship

Scholars have long debated the actual authorship of *Pericles* without resolution. It is likely that another playwright, George Wilkins, wrote the first nine scenes and Shakespeare wrote the remaining 13. Dual authorship is a good explanation for the stylistic differences between the two parts of the play. In the first part, the language closely reflects John Gower's 14th-century language, rather than that of Shakespeare or many of his contemporaries.

Though both Wilkins and Shakespeare use iambic pentameter, Wilkins uses more rhyming couplets to end lines, while Shakespeare relies on his characteristic use of enjambment, where a phrase or idea doesn't end at the end of a line, but carries over to the next. Structurally, the dual-author theory works as well, since the actions of the first half of the play repeat themselves for the most part in the second half.

Source Text

Another interesting problem with *Pericles* is the unreliability of its source text. Almost all of Shakespeare's other plays, first published in quarto form, draw directly on the author's manuscript or the actors' promptbooks. *Pericles,* however, was assembled out of reports from actors and spectators. Elizabethan citizens and actors lived in a world where relatively little printed material was available, so memorizing texts was common. For this reason no authoritative text of *Pericles* exists.

Various editors have tackled this problem by making greater or lesser efforts to increase the intelligibility of the play. Editors of the Oxford edition of the plays, for example, which many further versions draw from, decided to use a First Quarto version of this play, largely unchanged.

Other editors have drawn on another of Wilkins's plays about *Pericles* to add more to the story. But if the First Quarto edition was already based on reported speech, then any edition that tries to further reconstruct what the original *Pericles* may have been probably strays even further from any 'original text'.

It's important to remember that none of Shakespeare's texts are really word-for-word originals. Shakespeare worked in collaboration with a company of actors, and so his plays were constantly changing. Probably what he first wrote changed substantially during rehearsals, and again during performances.

The Play

Pericles goes to Antioch to court the Princess. He is given a riddle to solve, and correctly guesses that it reveals that Antiochus, the King, and his daughter are involved in an incestuous affair. Realizing that Pericles has guessed his secret, Antiochus determines to kill him. His life in peril, Pericles flees to save himself.

Antiochus is determined to nail Pericles. Knowing this, Pericles appoints his counsellor, Helicanus, to rule as regent, and then sails from Tyre for Tarsus, where he saves the people by bringing them much-needed supplies and wins the gratitude of the Governor, Cleon, and his wife, Dionyza. He then sets sail for Pentapolis. On the way, the vessel is shipwrecked, and Pericles is the sole survivor.

At Pentapolis, Pericles participates in a tournament for the hand of Thaisa, daughter of Simonides. He wins the tournament, and Pericles and Thaisa marry. In the meantime, news arrives that Antiochus is dead and the people of Tyre want their Prince back. Pericles and Thaisa, who is now pregnant with their child, set sail for Tyre. During a storm, Marina, their daughter, is born. Thaisa is believed to have died in childbirth. She is sealed in a watertight coffin and buried at sea. The coffin washes up on the shores of Ephesus, where Cerimon manages to revive Thaisa, who assumes that Pericles is lost at sea and promptly becomes a votaress (or 'nun') in the Temple of Diana. Pericles leaves the baby Marina at Tarsus with Cleon and his wife, Dionyza, and continues on to Tyre.

Sixteen years later, Dionyza becomes jealous of Marina and resolves to have her murdered. Dionyza's servant takes Marina to the shore, but cannot carry out the order. As he stands there indecisively, pirates capture Marina. The servant reports back that she is dead, and Cleon mournfully raises a monument to her memory. Pericles encounters the tomb on a visit to Tarsus and falls into a deep despair.

Pericles sails into Mitylene still depressed about losing his daughter. He encounters Marina, and eventually recognizes her as his child. The two are happily reunited. Lysimachus, the Governor, asks for Marina's hand, which Marina accepts. Then Pericles is visited by a dream that instructs him to visit Ephesus. There he is reunited with Thaisa (who is now the head priestess of the Temple of Diana), and the whole family is together again.

Commentary

Pericles is not one of Shakespeare's best works. The style of the play is so uneven that scholars suspect it is not the work of a single author. Yet the play was very popular in its day, and has been successfully performed since.

Unlike many of Shakespeare's works, there is little rapport between the nobility and peasants. The fishermen who help Pericles are forgotten, despite his promise to remember them. In the brothel in Mytilene, Marina constantly proves she is better than those who would patronise her, thanks to her royal blood. The lower characters are caricatures.

Ben Jonson, one of Shakespeare's contemporaries, attributed the play's success to its use of 'scraps out of every dish' – touches of fairy tales, the Bible, *The Tempest*, incest, a lost daughter and a wife presumed dead, several storms, several contests for the hand of a princess, and innumerable kingdoms ruled by men of greater or lesser stature.

Structurally, the play divides in two. In the first nine scenes, Pericles falls into unfortunate circumstances, and then his luck changes for the better. In the final 13 scenes, he repeats this pattern. One explanation for this repetition is that the authors change after Scene Nine.

Pericles's Sufferings

Pericles himself is something of a cipher, largely because Shakespeare does not delve into the workings of his psyche, as he did with characters in the tragic plays written immediately before. Overall, the play suggests that, like Job, enduring miseries heaped one on another, Pericles ultimately is rewarded for his stoicism: his family is reunited.

Pericles and his companions live in a pagan world, where even the goddess Diana becomes a character. Yet the complex plot is unwoven at the end to reveal a version of Christian providence, masquerading as the workings of the Greco-Roman gods. The trajectory from suffering to triumph is Christian in content.

Redemption

The journey to self-knowledge from a place of unawareness is a repeated narrative for Shakespeare's characters. But Pericles leaves one kingdom in fear for his life because of a contest for the hand of a princess, only to enter an identical contest quite soon after. He loses his wife, whom he barely knew, and then makes sure he won't know his daughter either, by leaving her in a different kingdom. At the end everyone is reunited, but Pericles divides the family again by sending Marina to Tyre and going to Pentapolis with Thaisa.

Meanwhile, most of Gower's monologues merely repeat the plot of scenes just past, or narrate events that take place offstage. Only through Gower's conclusion are we given any kind of sense of redemption in the plot. He explains to us, finally, that Antiochus and his daughter and Cleon and Dionyza are punished because they did evil, whereas Pericles and his family are rewarded. Gower also explains the role of the minor characters, who were living embodiments of various virtues, such as loyalty (Helicanus) and charity (Cerimon).

28 ❧ Romeo and Juliet

Main Characters

Romeo – A Montague. A teenager who falls in love with Juliet.
Juliet – A Capulet. Falls in love with Romeo.
Friar Laurence – A wise old priest.
Nurse – Juliet's second mother and confidante.
Benvolio – Romeo's cousin.
Mercutio – Romeo's best friend.
Tybalt – Juliet's hot-tempered cousin.
Capulet – Juliet's father.
Lady Capulet – Juliet's mother.
Paris – A nobleman. One of Juliet's suitors.
Prince Escalus – The ruler of Verona.
Montague – Romeo's father.
Lady Montague – Romeo's mother.

Introduction

Romeo and Juliet was written early in Shakespeare's career, probably in 1594 or 1595, and was first published in 1597. It is his first non-historical tragedy and, despite its poetic naiveté, in many ways it holds the promise of the mature plays Shakespeare would come to write in a few years' time.

The plot has become an archetypal love story for Western civilization. Scenes such as the balcony scene, for instance, are almost clichés now, and led to so many copies that a 19th-century French parody in Rostand's *Cyrano de Bergerac* was itself parodied in Steve Martin's film *Roxanne*.

The primary source was a poem entitled *The Tragicall Historye of Romeus and Juliet*, publishes in 1562 by Arthur Brooke. This, in turn, was a translation of a poem by a Frenchman, Pierre Boaistuau, published in 1559. The French poem, it seems, was derived from a 1554 story by an Italian writer named Mateo Bandello, which in turn was based on a version by Luigi Da Porto, published in 1530.

While the story of *Romeo and Juliet* was often told in the second half of the 16th century, Shakespeare's version has marked differences. His treatment has some of the greatest love poetry ever written in the English language, subtle and original characters (such as Mercutio and Tybalt, who are two of Shakespeare's most memorable early creations), and a fast pace (the action is compressed into five days).

The Play

In Verona, two feuding families, the Montagues and the Capulets, brawl constantly in the streets; the reason for the quarrel is never really made clear. In response to the constant fighting, the Prince of Verona issues an edict imposing the death penalty on anyone caught duelling.

Romeo, a young man of the house of Montague, has been infatuated with Rosaline, a niece of Capulet. He and his friends sneak into a masked ball at Capulet's house so that Romeo can see her. During the ball, Romeo catches sight of Juliet, Capulet's daughter, and quickly forgets about Rosaline.

That same night Romeo creeps under Juliet's bedroom window and professes his love for her. Juliet, who is standing on the balcony above him, overhears his sighs of love. She confesses she returns his feelings. With the aid of Friar Laurence, Romeo makes plans with Juliet for them to be married in secret.

The phrase 'Romeo, Romeo, wherefore art thou Romeo?' is probably second only to Hamlet's 'To be or not to be' as the most famous quotation from Shakespeare.

Tybalt, Juliet's cousin, discovers that Romeo attended the ball, and sets out to teach the young Montague a lesson. He challenges Romeo in the street. Romeo tries to avoid a duel because he is in love with Juliet. However, Romeo's best friend, Mercutio, takes up Tybalt's challenge and is killed by Tybalt. Before he realizes what he is doing, a distraught Romeo draws his sword and kills Tybalt in turn.

As a result of the bloodshed, despite the provocation, the Prince of Verona banishes Romeo. Romeo has time to consummate his marriage to Juliet and bid her goodbye. He hopes that they will soon be reunited.

Juliet's parents, meanwhile, press her to marry Paris. With Friar Laurence's help, Juliet comes up with a desperate plan to avoid her parents' wishes. She obtains a drug that will make her seem dead for 40 hours. While she is comatose, Friar Laurence will send word to Romeo so that he can rescue her from her family tomb.

Unfortunately, Friar Laurence's letter never gets to Romeo. Instead, he hears that Juliet has died. Grief-stricken, Romeo buys some poison with the intention of killing himself. Friar Laurence discovers that Romeo never received his letter, and in horror rushes to Juliet's tomb.

Too late. At Juliet's tomb, Romeo encounters Paris, who is mourning for his Juliet. In grief for Juliet's loss, the two men fight and Romeo kills Paris. Entering the tomb, Romeo discovers the 'dead' Juliet and, swallowing the poison, commits suicide at her side. Friar Laurence arrives at the scene just as Juliet wakes up. She discovers the body of her beloved Romeo beside her and, taking Romeo's dagger, stabs herself in the heart.

The Prince and the parents arrive, and Friar Laurence explains what has happened. Faced with the awful price their feud has cost them, the Montagues and Capulets swear to end the long bitterness between the two families.

Commentary

This is an early play written by a young poet with terrific talent. Despite its story, it is really quite optimistic, especially when compared to the latter tragedies and dark comedies. In modern times, critics have tended to disparage the play in favour of the great tragedies (*Hamlet*, *King Lear*, *Macbeth* and *Othello*). Certainly, when compared to these plays, *Romeo and Juliet* lacks psychological depth and structural complexity.

More recently, however, scholars have reconsidered their opinion, opting to judge *Romeo and Juliet* in its own right. Viewed in this light, the tragedy of the star-crossed teenagers is an extraordinary experimental play, featuring radical departures from long-standing conventions too complex to go into here.

Romeo

In Juliet, Romeo finds that rare gift, a soulmate – a lover of such purity and passion that when he learns she has died he cannot endure life without her. Initially this may seem an immature reaction. In fact, it can also be seen as a tragic sign of maturity. Romeo is the romantic in this couple. He grows up through 'the love of a good woman', who grounds his romantic notions, but it is Juliet who is the level-headed one of the pair. She inspires Romeo to utter some of the most beautiful and intense love poetry ever written.

The ardour and romantic intensity of *Romeo and Juliet*, as well as its theme of young lovers struggling against the oppressive values of their parents, make it an extremely youthful play. It represents a young playwright's first gropings toward the more mature and profound philosophical tragedies of *Hamlet*, *King Lear* and *Othello*.

At the beginning of the play Romeo pines for Rosaline, proclaiming her the paragon of women and despairing of her indifference toward him. His histrionics seem frankly juvenile, and he gets the teasing he deserves from his friends and relatives. Sure enough, Rosaline evaporates from Romeo's thoughts the first time he sees Juliet. But Juliet is not just another infatuation.

As Romeo's love matures from shallow desire to a profound passion, he also matures as a person. Against great provocation, he tries his best to avoid fighting with Tybalt, and only when Tybalt manages to include him in the death of his best friend, Mercutio, does Romeo 'lose it'. If only Romeo had restrained himself from killing Tybalt, or waited even a few hours before killing himself after seeing Juliet lying in her tomb, matters might have ended happily. But the same soaring passions that made his love for Juliet so powerful, condemned him to respond as he does in both cases.

Juliet

Juliet is a fascinating character. While Romeo is the romantic, Juliet is determined, strong and down-to-earth. Her growing love for Romeo propels her toward adulthood with the velocity of a rocket. She learns how to manage the adults on their own terms. She promises her mother, for example, that she will consider Paris as a possible husband with an outward show of obedience that is clearly meant to placate her mother.

Romeo and Juliet has been interpreted and adapted thousands of times in opera, ballet, novels, on stage, screen and television, and even so, the passage of time and changing cultural context do not seem to have diminished the play's innate innocence, youthful rebelliousness or capacity to shock, delight and move audiences.

Though profoundly in love with Romeo, Juliet is able to see and criticize his impetuosity and tendency to romanticize things. After Romeo is banished, she does not follow him blindly to Mantua, but calmly and rationally decides what the course of action should be for the two of them. She then cuts herself loose from her nurse and her parents in order to be reunited with her husband.

When she wakes up in the tomb to find Romeo dead beside her, she decides to kill herself out of the same intensity of love that overwhelmed Romeo. Juliet's suicide actually requires more nerve, as befits her character: while he swallows poison, she stabs herself through the heart with a dagger. Juliet's development from a wide-eyed teenager to a self-assured, loyal and capable woman is one of Shakespeare's early triumphs of characterization, and marks one of his most confident and rounded treatments of a female character.

Famous Lines

'The weakest goes to the wall' (Act I, Scene I).

'He that is strucken blind cannot forget
The precious treasure of his eyesight lost' (Act I, Scene I).

'True, I talk of dreams,
Which are the children of an idle brain,
Begot of nothing but vain fantasy' (Act I, Scene IV).

'But, soft! what light through yonder window breaks?
It is the east, and Juliet is the sun' (Act II, Scene I).

'See, how she leans her cheek upon her hand!
O, that I were a glove upon that hand,
That I might touch that cheek!' (Act II, Scene I).

'O Romeo, Romeo! wherefore art thou Romeo?' (Act II, Scene I).

'What's in a name? That which we call a rose
By any other name would smell as sweet' (Act II, Scene I).

'This bud of love, by summer's ripening breath,
May prove a beauteous flower when next we meet' (Act II, Scene I).

'Good night, good night! parting is such sweet sorrow,
That I shall say good night till it be morrow' (Act II, Scene I).

'These violent delights have violent ends' (Act II, Scene V).

'Too swift arrives as tardy as too slow' (Act II, Scene V).

'A plague o' both your houses!' (Act III, Scene I)

'Taking the measure of an unmade grave' (Act III, Scene III).

'Not stepping o'er the bounds of modesty' (Act IV, Scene II).

'Eyes, look your last!
Arms, take your last embrace!' (Act V, Scene III).

29   Sir Thomas More

Introduction

Anthony Munday wrote the original script of *Sir Thomas More* between 1592 and 1595. However, the Master of the Revels prevented its performance because scenes showing Londoners rioting might set a bad example. In previous years, plays that in the opinion of the authorities disparaged the established religion or the government were banned. Other writers later revised *Sir Thomas More*, making it less politically provocative, and among those writers, according to strong evidence, was William Shakespeare.

Sir Thomas More (1478–1535) was a leading Renaissance scholar whose opposition to Henry VIII's divorce from Catherine of Aragon, and subsequent refusal to swear that the King's authority superseded the Pope's, led to his execution in 1535.

Before clashing with Henry, More was a religious man of great principle. He was also the Sheriff of London, a position he assumed in 1510. After attracting Henry's attention, More rose further in the political ranks, serving as a diplomat, Speaker of the House of Commons, adviser to the King and finally Lord Chancellor of England. However, More's opposition to Henry's divorce effectively ended his career.

Two years after he resigned as Chancellor, the King imprisoned him, held a mock trial, and ordered his beheading. More was canonized a saint by the Roman Catholic Church in 1935.

Commentary

The play is sympathetic to Sir Thomas More, and presents him as a wise and worthy English citizen and public servant who exhibited honesty, right-thinking and courage. He paid with his head for sticking to his principles and opposing Henry VIII's marriage to Anne Boleyn.

Shakespeare's participation in the production of the play has added weight to the belief of some scholars that, like his mother, Shakespeare was a practising Roman Catholic, and not a member of the Church of England.

30 § The Comedy of Errors

Main Characters

Antipholus of Syracuse – The twin brother of Antipholus of Ephesus, and the son of Egeon.

Antipholus of Ephesus – The twin brother of Antipholus of Syracuse, and the son of Egeon. A well-respected merchant in Ephesus and Adriana's husband.

Dromio of Syracuse – The slave of Antipholus of Syracuse, and the twin brother of Dromio of Ephesus.

Dromio of Ephesus – The slave of Antipholus of Ephesus, and the twin brother of Dromio of Syracuse.

Adriana – The wife of Antipholus of Ephesus.

Luciana – Adriana's unmarried sister.

Solinus – The Duke of Ephesus.

Egeon – Husband of the Abbess (Emilia); father of the two Antipholuses. He is searching for the missing half of his family.

Abbess – Emilia, the long-lost wife of Egeon and the mother of both the Antipholuses.

Balthasar – A merchant in Syracuse.

Angelo – A goldsmith in Syracuse.

Merchant – A friend of Antipholus of Syracuse.

Second Merchant – A tradesman to whom Angelo is in debt.

Doctor Pinch – A schoolteacher and would-be exorcist.

Luce/Nell – Dromio of Ephesus's wife.

Courtesan – An expensive prostitute.

Introduction

The Comedy of Errors is an early play (some scholars think Shakespeare's first), with an emphasis on slapstick. It was first performed on 28 December 1594, at the Gray's Inn Christmas Revels, to an audience largely composed of lawyers and law students.

Shakespeare drew on the Roman comedy *Menaechmi* by Plautus (c.254–184 BCE) for his plot. Shakespeare had a grammar school education, and was possibly a schoolteacher before moving to London, so he may well have read the play in its original Latin. However, in 1594 an English translation was printed, though it had probably been floating around in manuscript form some time before that.

As usual, Shakespeare made a number of changes to the original story: a second set of identical twins (the Dromios); the expansion of Adriana's character; a new character, Luciana; and the subplot of Egeon and Emilia. The style of the comedy is modelled on *commedia dell'arte*, which developed in northern Italy after about 1550.

The Comedy of Errors is driven by coincidence and slapstick, its events confined within a single day. Characters are mistaken for one another, but do not pretend to be other than they are – there are no disguises here.

Typically of Shakespeare, there are also hints of tragedy – the story hinges on a threat of execution, and includes broken families, troubled marriages, slavery, beatings and a beheading.

The Play

The play is concerned with the separation and ultimate reunion of Egeon and his wife Emilia, and their twin sons, Antipholus of Ephesus (Antipholus E) and Antipholus of Syracuse (Antipholus S). The family is separated at sea during a storm, 33 years before the action of the play.

Egeon, Antipholus S and Dromio S survive the shipwreck together and grow up in Syracuse. Seven years before the action starts they decide to search, separately, for their lost family. Emilia survives with Antipholus E and Dromio E, only to have a 'rude' fisherman steal the boys from her. In sorrow, she becomes a nun. Eventually, Antipholus E and Dromio E move to Ephesus, though they don't know their mother Emilia is living there as well. Antipholus E marries Adriana.

Ignoring a law decreeing that strangers can be put to death, Egeon comes to the city looking for Antipholus E and his servant Dromio E. He is arrested and sentenced to death for entering enemy territory. Soon after, Antipholus S and his servant Dromio S enter the city on business. The identical twins are easily confused by the citizens of Ephesus, who think that the Antipholus and Dromio they know have gone mad. Doctor Pinch, a psychiatrist, even tries to exorcise the devil from Antipholus E.

As Egeon's execution draws near, Egeon recognizes his son Antipholus E, though Antipholus E doesn't recognize his father. Simultaneously, Emilia appears from the convent with Antipholus S and Dromio S, who have taken refuge there, and the family reunites. The Duke pardons Egeon for entering the city, Antipholus S begins to court Luciana, Adriana's sister, and Emilia holds a feast to celebrate the family's reunion.

Commentary

The Comedy of Errors is a comedy, so all the characters' confusion is cleared up at the end. The darker issues of imminent execution, cuckoldry and a broken marriage are easily resolved. Duke Solinus begins the play as almost a tyrant, but ends it as a forgiving father figure. The broken halves of Egeon's family, separated for more than 30 years, get put back together, and husband and wife reconcile as if time were unimportant. Even the poor abused slaves, the Dromios, quickly forget their beatings and embrace, emphasizing the play's main theme: love will triumph over all.

Famous Lines

'The pleasing punishment that women bear' (Act I, Scene I).

'A wretched soul, bruised with adversity' (Act II, Scene I).

'Every why hath a wherefore' (Act II, Scene II).

'Let's go hand in hand, not one before another' (Act V, Scene I).

31   The Merchant of Venice

Main Characters

Portia – A wealthy heiress from Belmont.
Shylock – A Jewish moneylender in Venice.
Antonio – A merchant and friend to Bassanio.
Bassanio – Antonio's friend, a gentleman of Venice.
Gratiano – A friend of Bassanio who is fiercely anti-Semitic.
Lorenzo – A friend of Bassanio and Antonio. In love with Jessica.
Jessica – Shylock's daughter. In love with Lorenzo.
Nerissa – Portia's lady-in-waiting.
Salerio and Solanio – Venetian gentlemen.
Launcelot Gobbo – Shylock's servant.
Old Gobbo – Launcelot's father.
The Prince of Morocco – One of Portia's suitors.
The Prince of Arragon – One of Portia's suitors.
Tubal – A Jew, one of Shylock's friends.

Introduction

Many people forget that *The Merchant of Venice* is a comedy because of the character of Shylock, and the theme of anti-Semitism, which are serious and are treated as such in the play. It was written in about 1596.

The Merchant of Venice weaves together two ancient folk tales, one involving a vengeful, greedy creditor trying to extract a pound of flesh, the other involving a suitor's choice among three chests to thereby win his mate.

The characters of the merchant, the suitor, the lady and the villainous Jew can be found in several contemporary Italian story collections. The cross-dressing heroine and the Italian location make *The Merchant of Venice* similar to earlier comedies. Portia is considered by many scholars to be Shakespeare's first great heroine, and Shylock's complex and not altogether unsympathetic villain makes the play one of Shakespeare's best.

While Shylock is clearly a stereotypical caricature of a money-obsessed, vicious medieval Jew, it is possible to argue that Shakespeare wanted to make anti-Semites peer into a mirror and see their own reflections. By merging the two stories, Shakespeare makes one a metaphor for the other.

Shylock is one of the most interesting Shakespearean characters for modern audiences. England had excluded communities of Jews for centuries, (though there were Portuguese Jews in London about this time), so all the moneylenders in London would have been Christian. Anti-Semitism was common in the 16th century throughout most of Europe, even when Catholics and Protestants were busy finding excuses to slaughter one another; Jews were also comic villains in Elizabethan theatre.

The Play

Antonio, a wealthy merchant, is feeling depressed, while his friend, Bassanio, needs his financial help so that he can court a wealthy woman, Portia, and win her hand in marriage. Antonio agrees to help Bassanio.

Portia complains to her servant, Nerissa, about the provisions of her father's will. The suitor who correctly chooses one of three chests (gold, silver and lead) may marry Portia and claim her money. If they fail, they must never marry. Portia doesn't like any of her suitors, except Bassanio, and prays that he chooses in time and correctly.

Back in Venice, Bassanio persuades Shylock the Jew to lend him 3,000 ducats. Antonio becomes his guarantor, putting up 'a pound of flesh' as the bond. Shylock hates Antonio, and lends the money hoping Antonio will default on the loan. Antonio is certain one of his ships will arrive before the three-month deadline is up.

Shylock's servant, Launcelot Gobbo, tells his father, old Gobbo, that he wants to leave Shylock and work for Bassanio. Shylock's daughter, Jessica, meanwhile, has fallen in love with Antonio's friend Lorenzo and intends to convert to Christianity in order to marry him.

Gratiano, Solario, Salerio and Lorenzo help Jessica elope with Lorenzo. They all head off to meet Bassanio. Solanio and Salerio gossip about Antonio's ship sinking and make fun of Shylock's losing his daughter.

Bassanio correctly chooses the lead casket and wins Portia's hand and fortune in marriage. To seal the deal, Portia gives Bassanio a ring, warning him never to lose it, or he'll risk losing her love. Gratiano then announces his intention to wed Nerissa.

Salerio, Lorenzo and Jessica arrive and tell Bassanio that Antonio has lost his ships. What's more, Shylock is determined Antonio should forfeit his bond. Bassanio immediately leaves for Venice to repay the loan. Meanwhile, Shylock has Antonio arrested for failure to honour the debt in time. Portia and Nerissa decide to disguise themselves as a lawyer and his clerk, and follow Bassiano to Venice.

Shylock's Petition

The Duke presides over Shylock's petition to cut 'a pound of flesh from Antonio's breast' since those were the terms of the bond, even though Bassanio offers him 6,000 ducats (rather than the 3,000 he originally lent) for repayment. Nerissa and Portia, disguised as a court clerk and Doctor of civil law, arrive at the court and join Gratiano, Bassanio and the Duke in trying to dissuade Shylock, to no avail. He will have his bond, no more, no less, that is what the law allows. Shylock seems to be victorious.

Then Portia points out that he's correct in that the law does indeed let him collect his pound of flesh, but he must be careful: no blood must be shed, and exactly one pound must be taken. Shylock realizes this is impossible. He tries to change his mind and take the money instead. Portia pounds home another nail: Shylock is himself guilty of conspiring to kill Antonio, a fellow citizen. As punishment, the Duke and Antonio decide that Shylock must give half his possessions to the court and promise to give the rest to his daughter and new son-in-law (Lorenzo) upon his death. What's more, he must become a Christian. Defeated, Shylock is forced to agree.

A Happy Ending

Still disguised as the lawyer, Portia asks Bassanio for his wedding ring. Despite his vow, and after some prodding by Antonio, Bassanio reluctantly hands it over. Nerissa (disguised as Portia's clerk) gets her husband (Gratiano) to do the same thing with his wedding ring.

Back at Portia's house, Bassanio and Portia and Gratiano and Nerissa reunite. After quarrelling over the loss of rings, the women admit their ruse and return the rings to their husbands. Antonio also discovers that three of his ships have come to port full of merchandise, and Jessica and Lorenzo learn that they will inherit Shylock's possessions on his death.

Shylock is, first and foremost, an anti-Semitic creation for an Elizabethan audience accustomed to seeing Jews as comic foils for Christian heroes. However, Shylock's eloquence is so great that modern productions elevate him to the level of tragic hero. But the play is ultimately a comedy, as Shylock's elimination at the end of Act IV and the happy ending in Act V show.

Commentary

The play is really two fairy tales that come together at the trial scene. Until this point, Shylock's story takes centre stage and Portia's courtships are something of a subplot. By the trial, Shylock has had enough. He has become a vengeful figure, blinded to humanity and compassion by the chance to finally exact revenge against those who have wronged him: 'I'll have my bond,' he gloats, ignoring pleas for mercy from all around him.

Portia sets up Shylock, offering him a chance to escape with the money. If he is merciful, it is a win-win situation for everyone. When Shylock refuses, she is justified in crushing him. But he threatens to turn the play into something other than it is, and must be disposed of once and for all so that the happy ending can take place.

Shylock seems almost too vivid for the rest of the characters in *The Merchant of Venice*. However, his determination to extract his pound of flesh at any cost is clearly the work of a comic villain whose downfall we will applaud. The good-humoured intrigue of the rings that ends the play is something of an anticlimax: love, mercy and compassion have conquered all.

Famous Lines

'I hold the world but as the world, Gratiano,—
A stage, where every man must play a part;
And mine a sad one' (Act I, Scene I).

'In my school-days, when I had lost one shaft,
I shot his fellow of the selfsame flight
The selfsame way with more advised watch,
To find the other forth; and by adventuring both,
I oft found both' (Act I, Scene I).

'God made him, and therefore let him pass for a man'
(Act I, Scene II).

'I will buy with you, sell with you, talk with you, walk with you, and so
following; but I will not eat with you, drink with you, nor pray
with you. What news on the Rialto?' (Act I, Scene III).

'The devil can cite Scripture for his purpose' (Act I, Scene III).

'You call me misbeliever, cut-throat dog,
And spit upon my Jewish gaberdine' (Act I, Scene III).

'Mislike me not for my complexion,
The shadow'd livery of the burnish'd sun' (Act II, Scene I).

'It is a wise father that knows his own child' (Act II, Scene II).

'Truth will come to light; murder cannot be hid long'
(Act II, Scene II).

'In the twinkling of an eye' (Act II, Scene II).

'But love is blind, and lovers cannot see
The pretty follies that themselves commit' (Act II, Scene V).

'All that glisters is not gold' (Act II, Scene VI).

'I am a Jew. Hath not a Jew eyes? Hath not a Jew hands, organs,
dimensions, senses, affections, passions?' (Act III, Scene I).

'The villainy you teach me I will execute, and it shall go hard, but I will
better the instruction' (Act III, Scene I).

'Tell me where is fancy bred,
Or in the heart or in the head?
How begot, how nourished?
Reply, reply' (Act III, Scene II).

'There is no vice so simple but assumes
Some mark of virtue in his outward parts' (Act III, Scene II).

'You take my house when you do take the prop
That doth sustain my house; you take my life
When you do take the means whereby I live' (Act IV, Scene I).

32 ✄ The Merry Wives of Windsor

Main Characters

Mistress Ford – Married to Ford and a friend of Mistress Page.

Mistress Page – A friend of Mistress Ford. She and her husband disagree about who should marry their daughter, Anne.

Falstaff – A knight and a scoundrel.

Ford – Husband of Mistress Ford. Calls himself Brooke.

Page – Husband of Mistress Page.

Sir Hugh Evans – The local clergyman. He is Welsh.

Caius – The local doctor. He is French.

Anne Page – Daughter of Page and Mistress Page.

Fenton – A suitor for Anne Page's hand.

Slender – A suitor for Anne Page's hand.

Shallow – A figure of the law, who is foolish.

Mistress Quickly – Caius's servant.

Bardolph, Pistol and Nym – Falstaff's men.

Host – Host of the Garter Inn.

William Page – Anne's brother and Page's son.

Simple – Slender's servant.

Introduction

The Merry Wives of Windsor was probably written around 1597. It is Shakespeare's most middle-class play in setting, subject matter and outlook. It's also one of his most farcical, using physical gags and linguistic jokes to establish a comic tone that influences the play's ultimate spirit of reconciliation. It is concerned with the phenomena of an emerging merchant/guild middle class filling the gap between agrarian peasant and landed gentry.

According to theatrical legend, Elizabeth saw *King Henry IV, Part I*, and liked the character of Falstaff so much she asked Shakespeare to write another play about him, allegedly giving him only 14 days. It's thought that Shakespeare may have put aside *King Henry IV, Part II* to complete *The Merry Wives of Windsor*, and he included several characters who appear in both plays, including Pistol, Nim, Bardolph, Mistress Quickly and Shallow. Falstaff and his entourage were supposedly good friends with Prince Hal, later Henry V, which lends a royal flavour to the archetypal suburban events of *The Merry Wives of Windsor*. Windsor, its castle still used as a residence by royalty today, has always been considered a royal town.

The Merry Wives of Windsor captures life in an English provincial town in the late 16th century and refers to other, older plays. The main plot closely resembles *Il Pecorone*, a 1558 Italian play by Ser Giovanni Fiorentino, which in turn draws on Ancient Roman comedy.

Scholars concur that the first performance was on 23 April 1597 at a feast of the Order of the Garter, which Elizabeth attended. There are two different versions: the First Quarto (1602) and the First Folio (1623). The Quarto is most likely a reconstruction from memory by actors and others. It is half the length of the Folio version, and is probably poorly remembered or trimmed for provincial performances. The Folio version is printed from a manuscript that was based on either a playhouse promptbook or an authorial manuscript, and has a close connection with the first performance of the play.

The Play

Sir John Falstaff, a rogue who is financially challenged, hatches a scheme to raise funds by seducing Mistresses Ford and Page at the same time in an attempt to get at their husbands' money. Falstaff, however, has overestimated his charm and his ingenuity. The two women are friends and, discovering his plot, decide to make him suffer for his impertinence. They send him letters encouraging his advances.

Mistresses Ford and Page enjoy their fun. Falstaff is in danger of being discovered and hides in a basket of dirty laundry, which is then tossed into the Thames. He is later dressed as a woman and beaten. Finally, the women tell their husbands what's going on, and all plot one final humiliation for the old knight.

Meanwhile, Page's daughter, Anne, is being courted by two suitors favoured by her parents, but she is in love with Fenton. It is decided that Sir Hugh Evans will lead Anne and the town's children dressed as fairies in a late-night attack on the knight as he waits in the woods for Mistresses Page and Ford. Anne's father, Page, tells Slender, one of Anne's suitors, that he should elope with his daughter after the prank. Mistress Page pulls her favourite suitor, Doctor Caius, aside and tells him the same thing. Because she will be in disguise, the two men will recognize Anne by the colour of her dress. Anne, meanwhile, makes plans of her own to elope with Fenton.

The Merry Wives of Windsor was a great favourite of Friedrich Engels, co-author with Karl Marx of the *Communist Manifesto*. No doubt he enjoyed the way Shakespeare made fun of the emerging bourgeoisie. With the exception of *The Comedy of Errors*, it is probably Shakespeare's most overtly farcical play.

Falstaff is persuaded to dress up as the god Herne (complete with antlers). While he waits in anticipation for the women to come to him, he is suddenly set upon and tormented by Anne and the children, dressed as fairies. The wives and husbands eventually reveal themselves to Falstaff, who is forgiven his roguish ways.

Slender and Doctor Caius reappear, chagrined. Both men erred on the colour of Anne's dress (Slender thought it was white; Caius thought it was green) and ran off with boys instead of Anne. Fenton arrives with Anne. The two of them are married, and Anne's parents begrudgingly accept the outcome.

Commentary

Mistresses Page and Ford determine that wives can lead boisterous, vivid lives (i.e. be merry) without having to betray their husbands. Page understands this, but Ford takes some convincing. The romance of Fenton and Anne Page affirms the idea of romantic love as a means of transcending class.

The Merry Wives of Windsor also exposes the provincial mindset by making fun of a community that in turn makes fun of outsiders. Slender's pretensions make him look like a fool. Justice Shallow, whose authority derives from the crown, ends up much the same. Sir Hugh Evans, the Welsh clergyman, is mocked for his foreign accent, as is Doctor Caius. Slender and Mistress Quickly speak in clichés, while Quickly hears sexual double entendres in Latin conjugations and declensions. The hostility of the locals to the aristocracy is clearly seen in Page's rejection of Fenton's request for Anne's hand, and in the continued abuse of the impoverished knight, Falstaff.

While the play celebrates the mistresses' autonomy (due in part to their husbands' wealth and social positions), the only woman who is 'liberated' is Anne, who avoids a marriage chosen for her by her parents in favour of a partnership of her own choosing, against their will.

Famous Lines

'If there be no great love in the beginning, yet heaven may decrease it upon better acquaintance, when we are married and have more occasion to know one another: I hope, upon familiarity will grow more contempt' (Act I, Scene I).

'This is the short and the long of it' (Act II, Scene II).

'This is the third time; I hope good luck lies in odd numbers.... There is divinity in odd numbers, either in nativity, chance, or death' (Act V, Scene I).

33   The Taming of the Shrew

Main Characters

Katherina – The shrew of the title. Also called Kate.

Petruchio – A gentleman from Verona.

Bianca – Kate's younger sister.

Baptista Minola – One of the wealthiest men in Padua. Father of the two girls.

Lucentio – A young student from Pisa. In love with Bianca.

Tranio – Lucentio's servant.

Gremio and Hortensio – Suitors for Bianca.

Grumio – Petruchio's servant.

Introduction

The Taming of the Shrew is an early comedy, loosely termed 'romantic', along with *Much Ado About Nothing* and *A Midsummer Night's Dream*, among others. The plays are lighthearted and often slapstick in style, filled with disguises and deception, and end happily. This is in sharp contrast to the later comedies, which are much darker and filled with cynicism and a sometimes bitter irony.

The Taming of the Shrew is clearly a young playwright's work, and focuses more squarely on marriage than almost any other of the early comedies. While the other plays end with a marriage, *The Taming of the Shrew* takes this almost as a starting point, following the early days of married life.

Elizabethan Marriages

The average 16th-century playgoer was interested in discussions about marriage, in part because Henry VIII's separation from the Catholic Church in 1536 was brought about by wrangling over a divorce. (Shakespeare dealt with this subject more directly in his play *King Henry VIII*. Henry named himself 'Defender of the Faith', a title still held by British monarchs, and formed the Church of England in order to get his own way.) The births of Mary and Elizabeth, his daughters, who became queens of England after Henry died, were directly responsible for this break with the Pope, who refused to grant Henry's request for a divorce so that he could remarry and produce a male heir. Henry desperately wanted a son. His eventual male heir, Edward, was sickly for most of his short life, and did not last long as king.

The plot was familiar to Elizabethan audiences, being drawn from popular folk tales and ballads such as *A Merry Jest of a Shrewde Curste Wyfe*, published in 1550. In the ballad the woman is thrashed to a bloody pulp and then wrapped in the salted skin of an old horse.

This recent history would be very much on the minds of an Elizabethan audience. Great pain, death and turmoil had resulted from the break with Rome. Unless you were a determined king of England willing to suffer excommunication, the late 16th and early 17th centuries offered few ways out of an unhappy marriage, so the resolution of marital disputes was a very hot topic in the popular literature of the era.

Elizabethan marriages were still being made along medieval lines – they were far more often made for money, land or power than for love. A woman had few options for survival if set adrift from the rule and support of a man, either her father or her husband, and less often her brother, and the fact that Elizabeth I never married was cause for great concern to Elizabethans because of its potential to undermine the long-established power structure of society.

The Shrew

Of particular worry to married men were 'shrews' or 'scolds', that is, cantankerous or gossipy wives who resisted or undermined the natural authority of their husbands. A large number of sermons, plays and pamphlets of the time address related topics: the taming of shrews by their husbands, or the public punishment of scolds (by repeated dunking in a river, for example). Some of this literature is very diplomatic, and some is clearly misogynistic. It's difficult to tell sometimes (perhaps deliberately so) what is meant as parody, and what is being presented as an ideal. This is also true for *The Taming of the Shrew*. Shakespeare's own marriage, at least at first, is thought not to have been the greatest match, and he spent many years of it living in London, while his family stayed in Stratford.

Viewing from a Distance

The main part of *The Taming of the Shrew* is set in Padua, a city in northern Italy. To Elizabethan England, Italy was a beautiful country of rich food, loose women, and generally materialistic and pleasurable living. It became a favourite setting of Shakespeare and his contemporaries for plays involving deceit, money, beautiful women, cross-dressing, or anything worth taking a little sinful pleasure in – but always at a very safe distance from England.

This idea of viewing from a distance is particularly true of *The Taming of the Shrew* because it has an 'outer' and an 'inner' play. The frame, or outer play, is actually set in the English countryside, and consists of only the first two scenes, called the Induction, where a group of English actors prepare to present the inner play, the story of Kate and Petruchio.

The Taming of the Shrew should not be confused with *The Taming of a Shrew*, published in 1594. That version has three sisters and Sly, a drunk appearing as a chorus throughout. It was probably reconstructed from the faulty memories of actors, and was a pirated or stolen play, called a bad quarto.

The Outer Play

Outside an alehouse, somewhere in England, a beggar named Christopher Sly is arguing with the hostess of the alehouse. The hostess leaves to fetch the local authorities, and Sly falls asleep, drunk.

A passing lord decides to have some fun with the comatose beggar. The lord decides to see if, with the right surroundings, he can convince a beggar that he is really of high birth. So he orders his servants to take Sly back to his house and treat him as if he were a lord.

At the house, the servants place Sly in the lord's bed with fine clothes and jewellery, and the lord disguises himself as one of the serving men. When Sly awakes, they present him with good wine and food and tell him that he is their master. He protests that he remembers being a poor tinker (an itinerant mender of pots). They tell him this memory is the result of a madness he has been in for 15 years. They put on quite a show, pleading and wailing in feigned distress at his continued illness, but despite this, Sly is still sceptical.

However, when his 'wife' is brought in – a male page dressed as a woman – he is finally convinced. The servants are overjoyed that his 'memory' has returned, and wish to entertain him. As luck would have it, a group of players happen to be in town and prepare to put on a play for the enjoyment of Sly and his wife.

The play within a play forms the main action of *The Taming of the Shrew*. The text only returns to Sly briefly after this Induction, and never concludes his story.

The Play within a Play

Lucentio arrives in Padua with his manservant Tranio to study at the university. Baptista, a wealthy merchant of Padua, has two daughters, Katherina and Bianca. Lucentio falls in love with Bianca, and becomes one of several suitors for the hand of the younger and kinder daughter. Lucentio and Tranio switch clothes, and thus disguised, Lucentio will offer his services as a tutor for Bianca in order to get closer to her.

However, because of her older sister Katherina's shrewish disposition, Bianca's father has declared that no one will marry Bianca until Katherina has a husband. The suitors are beside themselves. Enter Petruchio, in Padua to visit his friend Hortensio (one of Bianca's suitors). Petruchio is attracted to Katherina's large dowry, and Hortensio sees a potential solution to his problem, which will put him in good stead with Baptista.

Despite all the warnings he gets about the fiery Kate, Petruchio claims that he finds her charming and pleasant. The marriage is arranged, and Petruchio immediately sets out to tame Kate. He shows up late to his own wedding, constantly contradicts whatever she says, calling the sun the moon, refuses to give her food until she agrees with him, and so on. Finally, an exhausted Kate is 'tamed' into docility.

The matches of Kate and Petruchio and Lucentio and Bianca become contrasting versions of marriage. It is interesting to compare the concept of love and partnership in more mature men and women in *The Taming of the Shrew* with Benedick and Beatrice in *Much Ado About Nothing*.

Lucentio wins Bianca's heart, and Hortensio happily marries a rich widow in Padua. Petruchio and Kate return for Bianca's wedding. During the wedding feast, Petruchio makes a bet with the other two new husbands that he has the most obedient wife. Knowing her previous behaviour, the men take the bet, only to discover that Petruchio really has 'tamed' his wife. In a complete turnabout, Kate gives Bianca a lecture on how to be a good, loving and obedient wife.

Commentary

When you watch *The Taming of the Shrew*, it's important to remember the context of the play. In Elizabethan times marriages were far more often made for the convenience of fathers than because the potential bride and groom loved each other. People were married without ever having met previously. Spouses hoped to learn to love their partner once they were wed. There was no guarantee that 'love at first sight' brought greater happiness in marriage than the slowly developed, consistent love of a couple who learned to live with and for each other.

The fatal, overpowering passions of *Romeo and Juliet* are not the best basis for a marriage, Shakespeare suggests. Rather, marriage should be more pragmatic, allowing a man and woman to create a peaceful, supportive union. Petruchio and Kate end up being well matched. Only a happy-go-lucky, persistent, self-assured man like Petruchio could break through Kate's defences. It becomes clear that Kate wants a man – the right man – to say 'no' to her. Few, including her father, have been able to do so.

She is shocked when Petruchio is late for their wedding, and her reaction is not anger at being stood up, but fear she will die a lonely old maid. She wants a relationship of mutual respect. But to get there she must rethink her whole attitude toward men. Petruchio's attempts to stifle and humiliate her are meant only to force her to stop blindly lashing out. She must see him for who he is and what he can give her.

The result is that Kate can enjoy her married life with an equal partner and, as she finally reveals near the end of the play, love her husband in her married life without feeling she has somehow lost her earlier independence, which actually brought her only anger and distress – and it is this revelation that she tries to share with her younger sister at the end of the play.

Famous Lines

'I'll not budge an inch' (Induction, Scene I).

'And thereby hangs a tale' (Act IV, Scene I).

'Such duty as the subject owes the prince,
Even such a woman oweth to her husband' (Act V, Scene II).

'Who wooed in haste, and means to wed at leisure'
(Act III, Scene II).

34 § The Tempest

Main Characters

Prospero – Once Duke of Milan, overthrown by his brother, Antonio.
Alonso – The King of Naples.
Gonzalo – A well-meaning elderly counsellor to Alonso.
Ferdinand – The Prince of Naples, and Alonso's son.
Miranda – Prospero's daughter.
Ariel – A spirit controlled by Prospero, who rescued him from imprisonment
Sebastian – Alonso's brother.
Antonio – Prospero's brother.
Trinculo – Alonso's jester.
Stephano – Alonso's butler.
Caliban – Prospero and Miranda's slave. The son of a powerful witch.
Adrian and Francisco – Lords who attend Alonso.
Boatswain, Master and Sailors – Seamen.

Introduction

The Tempest is considered Shakespeare's last major play (written around 1611) and is a romantic comedy. It was probably performed at court as part of the celebration surrounding the marriage of Princess Elizabeth, the daughter of James I. It contains an unusual amount of spectacle – dances, songs, costumed plays-within-the-play – which would have made it especially appropriate as royal entertainment.

Shakespeare seems to have retired from full-time playwriting after *The Tempest*, although he probably collaborated on at least three more plays. As a result, some scholars consider *The Tempest* to be a farewell from a great playwright to his audience and a final, symbolic celebration of the magic of theatre. Many people consider Prospero a stand-in for Shakespeare himself, since he gives up his magic and manipulation of the natural and unnatural world (read, playwriting) at the play's conclusion.

The Survival of the *Sea-Venture*

In early June 1609, nine ships, carrying around 600 people to strengthen the new English colony in Virginia, set out from England. The *Sea-Venture* was the lead ship and carried Sir Thomas Gates, the newly appointed Governor of the colony, and Sir George Somers, the Admiral of the Virginia Company. On 25 July a violent storm (probably a hurricane) overtook the ships and raged for several days. When the storm had subsided, four of the nine ships found each other and proceeded on to Virginia. Three more eventually made it into port. The *Sea-Venture* never showed up and was presumed to be lost.

The setting of *The Tempest* draws on chronicles brought back from the early colonization of the American continents by travellers and explorers. Although the magic island of *The Tempest* is supposedly somewhere in the Mediterranean, it actually incorporates many myths and stories about Bermuda and other Caribbean islands.

The news, when it reached England by autumn, created a public sensation. But unknown to the rest of the world, the battered ship had run aground on Bermuda, with all aboard making it safely ashore. Bermuda had a reputation as a place of devils and wicked spirits, but the colonists found it to be very pleasant, and they lived there for the next nine months while building a new ship out of native wood under Somers's guidance.

They set sail on 10 May 1610, and reached Jamestown, Virginia, two weeks later. A ship carrying Governor Gates and others left Jamestown two months later and reached England in September. The news of their survival caused another public sensation.

The Tale Told

Several accounts of the wreck and survival of the *Sea-Venture* were rushed into print in autumn 1610. The first of these, *A Discovery of the Barmudas*, was written by Sylvester Jourdain, who had been aboard the *Sea-Venture* and had returned to England with Gates. A month later *A True Declaration of the Estate of the Colonie in Virginia* was published. This was edited together from various documents as a piece of pro-Virginia propaganda on behalf of the Virginia Company, the consortium of investors who had underwritten the trip. More important than either publication was William Strachey's *True Reportory of the Wrack, and Redemption of Sir Thomas Gates, Knight*. Shakespeare almost certainly read the pamphlets and used them in writing *The Tempest*.

Though it was not officially published until 1625, Strachey's account is dated 15 July 1610, and was circulated among those in the know. Shakespeare had connections to the Virginia Company and Strachey, and it is highly likely that he had access to Strachey's account in manuscript form prior to publication.

A number of later adaptations include John Dryden's *The Enchanted Island,* Thomas Shadwell's opera of the same name (1674), for which Henry Purcell wrote the score in 1690. An 1821 performance of *The Enchanted Island* included music by Purcell, Mozart and Rossini. It is also the basis of W. H. Auden's long poem, *The Sea and the Mirror*.

The Play

Prospero, a sorcerer and the rightful Duke of Milan, lives on an enchanted isle with his daughter, Miranda. Twelve years earlier, the Duke's brother, Antonio, and Alonso, the King of Naples, conspired to usurp his throne. Prospero and Miranda were set adrift in a boat and eventually washed up on the island. Using his magic, Prospero freed a spirit called Ariel from a tree.

As the play begins, Prospero has discovered that a ship carrying his old enemies home from a wedding is sailing nearby. Prospero conjures a storm to wreck their ship. The survivors make it to shore in scattered groups. Among these is Ferdinand, the son of Alonso, who meets Miranda. The two teenagers fall in love.

Meanwhile, Antonio, Alonso, Sebastian and Gonzalo search the island for Ferdinand. As they do, Antonio plots with Sebastian to murder Alonso. However, Ariel thwarts the plot. Elsewhere on the island, Stephano and Trinculo encounter the island's other native inhabitant, Caliban, son of the witch Sycorax. After the three drink together, Caliban persuades the two servants to help him kill Prospero. He even promises Miranda to Stephano. Ariel keeps Prospero apprised of what the various groups are doing.

The numerous film adaptations of *The Tempest* include at least one classic – the 1956 sci-fi movie, *Forbidden Planet*. Those who like art films may find Peter Greenaway's *Prospero's Books*, starring Sir John Gielgud, an interesting interpretation of the story.

Prospero makes Ferdinand work to win Miranda's love, and while that is going on, creates a magical banquet for Antonio and Alonso, which vanishes whenever they try to eat. He also sends Ariel to torment them for their crimes against him.

During a masque to celebrate the upcoming marriage of Miranda and Ferdinand, Prospero decides it's time to put an end to Caliban's plot, and sends Ariel to punish him and the servants. The spirit does this by setting on them other island spirits in the shape of hunting dogs that chase them around the island.

Finally, Prospero confronts his brother and Alonso, revealing his true identity as the rightful Duke of Milan. He demands that Antonio restore his throne; he also rebukes Sebastian for plotting against his own brother. He reveals Ferdinand as alive and well, playing chess with Miranda. Restored to his natural authority, Prospero abandons his magic and releases Ariel and Caliban from their servitude.

Commentary

The Tempest is simply not a play to be read – it must be seen or at least heard. With this, his last great play, Shakespeare decided to pull out all the stops. It is an inherently visual spectacle, which unfolds in a series of exotic, otherworldly and sometimes 'invisible' characters that the audience can see but other characters cannot. It is best described as a multi-sensory theatrical experience, with sound and music used to complement a somewhat simple story of retribution, and a lyrical text that is lush with exotic images.

The Tempest does not have the bitterness of the later tragicomedies, and yet it does combine elements of a pastoral (the city folk forced to live as natives in the country) and tragedy (Prospero's revenge) with romantic comedy (the young lovers Miranda and Ferdinand). As in *Measure for Measure*, one of the problem plays, *The Tempest* also poses profound questions that defy easy resolution. The extraordinary thematic complexity of the play is far too involved to try to summarize effectively here.

Modern critics often read the Caliban subtext from a postcolonial viewpoint, examining what the play can tell us about European colonization of the Americas in particular, and colonization in general. It is a play of great lyricism and heart that deserves careful and serious study.

Among other things, the play challenges our concepts of reality and illusion and our senses. On one level it is a self-conscious performance overtly orchestrated by the Shakespeare-like puppet-master Prospero – the master illusionist – as he and his creator take their final bow. There are a number of themes, notably nature versus civilization or art. From certain perspectives, however, *The Tempest* tackles an overarching question: what is humanity?

Famous Lines

'I would fain die a dry death' (Act I, Scene I).

'My library
Was dukedom large enough' (Act I, Scene II).

'Fill all thy bones with aches' (Act I, Scene II).

'Full fathom five thy father lies;
Of his bones are coral made;
Those are pearls that were his eyes:
Nothing of him that doth fade
But doth suffer a sea-change
Into something rich and strange' (Act I, Scene II).

'There's nothing ill can dwell in such a temple:
If the ill spirit have so fair a house,
Good things will strive to dwell with't' (Act I, Scene II).

'Misery acquaints a man with strange bedfellows' (Act II, Scene II).

'Deeper than e'er plummet sounded' (Act III, Scene III).

'Our revels now are ended. These our actors,
As I foretold you, were all spirits, and
Are melted into air, into thin air:
And, like the baseless fabric of this vision,
The cloud-capp'd towers, the gorgeous palaces,
The solemn temples, the great globe itself,
Yea, all which it inherit, shall dissolve,
And, like this insubstantial pageant faded,
Leave not a rack behind. We are such stuff
As dreams are made on; and our little life
Is rounded with a sleep' (Act IV, Scene I).

'Where the bee sucks, there suck I;
In a cowslip's bell I lie' (Act V, Scene I).

35   The Two Gentlemen of Verona

Main Characters

Proteus – Valentine's supposed best friend, and one of the title gentlemen of Verona.

Valentine – The other title gentleman of Verona.

Julia – Proteus's beloved, and mistress to Lucetta.

Silvia – Daughter to the Duke and beloved of Valentine.

Duke of Milan – Silvia's father.

Lucetta – Julia's servant.

Launce – Proteus's servant.

Speed – Valentine's page.

Thurio – A rival for Silvia's hand.

Sir Eglamour – The gentleman who helps Silvia escape the Duke's court.

Antonio – Father to Proteus and master to Panthino.

Host – Houses Julia.

Crab – Launce's dog.

Panthino – Antonio's servant.

Introduction

Critics are not certain exactly when *The Two Gentlemen of Verona* was written. Some believe it may be Shakespeare's first play, as it is clearly not one of his best, and is the work of a young writer. Authors such as Geoffrey Chaucer, Francis Bacon, John Lyly and George Peele had dramatized similar debates on romantic love versus male friendship prior to Shakespeare's own attempt to tackle the subject in *The Two Gentlemen of Verona*.

Some historians believe that the play was begun in 1592 and finished in 1593 for a specific performance date, which might explain the seeming addition of Launce and Crab, the inconsistent references to Milan and

Verona as the setting, and to Silvia's father, who is sometimes called the Duke and sometimes the Emperor.

The first historical mention of *The Two Gentlemen of Verona* is in 1598, though the presence of certain theatrical techniques and themes in the play suggests that it was a precursor to other early works, such as *As You Like It* and *Twelfth Night*.

While the date of the play's composition may be uncertain, its literary ancestors are not. The most significant source for the play is the story of Felix and Felismena from Portuguese writer Jorge de Montemayor's work *Diana*. Shakespeare may have either read *Diana* in a French translation or seen a version of it performed at court in 1585. In the original play, Silvia's equivalent is killed off and Valentine does not exist. As was often his way, Shakespeare changed the original story to create a happier, more symmetrical ending.

The Play

Valentine's father sends him to take up a position in the Duke of Milan's court, and his friend Proteus goes with him reluctantly because he doesn't want to leave his beloved Julia. Once in Milan, Valentine falls for the Duke's daughter, Silvia. However, Silvia is betrothed to Thurio, a wealthy courtier, although she clearly prefers Valentine. The two decide to elope, and Valentine confides in Proteus.

Proteus, however, also falls for Silvia, and in order to get Valentine out of the way and himself in her father's good graces, Proteus betrays his friend's plan to the Duke. Valentine is banished, Silvia is imprisoned, and Proteus becomes a confidant of the Duke.

Valentine comes across a band of outlaws and is elected their leader. Meanwhile, Julia, disguised as a boy page, enters Milan looking for Proteus, who is trying unsuccessfully to court Silvia. Silvia still loves Valentine. Julia, in disguise, becomes a page to Proteus, and ends up being an intermediary between Proteus and Silvia. Silvia finally seizes an opportunity to escape, and goes in search of Valentine. In the forest, Valentine's outlaws capture her.

The Duke, Proteus and Thurio set off to rescue Silvia, and Proteus recovers Silvia before the outlaws can take her to Valentine. As Proteus makes one last attempt to persuade Silvia to love him, he and Valentine meet up again.

The two men eventually make peace with each other, and in a gesture of reconciliation, Valentine offers Silvia to Proteus, which causes Julia (who is still disguised as a page) to faint. Proteus finally recognizes her, much to his shame. The Duke and Thurio now arrive on the scene. Thurio backs off from his claim to Silvia when challenged by Valentine, and Valentine and Silvia are united with the Duke's approval. Proteus and Julia are reconciled, and the Duke grants a pardon to the outlaws.

Commentary

The Two Gentlemen of Verona is about the conflict of loyalty and passion. While the play eventually decides that friendship is more important (that is, the love of friends is purer than romantic love), the twists and turns that each character takes in order to reach that conclusion involve a number of other issues.

The servants Launce, Speed and Lucetta act as foils to their respective masters Proteus, Valentine and Julia. The servants give us clues about their masters. Launce's pragmatic reasoning about love, for example, shows us that Proteus is more concerned with social position and money than romance.

By offering a view that challenged the works of such established writers as Chaucer, Lyly and Francis Bacon, it was with a certain hubris that the young Shakespeare attempted to distance himself from the accepted moral stance of the great writers of his time. It is a shame that he threw down the gauntlet with a play that does not match the quality of work for which he was later known.

The forest (and the countryside in general) plays an important role in Shakespeare's plays. From the magic of Prospero's island to the fairy-filled forest of Athens in *A Midsummer Night's Dream*, social status there becomes irrelevant. People are judged on their merits, not on their parentage. Such a breakdown encourages a rebellion that can include cross-dressing and even same-sex romance. When, for example, Proteus realizes he can't have Silvia, suddenly 'Sebastian' (Julia) is attractive to him. Valentine's friendship with Proteus, and how they eventually resolve the contentious issue of Silvia, examines further the nature of sexual identity.

Famous Lines

'That man that hath a tongue, I say, is no man,
If with his tongue he cannot win a woman' (Act III, Scene I).

'Is she not passing fair?' (Act IV, Scene IV).

'Come not within the measure of my wrath' (Act V, Scene IV).

36 ❧ The Two Noble Kinsmen

Main Characters

Theseus – Duke of Athens.

Palamon – Nephew of the King of Thebes.

Arcite – Nephew of the King of Thebes.

Pirithous – An Athenian general.

Artesius – An Athenian captain.

Valerius – A noble of Thebes.

A Jailer – Oversees the imprisonment of Palamon and Arcite.

A Doctor – Ordered by Theseus to tend to the wounds of Palamon and Arcite.

Gerrold – A schoolmaster.

Hippolyta – Wife of Theseus.

Emilia – Theseus's sister.

Three Queens – Their husbands were killed by Creon, ruler of Thebes.

Jailer's Daughter – In love with Palamon and frees him from the jail.

Introduction

Based on Chaucer's *Knight's Tale*, *The Two Noble Kinsmen* was written at the end of Shakespeare's career, as a collaboration with the rising young dramatist John Fletcher. Chaucer's story of Palamon and Arcite was based on Boccaccio's *Teseide*. Boccaccio in turn based his work on material by Statius. Richard Edwards wrote *Palamon and Arcyte* as early as 1566, and it was performed before Elizabeth I by Oxford students on the occasion of the Queen's visit to the university in that year. The account of this lost comedy, published in Nichols's *Progresses of Elizabeth,* suggests that it was a very different kind of play from *The Two Noble Kinsmen*. Nothing is known of the *Palamon and Arsett* mentioned by Henslowe as having been acted at the Newington Butts theatre in 1594.

The Two Noble Kinsmen was first published in 1634 in quarto format, although scholars date it sometime around 1613. The title page ascribes the play to 'the memorable Worthies of their time; Mr John Fletcher, and Mr William Shakspeare' (sic) at the Blackfriars Theatre. Most modern critics accept this attribution.

Because the play was excluded from the 1623 First Folio some critics dispute Shakespeare's role in the play's composition. However, *Pericles* was also excluded from the First Folio, and *Troilus and Cressida* was included in only some editions, having been stitched into the binding between *King Henry VIII* (another co-authored play) and *Coriolanus*, and is subsequently absent from the title pages of those editions. When the second Beaumont and Fletcher folio was published in 1679, it contained an additional 18 plays, including *The Two Noble Kinsmen*.

It was not included in a complete Shakespeare edition until 1841 (*The Pictorial Shakespeare*), and only during the 20th century was it accepted into most of the major modern collections of Shakespeare's works, particularly the Oxford, Riverside, Arden, Norton, Cambridge and Penguin editions.

Curiously, of all the single-edition versions of the play in the 20th century, only one, the Regents Renaissance Drama edition (edited by Richard Proudfoot, 1970), bears the names of both Shakespeare and Fletcher on the front cover.

The Play

The Two Noble Kinsmen is essentially an adaptation of Chaucer's *Knight's Tale*. In this story, the two kinsmen are Palamon and Arcite, who are captured while fighting for Thebes against Athens. While imprisoned, the two cousins find themselves attracted to Emilia, Theseus's unmarried sister-in-law. Their professed 'eternal friendship' is severely tested as the two cousins woo her. Theseus finds out what's going on, exiles Arcite from Athens and leaves Palamon in jail.

Once he is free, Arcite disguises himself as a peasant in order to keep an eye on Emilia. Meanwhile, the jailer's daughter has fallen in love with Palamon and helps him to escape and hide in the forest.

He runs into Arcite again, and the two men resume their argument over Emilia. They decide to fight a duel for her. However, as they prepare for the duel, the two cousins are discovered by Theseus. He condemns both to death, but after pleading from both Emilia and her sister, Hippolyta, the Duke decides to banish them both.

The Two Noble Kinsmen is a play that needs to be seen ifr that the masque-like splendour of some of its scenes is to be fully appreciated. It contains elements of classic legend, medieval romance, Elizabethan comedy and Jacobean masque, and in the union of these varying elements we can perceive the genius of a dramatist who could subdue all things to harmony.

Both Palamon and Arcite refuse. Theseus tells Emilia she must choose between them, and the loser will be put to death. Emilia, however, can't make up her mind, so Theseus declares that the matter will be settled by combat after all. In one month, Palamon and Arcite will fight for Emilia's hand, and the loser will be executed.

Meanwhile, the jailer's daughter has gone mad because of her unrequited love for Palamon. Theseus pardons the jailer, realizing he had no part in Palamon's escape, and forgives the deranged daughter. A doctor tries to help restore her sanity by getting her fiancé to pretend he's Palamon.

The time for the contest comes about, and Arcite defeats Palamon. However, while Palamon awaits execution, a messenger arrives bringing news that Arcite has fatally injured himself in a horse-riding accident. Arcite gives Emilia's hand to Palamon before he dies.

Commentary

Neglected until recently by directors and teachers, the play deserves to be better known for its moving dramatization of the conflict of love and friendship. While one of the kinsmen braces himself for execution, the shocking accident that frees him seems to make a nonsense of the belief that we are responsible for our own fate. This concept is reinforced by

Theseus's closing speech in the last scene, where he tries to convince us that Palamon had the better right to the lady because he saw her first. The enduring impression the play leaves is that humans are but puppets of fortune.

The Two Noble Kinsmen follows Chaucer's *Knight's Tale* closely, but the dramatists, deferring to the 17th-century taste for a realistic subplot to a romantic theme, added the story of the jailer's daughter. The play has problems, however: Palamon and Arcite are not particularly distinguished from each other; Theseus is a stilted and vacillating figure; and Emilia is a poor copy of Chaucer's 'Emelye the sheene'. Finally, the subplot reminds us of a poorly revisited Ophelia (in *Hamlet*).

The authorship is clearly a problem. But to the play's credit, it's tough to say who wrote what exactly. Critics are agreed that one of the two authors was Fletcher, and that to him may be allotted most of Acts II, III and IV, including the whole of the subplot, with the possible exception of the two prose scenes, but only a small, and comparatively unimportant, part of the main story.

The whole of the Act I, the first scene in Act III, and almost the whole of the last act are clearly not by Fletcher, and the choice of authorship seems to fall to Shakespeare. The profusion of striking metaphors, the profound thoughts and the extreme conciseness of writing in these scenes bears a marked resemblance to Shakespeare's later plays.

37 ❦ The Winter's Tale

Main Characters

Leontes – The King of Sicilia.

Hermione – Leontes's Qsueen.

Perdita – The daughter of Leontes and Hermione.

Polixenes – The King of Bohemia, and Leontes's boyhood friend.

Florizel – Polixenes's only son and heir.

Camillo – A Sicilian nobleman.

Paulina – A noblewoman of Sicily.

Autolycus – A roguish peddler.

Shepherd – He finds Perdita as a baby and raises her as his own daughter.

Antigonus – Paulina's husband.

Clown – Perdita's adopted brother.

Mamillius – The young Prince of Sicilia.

Cleomenes – A lord of Sicilia.

Dion – A Sicilian lord.

Emilia – One of Hermione's ladies-in-waiting.

Archidamus – A lord of Bohemia.

Introduction

The Winter's Tale is one of Shakespeare's last plays, written and performed around 1611. It joins *Pericles*, *Cymbeline* and *The Tempest* in a list of genre-defying plays that are usually referred to as tragicomedies or bitter comedies.

There is no one source for *The Winter's Tale*, although Shakespeare relied heavily on *Pandosto*, a 1588 prose romance by Robert Greene, a university-trained London writer, who in 1592 wrote a pamphlet accusing a young Shakespeare of being an untalented, 'upstart Crow' who stole from other writers (which makes this borrowing somewhat ironic). The story of the abandoned royal baby probably comes from popular folklore, while Hermione's resurrection at the end of the play is obviously from the Greek myth of Pygmalion, in which a sculptor's work comes to life.

The Play

Leontes's friend Polixenes of Bohemia thinks he should return to his kingdom after spending time with his old school friend. Leontes asks his wife, Hermione, to try to persuade Polixenes to stay longer. Because Hermione succeeds, Leontes starts to think she is having an affair with Polixenes. His jealousy gets the better of him, and Leontes decides to kill Polixenes.

The play has been a favourite of directors and audiences since it was first presented. In a number of productions the roles of Hermione and Perdita have been played by the same actress, notably Dame Judi Dench in 1969. Other recent productions have starred Patrick Stewart, Sir Ian McKellen and Jeremy Irons.

Camillo, however, warns Polixenes, and the two men escape to Bohemia. Leontes has Hermione tried for adultery, despite the fact that the Delphic oracle proclaims her innocent. While in prison, Hermione gives birth to a daughter, which Leontes orders killed. He is persuaded to save the child's life, and orders Antigonus to abandon the baby in the desert. Antigonus does so, but is devoured soon after by a bear. (This gives rise to one of Shakespeare's classic stage directions: 'Exit, pursued by a bear'.)

Leontes's son, Mamillius, dies from grief over his mother's predicament. Hermione is next reported dead by her maid, Paulina. The shock seems to bring Leontes to his senses. He is overcome by grief and guilt and goes into seclusion.

The abandoned baby, Perdita, is found by a shepherd, who raises her as his daughter. Sixteen years later, Florizel, Polixenes's son, meets Perdita, and the teenagers fall in love. Polixenes, however, is not happy that his son is in love with a peasant girl, so Florizel and Perdita decide to flee to Sicilia, aided by old Camillo.

Florizel and Perdita are welcomed at the court of Leontes. Polixenes follows them, and is reconciled with Leontes. Perdita is revealed to be a princess, and Leontes and Polixenes are delighted that their children are in love.

Leontes's happiness is tempered by the bitter memory of Hermione's death. Paulina takes Leontes and the court to see a statue of the Queen, which magically comes to life. It seems the Queen has been hiding for the past 16 years. Thus Leontes is finally reunited with his wife, daughter, best friend, and closest adviser, Camillo. Even Paulina gains a husband when Leontes agrees to marry her to Camillo.

Commentary

The Winter's Tale is perhaps Shakespeare's best tragicomedy. It is set in an imaginary world where ancient Greek oracles co-exist with Renaissance sculptors, and offers an *Othello*-like tragedy that magically culminates in the all's-well-that-ends-well finale of *A Midsummer Night's Dream* or *The Tempest*.

Leontes is both Othello and Iago. His paranoia illustrates the terrifying destructive power of the whims of princes, and subtly emphasizes the need for the middle classes (through the growth of the power of parliament and the guilds) to take more control of their own lives.

The play is almost seasonal in structure. The first half is wintry and chilly, emotionally cold, and dominated by a fit of jealous madness and rage that seems so destructive even an innocent child may not escape.

But 16 years go by, and Leontes's madness passes. The second half of the play is spring-like, and the destruction created by the King's madness is ploughed under so that through coincidence, goodwill, and the magic of new life springing forth from previously hard and barren ground, a statue of his 'dead wife' comes to life and embraces him.

The problem plays are concerned with death and the power of evil, and in *The Winter's Tale* we are given an ending where death is literally banished from the stage.

Like *King Lear*, this play deals with the anarchy unleashed because of the main character's self-absorbed madness. When Leontes is told that there is 'nothing' between Hermione and Polixenes, he declares, 'Why, then the world and all that's in 't is nothing.' When he finally comes to his senses, all Leontes can offer by way of explanation for his behaviour is, 'I have drunk, and seen the spider'.

If Leontes is a tragic hero, Perdita is clearly a fairy-tale princess reared among commoners who falls in love with a prince and discovers her nobility quite naturally. The 'miracle' of Hermione's resurrection at the play's close is an appropriate ending to a play about death (winter) and rebirth (spring).

Famous Lines

'They say we are
Almost as like as eggs' (Act I, Scene II).

'To unpathed waters, undreamed shores' (Act IV, Scene III).

38 ꙮ Timon of Athens

Main Characters

Timon – A wealthy man who enjoys giving gifts to his friends and sharing his wealth.

Apemantus – One of Timon's guests.

Alcibiades – An acquaintance of Timon.

Flavius – One of Timon's servants.

Lucullus, Lucius, Sempronius and Ventidius – Timon's fair-weather friends.

Lucilius, Flaminius and Servilius – Timon's servants.

Caphis, Varro's servant, Isidore's servant – Servants of creditors who demand repayment of their loans.

Poet – One of Timon's hangers-on.

Painter – One of Timon's hangers-on.

Jeweller – One of Timon's hangers-on.

Fool – The Fool appears with Apemantus outside Timon's house while servants of creditors wait for their payments.

Bandits – Thieves Timon meets in the wilderness.

Senators – Members of the Athenian Senate.

Lords – Among Timon's many friends who attend his feasts and accept his gifts.

Introduction

Timon of Athens was probably written between 1605 and 1608, but is not known to have been produced, probably because, as many scholars argue, it was never finished. An alternative theory is that it focused on too controversial a topic for the years directly after James I's accession to the English throne in 1603.

In the early part of the 17th century there was growing condemnation of the almost profligate spendthrift behaviour of the English aristocracy, most of whom could not afford the lifestyles they tried to maintain.

Nobles constantly competed to outdo one another, but lacked the cash to back up their behaviour. As a result, a new credit market arose.

> Some scholars think Shakespeare co-authored this play with a dramatist named Thomas Middleton. Nevertheless, some Shakespearean characteristics are unmistakable, such as the story's derivation from Plutarch's *Lives of Noble Greeks and Romans*, one of Shakespeare's favourite sources.

James I was well known for extravagant behaviour, giving his friends expensive gifts and generally spending money on fashionable things until he had incurred huge deficits at the royal treasury. Much of the aristocracy followed his example. The play draws attention to the irresponsible behaviour of the upper classes, a criticism which may have contributed to keeping the play from being sponsored or performed.

The Play

Timon is a generous aristocrat of Athens. Everyone loves him because of his generosity, and he just hasn't wanted to hear what his steward, Flavius, has been trying to tell him. When Timon finds creditors knocking on the door, Flavius is finally able to tell him he is bankrupt.

Timon then sends his servants to his 'friends', only to find that no one will lend him money to repay his debts except his steward, who gives what little he has to his master. Incensed at this betrayal, Timon invites everyone to one last feast. The only dish, to everyone's surprise, is warm water. Timon then denounces not only his former comrades but also humankind as a whole.

In the meantime, Alcibiades, a captain of Athens, is banished for pleading for the life of one of his men, under sentence of death by the Senate. Alcibiades seriously considers turning his army against Athens in revenge.

He hears about Timon who, while living as a hermit in the forest, digging for roots to eat, stumbled upon a buried trove of gold. Alcibiades decides to visit Timon, who in turn offers Alcibiades gold if he will sack Athens. Alcibiades accepts his offer and marches on Athens.

Timon receives more visitors, some of whom are bandits. Timon pays them gold to wreak havoc on Athens. The bandits accept the gold, but Timon's ranting, ironically, persuades them to stop stealing. Timon also sends away his only loyal friend, his former steward, Flavius, but with gold in his pockets and more kindness than he has shown to anyone else.

Despite his apparent goodness at the start of the play, Timon is a self-absorbed character who sets himself up as a god of generosity and, when he loses his wealth through his own foolishness, becomes a god of vitriol and revenge, cursing humankind with the same kind of enthusiasm with which he earlier praised it.

Alcibiades takes Athens. Knowing he is a friend of Alcibiades, the Athenians beg Timon for help. Timon offers them a tree outside his cave – on which they can hang themselves. The senators ingratiate themselves with Alcibiades by giving up his enemies and those who refused to help Timon when he was in debt. Alcibiades accepts, vowing to restore peace to Athens. A soldier enters with the news that Timon has died alone in his cave.

Commentary

Timon of Athens focuses exclusively on the question: is material well-being inextricably linked to love and friendship? It is, in some ways, almost a proto-Marxist play, and has a number of things to say which counter what we may see as a modern, buy-now-pay-later mentality.

A Poor Judge of Character

Timon enjoys sharing his wealth, but doesn't pick his friends very well. Almost certainly the only reason they have stuck around is in sthe hope that Timon will give them a gift. Apemantus may think Timon's friends are all worthless flatterers, but he hangs around as well, although without eating or accepting gifts, just to see how long things will go on before they come crashing to a halt.

Timon likes his friends' affection and seems to get some sense of status merely from spending. Perhaps he believes his generosity will solidify his friendship with the various Athenian lords who surround him. He is astonished to see the intangible bonds of 'friendship' disintegrate when he needs loans from his friends.

Possession and Financial Gain

Apemantus takes the opposite tack to Timon at every stage. He believes people are naturally greedy, and that generosity is an attempt to control and influence others and gain a return later. Yet both men believe that possessions, or lack thereof, determine how we think of ourselves.

Like the earlier play *The Merchant of Venice*, *Timon of Athens* concerns itself with the connection between ties of affection and monetary bonds. Timon must discover how much friendship has to do with self-interest, how material goods compare to intangible feelings, and how much people are esteemed for their personal characteristics versus their possessions.

The play is almost exclusively about financial exchanges between men (there is no significant female part), and can seem to suggest that such dealings are almost depraved . The Fool at one point actually draws parallels between those who go to creditors and those who go to prostitutes. The play draws on the ancient portrait of moneylending as an unnatural practice where money is bred for interest.

Friends: Fair-weather or True?

Timon begins the play as a generous but foolish man, and ends it as an angry and foolish man. He takes the behaviour of a few people he should have realized were fair-weather friends as a sign that the whole of humanity is rotten. Yet he fails to see that many people who come to see him in his cave prove his assumption false. Flavius, who echoes Timon's philosophy of generosity, but in a sensible way, shares his remaining funds with Timon's servants, proving himself an honourable man; Apemantus and Timon argue, but clearly enjoy each other's company; and Alcibiades, in a subplot involving a condemned friend, which may have been one of the casualties of an unrevised play, prepares to attack Athens in order to rehabilitate Timon's honour in the city. At the end of the play Timon learns from the senators that many Athenians want to make amends for the way Timon has been treated. Still he rejects them.

When Alcibiades arrives at the gates of Athens with his army, the senators persuade him not to attack by saying that those who were cruel to Timon and to Alcibiades make up only a small portion of the population, and will be easy to single out and punish. The play suggests that the wholesale villainy that sTimon thought made up the world is really only limited to some badly chosen friends.

Famous Lines

'Here's that which is too weak to be a sinner, – honest water, which ne'er left man i' the mire' (Act I, Scene II).

'Every man has his fault, and honesty is his' (Act III, Scene I).

'Nothing emboldens sin so much as mercy' (Act III, Scene V).

'We have seen better days' (Act IV, Scene II).

'Life's uncertain voyage' (Act V, Scene I).

39   Titus Andronicus

Main Characters

Titus Andronicus – General of Rome and tragic hero of the play.
Tamora – Queen of the Goths, mother of Chiron and Demetrius.
Aaron – Tamora's Moorish lover.
Lavinia – The only daughter of Titus Andronicus. In love with Bassianus.
Marcus Andronicus – Roman tribune. Brother of Titus Andronicus.
Saturninus – The eldest son of the late Emperor of Rome.
Bassianus – The younger brother of Saturninus.
Lucius – Titus's only surviving son.
Chiron and Demetrius – Goth princes. Sons of Tamora.
Young Lucius – Titus's grandson, and Lucius's son.

Introduction

Elizabethan written accounts testify to audiences with particularly bloodthirsty tastes, and *Titus Andronicus* was received with great applause, remaining a favourite for over a decade. However gruesome we may find *Titus Andronicus* today, it's worth recalling that, competing with the burgeoning theatre, bloodsports such as public bear-baiting were very popular in Elizabethan times.

Saving Shakespeare's Good Name

In 1687, some 100 years after the first performance of *Titus Andronicus*, Edward Ravenscroft adapted the play for a different audience and called it *The Rape of Lavinia*. In an introduction to his more refined version, he wrote, 'I have been told... that it was not originally [Shakespeare's], but brought by a private author to be acted, and [Shakespeare] only gave some Master-touches to one or two of the principal parts of characters. This I am apt to believe, because 'tis the most incorrect and indigested piece in all his works. It seems rather a heap of Rubbish than a structure.'

What's particularly interesting about Ravenscroft's comment is his need to try and rescue Shakespeare's good name. It's as though a brutal, pornographic early novel by Samuel Beckett surfaces and scholars feel compelled to justify something they would otherwise condemn with disdain as low popular trash. *Titus Andronicus* is an Elizabethan *Texas Chainsaw Massacre*. Yet, knowing the author, we can't help but think that its massive excess may be less an imitation of the Elizabethan revenge drama than a parody of that form.

During Elizabethan times, those found guilty of treason were publicly hanged, cut down while still alive and disembowelled (drawn), and their bodies then cut up, or 'quartered', and sent off to different parts of the realm; heretics were publicly burned alive.

In some ways this explanation makes sense of the history of *Titus Andronicus*. Shakespeare's admirers half-heartedly try to deny his authorship of what is probably his worst play. The debate has gone on for centuries. In 1614, Ben Jonson claimed it was as popular a play as Thomas Kyd's equally bloody *The Spanish Tragedy*. Samuel Johnson theorized that Shakespeare 'play-doctored' someone else's work.

If scholars acknowledge the hand of the great master in this work at all, they usually point to his youth as an excuse. Shakespeare would have been about 26 when he wrote *Titus Andronicus*, and it marked his first attempt at writing tragedy. This controversy rages despite the fact that Meres publicly named Shakespeare as the play's author in *Palladis Tamia* (1598), and that the play is included in the First Folio.

Sources

The play was probably written between 1590 and 1593. While there are no clear main sources for the story, critics think that they included *Hecuba* by Euripides, *The Metamorphoses* by Ovid, and *Thyestes and Troades* by Seneca. A tutor to the emperor Nero, Seneca wrote plays that described the grisly horror of murder in elaborate detail. When Elizabethans began translating Seneca's works from Latin in 1559, writers relished them and wrote plays 'in the classical style' imitating them. Shakespeare appears to have seasoned *Titus Andronicus* and, later, *Macbeth* and parts of *King Lear* with some of Seneca's ghoulish spice.

The poetry of *Titus Andronicus* displays definite Shakespearean traits, and in the character of Aaron we see the seeds of Othello, Iago and Richard III, while Tamora can be seen as an early version of Margaret in the *King Henry VI* plays. It is the only Shakespeare play for which we have a contemporary illustration, by Henry Peacham, which shows characters in a mix of Roman and Renaissance costumes.

The Play

Titus, a Roman general, returns to Rome after a victorious campaign against the Goths. In tow as captives are Tamora and her sons, one of whom, Alarbus, is sacrificed by Titus's sons. Saturninus, the newly declared Roman emperor, is feuding with his younger brother, Bassianus. Lavinia, Titus's daughter, chooses Bassianus over Saturninus, and the Emperor is seduced by the captive Queen Tamora who, with her Moorish lover, Aaron, is plotting to get revenge against Titus.

Before performing a bloody play such as *Titus Andronicus*, Elizabethan actors would fill vessels such as pigs' bladders with blood and hide them under their costumes. Onstage, they had only to pound a fist against the bladder to release the blood.

Demetrius and Chiron come across Bassianus in the woods. They murder him then rape and mutilate Lavinia, leaving her without a tongue to speak or hands to write. Aaron now frames Titus's sons (Quintus and Martius) for Bassianus's murder, and they are condemned to death. Titus's remaining son, Lucius, tries to rescue his brothers and is banished from Rome.

Aaron tells Titus that the Emperor will spare Quintus and Martius if Titus cuts off a hand and sends it to him. Titus does so. However, his hand is returned to him along with the heads of his two sons. Lucius, meanwhile, raises an army of Goths to sack Rome.

Titus is finally able to communicate enough with a half-crazed Lavinia to discover that Demetrius and Chiron were responsible for attacking her. Titus kills them, and serves them up as a pie!

When Tamora and Saturninus arrive to try to persuade Titus to call off Lucius and his Goths, Titus serves them dinner, featuring pie as the main course. In the middle of the feast, Titus kills Lavinia to put her out of her misery, reveals the secret ingredient of his pie, then butchers Tamora. Saturninus in turn slays Titus. Lucius, who has just arrived, kills Saturninus.

Lucius is elected Emperor of Rome and orders Aaron (who refuses to ask forgiveness for his crimes) to be buried up to his chest and left to starve, and for Tamora to be left unburied for scavengers to feast on.

Commentary

Titus Andronicus falls between two stools: it is neither history (i.e. not based on real events), nor a Roman play with elements of a tragedy, because it is clearly a melodrama. The play is best described as Elizabethan revenge tragedy, a genre defined by a hero who doggedly pursues vengeance and perishes at the moment of his success. *Titus Andronicus* also features one of the few genuinely evil characters in Shakespearean literature, Aaron the Moor. Aaron orchestrates all the evil in the play, and his only regret is that he wasn't able to commit more evil. And yet even this personification of evil has one soft spot, his newborn son.

Titus is a paradoxical character. His behaviour is hard for us to understand, but we can admire his concepts of honour and justice. As Rome's greatest general, Titus will allow nothing to compromise his honour or that of his family, even if he has to kill one of his sons to maintain it.

The revenge tragedy is not just about Titus taking revenge on those who wronged him and his family. It is also about Tamora getting revenge on Titus because his sons killed her son at the start of the play. She pushes Titus to the point where he has been stripped of all he holds dear, but fails to administer the *coup de grâce*, leaving him a wounded and dangerous creature.

While *Titus Andronicus* is clearly an archetypal gore-filled Elizabethan revenge tragedy, the story of *Hamlet* has a superficial resemblance to *Titus Andronicus*. Yet, clearly, the more mature playwright – with years of theatrical experience and first-hand knowledge of real personal tragedy (the death of his young son) – who wrote *Hamlet,* decided to revisit a popular genre in order to turn it on its head and put it to rest. In *Hamlet* he is not content with just piling up the bodies. Instead, the horror of *Hamlet* is a spiritual one, and it takes the expectations of an audience for a genre play like *Titus Andronicus* and forces them to consider what all this violence and blood does to our souls.

Famous Lines

'Sweet mercy is nobility's true badge' (Act I, Scene I).

'The eagle suffers little birds to sing' (Act IV, Scene IV).

40 ❧ Troilus and Cressida

Main Characters

Troilus – A prince of Troy. The younger brother of Hector and Paris.

Cressida – A beautiful young Trojan woman.

Hector – A prince of Troy.

Ulysses – One of the Greek commanders.

Pandarus – Cressida's uncle.

Thersites – A deformed slave serving Ajax.

Achilles – The greatest of the Greek warriors.

Ajax – A Greek warrior.

Agamemnon – A Greek general, brother of Menelaus.

Diomedes – A Greek commander.

Paris – A prince of Troy.

Menelaus – A Greek commander.

Helen – Menelaus's wife.

Calchas – A Trojan priest, and Cressida's father.

Aeneas – A Trojan commander.

Nestor – The oldest of the Greek commanders.

Cassandra – A Trojan princess and prophetess; she is considered mad.

Patroclus – A Greek warrior. Achilles's best friend, and maybe his lover.

Priam – The King of Troy, and the father of Hector, Paris and Troilus, among others.

Antenor – A Trojan commander.

Helenus – A prince of Troy.

Andromache – Hector's wife.

Introduction

Troilus and Cressida is one of Shakespeare's later plays, written shortly after *Hamlet* but before the other great tragedies. It is a sort of anti-*Romeo and Juliet*. Composed around 1602, it was probably performed in winter

1602–03, but no record of the performance survives, and the play itself was not published in a collection for a further six years.

The genre classification of *Troilus and Cressida* has been in dispute from the beginning. Labelled a history in an early folio, it is not really a tragedy and is sometimes grouped with the so-called 'problem comedies', *Measure for Measure* and *All's Well That Ends Well*. All three share a dark, bitter wit and a pessimistic view of human relations.

> It's important to remember the popularity of Greek and Roman mythology in Shakespeare's time. The story of Troy was well known, and the events of the play, including the denouement, would have been expected from the beginning – Cressida's treachery and Hector's death would have been as predictable as the sinking of the *Titanic* is for cinema-goers today.

Sources for the play include classical mythology and Homer's *Iliad*, which contains the Achilles–Hector story. The romance of Troilus and Cressida is principally derived from Chaucer's great 14th-century epic, *Troilus and Criseyde*. Typically, Shakespeare took only the bare bones of this story, combined with other medieval retellings of the tale, and emphasized the Elizabethan idea of Cressida's falseness over Chaucer's more sympathetic interpretation of her.

The Play

The Trojan War is in its seventh year. The Greeks besieging Troy are bickering among themselves. When Hector, a Trojan hero, issues a challenge to fight any Greek in one-to-one combat, Ulysses arranges for Ajax to be the Greek champion. Ulysses hopes to spur Achilles out of his lethargy and thus reinvigorate the Greek armies.

Calchas deserts Troy for the Greek encampment. In exchange for intelligence about the Trojan forces, Calchas asks the Greeks to exchange a Trojan prisoner for Cressida. Agamemnon, commander of the Greek army, agrees to this, and Cressida is soon parted from Troilus, who is devastated.

Once inside the Greek encampment, Cressida meets – and flirts with – all the Greek generals. Hector and Ajax battle each other to a standstill and eventually call a truce. The Trojan and Greek generals dine together at a feast.

Diomedes has been courting Cressida since her arrival in the Greek camp. While accompanying Ulysses, the heartbroken Troilus sees Cressida give Diomedes the love token Troilus gave her when she left Troy. He vows to kill Diomedes in battle.

During the battle, next day, Hector slays Achilles's friend (and perhaps lover) Patroclus. When Achilles meets Hector on the field of battle he is so incensed that he orders his men to kill Hector while he is unarmed and resting. Troy has suffered a grave defeat, and an enraged Troilus hurls curses at Achilles and Pandarus alike from the city walls.

Commentary

Troilus and Cressida is one of Shakespeare's more difficult plays. It's a romance set against the backdrop of an interminable war that is draining the humanity out of all who are engaged in it.

The play has a cast of generally unsympathetic characters, but tackles the broad theme of conflict between an individual's interests and those of the state – in this case, the conflict between the romance of the title characters and the wartime politics that puts Cressida in the Greek camp, where she is forced to make the best of her situation.

The play's general pessimism is matched only by that found in *Timon of Athens*. Heroes such as Achilles and Ajax are presented as self-absorbed thugs, and the central romance of Troilus and Cressida is reduced to a roll in the grass that passes for love amid boredom and bloodshed. In the words of the arch-cynic Thersites, 'all the argument is a whore and a cuckold', which rather sums up the Trojan War.

Structurally, the play feels disjointed. Shakespeare uses anticlimax throughout the play, so that scenes that we think will be critical turn out to be letdowns. This is especially true of the duel between Hector and Ajax, which ends in a draw, and again in the final battle, in which the events we expect do not transpire: Troilus is not avenged for the loss of his beloved, and Hector does not have a climactic duel with his great adversary, Achilles, but is ambushed and killed while he's unarmed.

> Some critics have suggested that this play was performed only once, or not at all – possibly because some of the characters in the Greek and Trojan armies were thinly disguised caricatures of contemporaries, either other playwrights or members of James I's court.

The play is almost defiantly philosophical. The argument between Hector and Troilus over the value of fighting to keep Helen in Troy is rich in insight, while Ulysses, one of the play's most interesting characters, discusses the role of order in society. Thersites is another interesting character. For all his abusiveness to the people around him, he emerges as being the only moralist, even if that morality is delivered in bitter language about a futile situation made worse by uncaring, scheming heroes.

Famous Lines

'The common curse of mankind, – folly and ignorance'
(Act II, Scene III).

'All lovers swear more performance than they are able, and yet reserve an ability that they never perform; vowing more than the perfection of ten, and discharging less than the tenth part of one' (Act III, Scene II).

'The end crowns all,
And that old common arbitrator, Time,
Will one day end it' (Act IV, Scene V).

41   Twelfth Night

Main Characters

Viola (Cesario) – A young woman.

Duke Orsino – A powerful nobleman in the coastal country of Illyria.

Olivia – A wealthy lady.

Sebastian – Viola's lost twin brother.

Malvolio – Lady Olivia's straitlaced steward.

Feste – A clown; in the service of Olivia.

Sir Toby Belch – Olivia's uncle.

Sir Andrew Aguecheek – A friend of Sir Toby.

Maria – Olivia's witty, clever servingwoman.

Antonio – A gentleman who rescues young Sebastian.

Introduction

Twelfth Night was written in 1601, around the middle of Shakespeare's career. Many critics consider it one of his great comedies, along with *As You Like It*, *Much Ado About Nothing* and *A Midsummer Night's Dream*.

What does 'twelfth night' refer to?
Twelfth night refers to the last night of the Christmas celebrations – usually 6 January – and was very popular in Elizabethan times, a day given to madcap fun, disguises and pranks. it is also known in the xchurch calendars as Epiphany.

Twelfth Night is about illusion, deception, disguises, madness and perhaps homosexuality – it is certainly concerned with the extraordinary things we do in the name of love. It's a funny and entertaining play, and one of the most accessible of several film adaptations is arguably Trevor Nunn's 1996 version, starring Helena Bonham Carter. Music has been written for and about the play, including an opera composed by Smetana, and works by Brahms, Schubert and Sibelius.

The Play

Viola and her twin brother, Sebastian, are shipwrecked in a violent storm off the coast of Illyria. They lose contact, with each thinking the other is dead. Viola disguises herself as a boy named Cesario and becomes a page in the service of Duke Orsino.

Lost in Love

Olivia is in mourning for her father and brother, and is not interested in being courted. Orsino, however, is determined to woo her. He sends Cesario to Olivia with love letters. Cesario insists on being allowed to see Olivia. Olivia finally agrees, and on meeting the boy messenger takes a fancy to Cesario.

She sends her steward, Malvolio, after Cesario with a ring that she says Cesario left behind by mistake. Viola finds herself in a bind: she realizes, to her dismay,s that Olivia has fallen for Cesario – and Viola herself has a stirring of affection for Orsino, who is still besotted with Olivia.

Sebastian (Viola's twin) is rescued by Antonio and they become fast friends. At some risk to himself, because he fell foul of the Duke, Antonio helps Sebastian.

Back in Olivia's house, Sir Toby Belch (her uncle, who has shades of Falstaff about him) has hoodwinked a foppish wealthy friend, Sir Andrew Aguecheek, into supporting him by convincing him that Olivia might be interested in marrying him. Malvolio is a pompous and bossy steward who has a running feud with Sir Toby. With the help of Maria, Olivia's maid, and Feste, a clown, Sir Toby plots to bring Malvolio down a peg or two.

Maria writes a love letter to Malvolio that makes him think Olivia has fallen for him. Malvolio's self-importance makes him fall for the trick, which eventually leads to his being locked up as a madman.

Confusion Abounds

Meanwhile, Sir Toby is urging Sir Andrew into a duel with Cesario. Olivia is now in love with Cesario, even though Cesario continues to press Orsino's cause. As Cesario and Sir Andrew prepare for a duel that neither wants, Antonio happens upon the scene. Believing Viola to be Sebastian, he intervenes and is arrested. Viola, of course, does not recognize Antonio, who now thinks his newfound friend has abandoned and betrayed him.

Sir Andrew encounters Sebastian, thinking he is Cesario. This time 'Cesario' doesn't back down when Aguecheek challenges him, and resoundingly beats him. Olivia intervenes just in time and, mistaking Sebastian for Cesario, continues to press her suit for him. A bemused Sebastian agrees to marry her.

Antonio is brought before the Duke for questioning, and Viola relates the events of the duel. Pointing to Cesario, Antonio tells everyone how he dragged 'this man' from the surf, saving his life. Olivia now enters, searching for her new husband, whom she mistakes for Cesario. Adding to this confusion, Sir Toby and Sir Andrew enter, claiming that Cesario has violently assaulted them.

In the middle of Viola's denials, Sebastian appears. The brother and sister recognize one another and are reunited. Sebastian helps to clear the confusion as to who fought and married whom. At the end, Orsino and Viola pledge their love, Olivia and Sebastian remain happily married, and Olivia rebukes Sir Toby and Maria for their abuse of Malvolio, who vows his revenge upon the whole lot. Sir Toby agrees to marry Maria to make up for getting her in trouble, and all, except the disgruntled Malvolio, live happily ever after.

Commentary

Twelfth Night is one of Shakespeare's 'transvestite comedies', a category that also includes *As You Like It* and, to a lesser degree, *The Merchant of Venice*. These plays feature female protagonists who, for one reason or another, have to disguise themselves as young men.

It's worth remembering that in Shakespeare's day all the parts were played by men, so Viola would actually have been a boy pretending to be a girl pretending to be a boy. Some contemporary critics have also found a great deal of interest in the homoerotic implications of these comedies.

Some scholars think the play was first performed on 6 January 1601 at Whitehall for an Italian nobleman, Duke Orsino of Bracciano. Others think it was first performed on 2 February 1602.

Twelfth Night is the only Shakespeare play to have an 'alternative' title – *Twelfth Night: or, What You Will* – although critics are not quite sure what the play's two titles mean. *Twelfth Night* is a reference to the 12th night of the Christmas celebrations, a holiday characterized by a festival in which everything was turned upside-down – much like the topsy-turvy world of Illyria.

Famous Lines

'If music be the food of love, play on;
Give me excess of it, that, surfeiting,
The appetite may sicken, and so die.
That strain again! it had a dying fall:
O, it came o'er my ear like the sweet sound
That breathes upon a bank of violets,
Stealing and giving odour!' (Act I, Scene I).

'We will draw the curtain and show you the picture'
(Act I, Scene V).

'He does it with a better grace, but I do it more natural'
(Act II, Scene III).

'Is there no respect of place, persons, nor time in you?'
(Act II, Scene III).

'My purpose is, indeed, a horse of that colour' (Act II, Scene III).

'She never told her love,
But let concealment, like a worm i' the bud,
Feed on her damask cheek: she pined in thought,
And with a green and yellow melancholy
She sat like Patience on a monument,
Smiling at grief' (Act II, Scene IV).

'I am all the daughters of my father's house,
And all the brothers too' (Act II, Scene IV).

'Some are born great, some achieve greatness, and some have
greatness thrust upon 'em' (Act II, Scene V).

'Love sought is good, but given unsought is better' (Act III, Scene I).

'Still you keep o' the windy side of the law' (Act III, Scene IV).

'Out of the jaws of death' (Act III, Scene IV).

'For the rain it raineth every day' (Act V, Scene I).

APPENDIX A

Resources for Further Study

Reading Resources

All these titles should be available at Amazon.com or from your local bookseller.

Acting Shakespeare by John Gielgud.

Acting with Shakespeare: The Comedies by Janet Suzman.

Adaptations of Shakespeare: A Critical Anthology by Daniel Fischlin and Mark Fortier (eds).

Clues to Acting Shakespeare: Skills Clarified for the Actor, Student and Reader by Wesley Van Tassel.

Cleopatra by Michael Grant.

Lectures on Shakespeare by W.H. Auden.

William Shakespeare: The Man Behind the Genius: A Biography by Anthony Holden.

Brightest Heaven of Invention: A Christian Guide to Six Shakespeare Plays by Peter J. Leithart.

The Cambridge Companion to Shakespeare by Margreta De Grazia and Stanley W. Wells (eds).

Coined by Shakespeare: Words and Meanings First Used by the Bard by Jeffrey McQuain and Stanley Malless.

A Companion to the Shakespearean Films of Kenneth Branagh by Sarah Hatchuel.

The Arden Shakespeare Complete Works by Richard Proudfoot, Ann Thompson and David Scott Kastan (eds).

A Shakespeare Glossary by C.T. Onions.

A Dictionary of Shakespeare by Stanley Wells and James Shaw.

Shakespeare Lexicon and Quotation Dictionary by Alexander Schmidt.

The Arden Dictionary of Shakespeare Quotations compiled by Jane Armstrong.

Daily Life in Elizabethan England by Jeffrey L. Singman.

Shakespeare's England: Life in Elizabethan and Jacobean Times by Ron Pritchard.

The Reader's Encyclopedia of Shakespeare by Oscar James Campbell and George Quinn (eds).

From Shakespeare to Existentialism by Walter Kaufmann.

The Cambridge Companion to Shakespeare on Film by Russell Jackson (ed.).

A History of Shakespeare on Screen: A Century of Film and Television by Kenneth S. Rothwell.

Interpreting Shakespeare on Screen by Deborah Cartmell.

Orson Welles, Shakespeare and Popular Culture by Michael Anderegg.

Shakespeare in the Movies: From the Silent Era to Shakespeare in Love by Douglas C. Brode.

Shakespeare, the Movie: Popularizing the Plays on Film, TV and Video by Lynda E. Boose and Richard Burt (eds).

The Friendly Shakespeare: A Thoroughly Painless Guide to the Best of the Bard by Norrie Epstein.

Shakespeare's Mystery Play: The Opening of the Globe Theatre 1599 by Steve Sohmer.

The Purpose of Playing: Shakespeare and the Cultural Politics of Elizabethan Theatre by Louis Montrose.

Shakespeare's Globe Rebuilt by J.R. Mulryne and Margaret Shewring (eds).

Shakespeare's Theatre by Andrew Langley.

Staging in Shakespeare's Theatres by Andrew Gurr and Mariko Ichikawa.

Welcome to the Globe: The Story of Shakespeare's Theatre by Peter Chrisp (children's book).

William Shakespeare & the Globe by Aliki.

Understanding Hamlet by Don Nardo.

Understanding Hamlet: A Student Casebook to Issues, Sources and Historical Documents by Richard Corum.

What Happens in Hamlet by John Dover Wilson.

Henry V, War Criminal? and Other Shakespeare Puzzles by John Sutherland, et al.

The Children of Henry VIII by Alison Weir.

Thy Father Is a Gorbellied Codpiece: Create over 100,000 of Your Own Shakespearean Insults by Barry Kraft.

Shakespeare and the Jews by James Shapiro.

Understanding Shakespeare's Julius Caesar by Thomas J. Derrick.

The Lives of the Kings and Queens of England by Antonia Fraser.

Shakespeare's Kings: The Great Plays and the History of England in the Middle Ages: 1337–1485 by John Julius Norwich.

Understanding Macbeth: A Student Casebook to Issues, Sources and Historical Documents by Faith Nostbakken.

The Military Campaigns of the Wars of the Roses by Philip A. Haigh.

The Merchant of Venice: Choice, Hazard and Consequence by Joan Ozark Holmer.

The Merchant of Venice Study Guide by Bethine Ellie.

Bulfinch's Mythology by Thomas Bulfinch.

Dictionary of Classical Mythology by John Edward Zimmerman.

Greek Gods and Heroes by Robert Graves.

The Greek Myths by Robert Graves.

Heroes, Gods and Monsters of the Greek Myth by Bernard Evslin.

Mythology: Timeless Tales of Gods and Heroes by Edith Hamilton

Othello: A Guide to the Play by Joan Lord Hall (ed.).

Understanding Othello: A Student Casebook to Issues, Sources and Historical Documents by Faith Nostbakken.

Romeo and Juliet Study Guide by Bethine Ellie.

Understanding Romeo and Juliet by Thomas E. Thrasher.

Understanding Romeo and Juliet: A Student Casebook to Issues, Sources and Historical Documents by Alan Hager (ed.).

Shakespeare After Theory by David Scott Kastan.

Shakespeare: The Invention of the Human by
Harold Bloom.

*Shakespearean Tragedy: Lectures on Hamlet, Othello,
King Lear and Macbeth* by A.C. Bradley.

Shakespeare's Women in Love by Alice Griffin.

Shakespeare's Sonnets: Critical Essays edited by
James Schiffer.

The Art of Shakespeare's Sonnets by Helen
Hennessy Vendler.

The Tempest: Complete Study Edition by Sidney
Lamb (ed.).

Twelfth Night: A User's Guide by Michael
Pennington.

*Understanding The Merchant of Venice: A Student
Casebook to Issues, Sources and Historical
Documents* by Jay L. Halio.

Shakespeare on Film

Nothing compares with watching a
wonderfully envisioned and acted version of
a Shakespeare play. Type in Shakespeare at the
Internet Movie Database (*www.imdb.com*) and
you will get many listings for Shakespeare on
DVD and videotape, going back to a silent
version of *King John* in 1899, starring Sir
Herbert Beerbohm Tree. Most of these are
available for hire or purchase. A great resource
to start with is local libraries, many of which
now have movie rental sections, and in some
cases they can get inter-library loans for films
they don't have.

When watching Shakespeare on film, you
will enhance your experience if you pay
attention to the following ten viewers' clues:

1. Things happen in a live performance that
   are sometimes unrehearsed and
   unscripted. But everything in a film is
   meant to be there. If something stands out,
   the chances are it was supposed to, so pay
   attention. In general, ask yourself why a
   director would use that music or focus on
   that thing?

2. Watch the film a couple of times and then
   follow it with a copy of the original play on
   your lap. Try and spot which scenes have
   been cut or merged, and which lines cut or
   reordered. Play performances are often
   rearranged and edited as well, but not to the
   same degree. What is the director trying to
   tell you about the play? To really see the
   difference a director can make, watch two
   different versions of the same play.

3. Who's in the cast? Are they popular actors?
   Do they specialize in something? For
   example, is Ice T playing Othello?
   How does this affect the way you see this
   character? Is the director relying on star
   appeal? Shock appeal? Can you explain any
   of the director's casting decisions?

4. Where is the film set? In what era? Does
   the play need a historically 'accurate'
   setting, for example, Renaissance England,
   rather than fascist Italy in the 1930s for
   Richard III?

5. What do the costumes tell you? Are they
   being used to convey a general impression
   or to establish a historical era, or both?

6. How knowledgeable are we expected to be

about the original play? Have any sub-plots or characters been dropped for this film? Why?

7. Has the genre of the film been changed? *Hamlet* became Disney's *The Lion King; The Tempest* became the 1956 sci-fi classic *Forbidden Planet*. What does this change tell you about the play you hadn't thought of before?

8. What does the music in the film tell you about it? Music expresses the emotional undercurrent in the story. How does the score affect how you experience the dialogue? Is it intrusive?

9. What did this film teach you about this play? What would you change?

10. When a new film comes out, watch how it's promoted. Catch interviews with the cast and the director. What they thought they were doing, and what actually ended up on film, may be very different.

The following is a partial list of films of Shakespeare plays, of dramas inspired by his plays, or about Shakespeare the man, that are worth watching.

The Taming of the Shrew (1929), featuring Douglas Fairbanks and Mary Pickford.

Romeo and Juliet (1935), directed by George Cukor.

A Midsummer Night's Dream (1935), directed by Max Reinhardt and William Dieterle.

As You Like It (1936), directed by Paul Czinner.

Swinging the Dream (1938), featuring Louis Armstrong and Benny Goodman (based on *A Midsummer Night's Dream*).

Henry V (1945), directed by Lawrence Olivier.

A Double Life (1948), directed by George Cukor, starring Ronald Coleman (based on *Othello*).

Macbeth (1948), directed by Orson Welles.

Hamlet (1948), directed by Lawrence Olivier.

Othello (1952), directed by Orson Welles.

Julius Caesar (1953), directed by Joseph L. Mankiewicz.

Romeo and Juliet (1954), directed by Renato Castellani.

Richard III (1955), directed by Lawrence Olivier.

Forbidden Planet (1956), directed by Fred M. Wilcox (based on *The Tempest*).

West Side Story (1961), starring Natalie Wood and Richard Beymer (based on *Romeo and Juliet*).

Hamlet (1964), starring Richard Burton and directed by Bill Colleran and John Gielgud.

Hamlet (1964), directed by Grigori Kozintsev.

Chimes at Midnight (1965), directed by Orson Welles (a fictional biography of Falstaff, lifted from the histories).

Othello (1965), starring Lawrence Olivier, Maggie Smith and Frank Finlay.

The Taming of the Shrew (1967), starring Elizabeth Taylor and Richard Burton, and directed by Franco Zeffirelli.

Romeo and Juliet (1968), directed by Franco Zeffirelli.

King Lear (1970), directed by Peter Brook.

King Lear (1970), directed by Grigori Kozintsev.

Macbeth (1972), directed by Roman Polanski.

Antony and Cleopatra (1974), starring Patrick Stewart and Ben Kingsley, and directed by Trevor Nunn and John Schoffield.

The Comedy of Errors (1978), starring Judi Dench and Francesca Annis, and directed by Philip Casson and Trevor Nunn.

Richard II (1978), starring Derek Jacobi, John Gielgud and Wendy Hiller.

Hamlet, Prince of Denmark (1980), starring Patrick Stewart, and directed by Rodney Bennett.

The Merry Wives of Windsor (1982), starring Ben Kingsley, and directed by David Hugh Jones.

The Tempest (1982), directed by Paul Mazursky.

Ran (1985), directed by Akira Kurosawa (based on *King Lear*).

King Lear (1987), directed by Jean-Luc Godard.

Henry V (1989), directed by Kenneth Branagh.

Rosencrantz and Guildenstern Are Dead (1990), featuring Richard Dreyfuss (based on *Hamlet*).

Romeo and Juliet (1990), starring Francesca Annis, Vanessa Redgrave and Ben Kingsley, and directed by Armando Acosta II.

Hamlet (1991), directed by Franco Zeffirelli.

Prospero's Books (1991), directed by Peter Greenaway (based on *The Tempest*).

As You Like It (1992), directed by Christine Edzard.

Much Ado about Nothing (1993), directed by Kenneth Branagh.

Othello (1995), directed by Oliver Parker.

Richard III (1995), directed by Richard Loncraine, and featuring Ian McKellen.

Hamlet (1996), starring Kenneth Branagh, Richard Attenborough, Judi Dench, Billy Crystal and Kate Winslet, and directed by Kenneth Branagh.

Twelfth Night (1996), starring Helena Bonham Carter, Nigel Hawthorne, Ben Kingsley, Imogen Stubbs and Mel Smith, and directed by Trevor Nunn.

Looking for Richard (1996), directed by Al Pacino.

Romeo and Juliet (1996), featuring Leonardo DiCaprio and Claire Danes.

Shakespeare in Love (1998), starring Joseph Fiennes, Gwyneth Paltrow, Geoffrey Rush and Judi Dench, and directed by John Madden.

10 Things I Hate About You (1999), starring Julia Stiles and Heath Ledger, and directed by Gil Junger (based on *The Taming of the Shrew*).

A Midsummer Night's Dream (1999), starring Calista Flockhart and Michelle Pfeiffer, and directed by Michael Hoffman.

Titus (1999), starring Anthony Hopkins and Jessica Lange. directed by Julie Taymor.

Othello (1999), featuring Lawrence Fishburne and Kenneth Branagh.

Love's Labour's Lost (2000), directed by Kenneth Branagh.

Shakespeare on the Web

There are quite literally thousands of Web sites about Shakespeare. Below are a handful that are interesting and useful. They have been categorized by topic to help you find your way around. No doubt your search will find many more.

Complete Texts

www.ipl.org/reading/shakespeare/shakespeare.html
www.groundling.com/Edward3/index.shtml
http://shakespeare.about.com/mbody.htm
www.chemicool.com/Shakespeare/
http://theplays.org/
*http://htf-puppy.mit.edu/research/shakespeare/
    sea.html*
*www.btinternet.com/~steveaj/Shakespeare/
    works.htm*

Summaries and Plot Guides

A.C. Bradley's Shakespearean Tragedy:
    www.clicknotes.com/bradley/welcome.html
All Shakespeare:
    www.allshakespeare.com/index.php
Shakespeare Resource Center – Synopsis Index:
    www.bardweb.net/plays/index.html
Shakespeare Magazine: *www.shakespearemag.com*
SparkNotes Shakespeare:
    www.sparknotes.com/shakespeare/.dir/
The Seven Ages Shakespeare's Life:
    *http://web.uvic./shakespeare/Library/
    SLTnoframes/life/lifesubj.html*
The Shakespeare Classroom:
    www.jetlink.net/~massij/shakes/

Shakespeare Play Summaries–Synopses:
    *www.unc.edu/~monroem/shakespeare/
    shakespeare.html*
Shakespeare Study Guide with Plot Summaries:
    *http://zekscrab.users.50megs.com/Cummings/
    Shakespeare*

Shakespeare Performed

Romeo and Juliet: *www.romeoandjuliet.com*
IMS William Shakespeare, HarperAudio:
    *http://town.hall.org/Archives/radio/IMS/
    HarperAudio/020994_harp_ITH.html*
Shakespeare Wired for Books:
    www.tcom.ohiou.edu/books/shakespeare
Village Story Tapes:
    www.storytapes.net/index.html
Shakespeare Film: *www.jetlink.net/~massij/
    shakes/films/movilist.html*
Lynch Multimedia–Shakespeare:
    www.lynchmultimedia.com/shakespeare.html
Shakespeare and the Globe Then and Now:
    http://shakespeare.com/shakespeare/ind_.html
The Play's the Thing audio files and
    information:
    www.eamesharlan.org/tptt/audio.html
Taste Shakespeare: *www.atasteofshakespeare.com*
Virtual Globe Theatre – Opening Page:
    *www.holycross.edu/departments/theatre/
    wrynders/globe/globe.htm*
The Official RSC Web site: *www.rsc.org.uk*
Shakespeare's Globe Theatre, Bankside,
    Southwark, London:
    www.shakespeares-globe.org
Shakespeare Film–Miami University: *www.
    mucmuohio.edu/~shakespeare/index2.html*

How to Curse in Shakespeare

Do you find yourself cursing with the same words too often? Can't think of any alternatives? You're still stuck in Anglo-Saxon times. Be modern: think Elizabethan English.

Elizabethans took a delight in clever use of language, and wove together words to make stinging but witty insults ('You mammering plume-plucked maggot!', for example). Certainly, Elizabethans used words like 'fie', and swore by Christ's wounds (''Zwounds' became 'Zounds'), and if an occasion arose where they felt the only suitable expression would involve the F word, more often than not they would use the verb 'swive', which has vanished from the language today.

Name-calling was an art in Shakespeare's day, and some of his best comes from family members insulting other family members. 'Thou art a boil, a plague sore!' Lear screams at his daughter Goneril. 'Thou toad,' the Duchess of York yells at her son Richard III.

Instead of just calling Falstaff a fat liar, Prince Hal calls him 'A huge hill of flesh' and then goes on:

A trunk of humours,
that bolting-hutch of beastliness, that swollen parcel
of dropsies, that huge bombard of sack, that stuffed
cloak-bag of guts, that roasted Manningtree ox with the
pudding in his belly.

To create your own curses, memorize some choice terms from the list overleaf, with two adjectives and a noun, minimum, per curse, please. For example, try 'Thou bawdy bat-fowled barnacle', or, to sound more modern, try 'You surly sheep-biting puttock'.

Combine words from each of the three columns below.

Adjective	Adjective	Noun
artless	base-court	apple-john
bawdy	bat-fowling	baggage
beslubbering	beef-witted	barnacle
bootless	beetle-headed	bladder
churlish	boil-brained	boar-pig
clouted	clay-brained	bum-bailey
cockered	clapper-clawed	bugbear
craven	common-kissing	canker-blossom
currish	crook-pated	clack-dish
dankish	dismal-dreaming	clotpole
errant	dread-bolted	death-token
fawning	earth-vexing	dewberry
fobbing	elf-skinned	flap-dragon
frothy	fen-sucked	flirt-gill
froward	fat-kidneyed	flax-wench
gleeking	flap-mouthed	foot-licker
goatish	fly-bitten	fustilarian
gorbellied	folly-fallen	giglet
infectious	full-gorged	haggard
loggerheaded	half-faced	hedge-pig
lumpish	hasty-witted	horn-beast
mammering	hedge-born	hugger-mugger
mangled	hell-hated	joithead

Adjective	Adjective	Noun
mewling	idle-headed	lewdster
paunchy	ill-breeding	lout
pribbling	ill-nurtured	maggot-pie
puking	knotty-pated	malt-worm
puny	milk-livered	mammet
rank	onion-eyed	minnow
reeky	plume-plucked	miscreant
roguish	pottle-deep	moldwarp
ruttish	pox-marked	mumble-news
saucy	reeling-ripe	nut-hook
spleeny	rough-hewn	pigeon-egg
spongy	rude-growing	pignut
surly	rump-fed	pumpion
tottering	shard-borne	puttock
unmuzzled	sheep-biting	rascal
vain	spur-galled	ratsbane
venomed	swag-bellied	scut
villainous	tardy-gaited	skainsmate
warped	tickle-brained	strumpet
wayward	toad-spotted	varlet
whoreson	wart-necked	vassal
weedy	unchin-snouted	whey-face
yeasty	weather-bitten	wagtail

Need more? Look up Shakespearean insults on the Internet. Or you can always read Shakespeare's plays and then make them up. For references on such terms, try *Shakespeare's Bawdy* by Eric Partridge; *Shakespeare's Insults: Educating Your Wit* and *Insults for Teachers*, both by Wayne F. Hill and Cynthia Öttchen; and more generally, *Opus Maledictorum: A Book of Bad Words and Talking Dirty* by Jeremy Ellis.

Index